WHAT WOULD CERVANTES DO?

McGill-Queen's Iberian and Latin American Cultures Series
SERIES EDITOR: NICOLÁS FERNÁNDEZ-MEDINA

The McGill-Queen's Iberian and Latin American Cultures Series is committed to publishing original scholarship that explores and re-evaluates Iberian and Latin American cultures, connections, and identities. Offering diverse perspectives on a range of regional and global histories from the early modern period to twenty-first-century contexts, the series cuts across disciplinary boundaries to consider how questions of authority, nation, revolution, gender, sexuality, science, epistemology, avant-gardism, aesthetics, travel, colonization, race relations, religious belief, and media technologies, among others, have shaped the rich and complex trajectories of modernity in the Iberian Peninsula and Latin America.

The McGill-Queen's Iberian and Latin American Cultures Series promotes rigorous scholarship and welcomes proposals for innovative and theoretically compelling monographs and edited collections.

1 Populism and Ethnicity
  Peronism and the Jews of Argentina
  Raanan Rein
  Translated by Isis Sadek

2 What Would Cervantes Do?
  Navigating Post-Truth with Spanish Baroque Literature
  David Castillo and William Egginton

What Would Cervantes Do?

Navigating Post-Truth with Spanish Baroque Literature

DAVID CASTILLO
and
WILLIAM EGGINTON

McGill-Queen's University Press
Montreal & Kingston • London • Chicago

© McGill-Queen's University Press 2022

ISBN 978-0-2280-0814-9 (cloth)
ISBN 978-0-2280-0815-6 (paper)
ISBN 978-0-2280-0930-6 (ePDF)
ISBN 978-0-2280-0931-3 (ePUB)

Legal deposit first quarter 2022
Bibliothèque nationale du Québec

Printed in Canada on acid-free paper that is 100% ancient forest free (100% post-consumer recycled), processed chlorine free

---

Library and Archives Canada Cataloguing in Publication

Title: What would Cervantes do?: navigating post-truth with Spanish Baroque literature / David Castillo and William Egginton.

Names: Castillo, David R., 1967– author. | Egginton, William, 1969– author.

Series: McGill-Queen's Iberian and Latin American cultures series; 2.

Description: Series statement: McGill-Queen's Iberian and Latin American cultures series; 2 | Includes bibliographical references and index.

Identifiers: Canadiana (print) 20210301 66X | Canadiana (ebook) 20210306009 | ISBN 9780228008156 (softcover) | ISBN 9780228008149 (hardcover) | ISBN 9780228009306 (PDF) | ISBN 9780228009313 (ePUB)

Subjects: LCSH: Cervantes Saavedra, Miguel de, 1547–1616—Criticism and interpretation. | LCSH: Truthfulness and falsehood. | LCSH: Truthfulness and falsehood in literature. | LCSH: Fake news. | LCSH: Mass media—Objectivity. | LCSH: Information literacy. | LCSH: Spanish literature—Classical period, 1500–1700—History and criticism.

Classification: LCC PQ6351 .C37 2022 | DDC 863/.3—dc23

This book was typeset by Marquis Interscript in 10.5/13 Sabon.

Contents

Acknowledgments vii

Prologue: The Deadly Devolution of Language 3

PART ONE TRUE LIES AND OTHER RULES OF ENGAGEMENT

1 Reality Entitlement 17
2 The Imagination of the Possible 26
3 The Art of the Real 34
4 The Apocalypse Will Not Be Televised! 43
5 From Breaking Bad to Breaking Worse 50
6 Playing the Game 58

PART TWO HE SAID, SHE SAID

7 Not Your Father's Classroom 73
8 The Poison of Purity 81
9 Her Weapon 98
10 A Homeopathic Cure for Patriarchy 109

PART THREE A CERVANTINE TOOLKIT FOR THE POST-TRUTH AGE

11 Revelations of a Glass Man 121
12 A Posthumous Lesson 129

13 Surviving the Post-Truth Age   148

Epilogue: Looking for Relevance in All the Right Places   159

Notes   169

Bibliography   183

Index   199

Acknowledgments

We owe a profound debt of gratitude to all those who have responded to our work and whose own work we have read with such pleasure and to such personal benefit, including but certainly not limited to Mercedes Alcalá-Galán, Palmar Álvarez-Blanco, Luis Avilés, Mindy Badía, Julio Baena, Marina Brownlee, Bruce Burningham, Anthony Cascardi, Moisés Castillo, Crystal Chemris, William Childers, Robert Davidson, Fred de Armas, Julia Domínguez, Javier Domínguez García, the late Edward Dudley, the late David Foster, Edward Friedman, Timothy Frye, Charles Ganelin, Bonnie Gasior, Michael Gerli, Stephen Hessel, David Hildner, Steven Hutchinson, the late Carroll Johnson, Ana Laguna, Massimo Lollini, Howard Mancing, Michael Marder, Adrienne Martín, Luís Martín-Estudillo, Leah Middlebrook, Alberto Moreiras, Carmen Moreno-Nuño, John Mowitt, Jesús Muñoz Merchán, Bradley Nelson, Andrea Pérez Mukdsi, Brian Phillips, Amanda Powell, Adriana Primo-Mckinley, Chris RayAlexander, Thomas Regele, Nieves Romero Díaz, Marcella Salvi, Eva Santos García, Rachel Schmidt, Barbara Simerka, Fernando Simón Abad, David Souto Alcalde, Nicholas Spadaccini, Luis Verano, Patricia Vieira, Lisa Vollendorf, Julian Weiss, Amy Williamsen, Kari Winter, and Santiago Zabala. Special thanks are owed to Troy Tower for his eagle eyes and editorial skills in helping us prepare the final manuscript.

We also owe our thanks to the journals, book series, and essay collections from which we have adapted some portions of this work as we were writing it. These include David Castillo, "Not Your Father's Classroom: Looking Back at the Golden Age through the Lens of the #MeToo Movement," in *Reconsidering Early Modern Spanish Literature through Mass and Popular Culture: Contemporizing the*

Classics in the Classroom, ed. Mindy Badia and Bonnie Gasior (Juan de la Cuesta, 2021); David Castillo, "Clarividencia tangencial y excentricidad en *El licenciado Vidriera*: nueva interpretación de un motivo clásico," in *Estas primicias del ingenio. Jóvenes cervantistas en Chicago*, ed. Francisco Caudet and Kerry Wilks (Castalia, 2003); David Castillo, "Literature to the Rescue! A Cervantine Survival Kit for the Post-Truth Age," *Cervantes* 40, no. 1 (2020); David Castillo, "Monumental Landscapes in the Society of the Spectacle: From Fuenteovejuna to New York," in *Spectacle and Topophilia: Reading Early Modern and Postmodern Hispanic Cultures*, ed. David Castillo and Bradley Nelson (Vanderbilt University Press, 2012); David Castillo and William Egginton, "The Screen Behind the Screen: A Penultimate Response to a Polemical Companion," in *A Polemical Companion to Medialogies*, ed. Bradley Nelson and Julio Baena, *Hispanic Issues On Line* 8 (2017); David Castillo and William Egginton, "The Apocalypse Will Not Be Televised! Baroque Lessons in Apocalypticism, Demagoguery, and Reality Literacy," in *Writing in the End Times: Apocalyptic Imagination in the Hispanic World*, ed. David Castillo and Bradley Nelson, *Hispanic Issues On Line* 23 (2019); David Castillo and William Egginton, "All the King's Subjects: Honor in Early Modernity," *Romance Languages Annual* 6 (1995); David Castillo and William Egginton, "The Rules of Chanfalla's Game," *Romance Languages Annual* 6 (1995); David Castillo and William Egginton, "Hispanism(s) Briefly: A Reflection of the State of the Discipline," in *Debating Hispanic Studies: Reflections on Our Disciplines*, ed. Luís Martín-Estudillo and Nicholas Spadaccini, *Hispanic Issues On Line* 1 (2006); David Castillo and William Egginton, "Cervantes's Treatment of Otherness, Contamination, and Conventional Ideals in *Persiles* and Other Works," in *Si ya por atrevido no sale con las manos en la cabeza: el legado poético del "Persiles" cuatrocientos años después*, ed. Mercedes Alcalá Galán, Antonio Cortijo Ocaña, and Francisco Layna Ranz, *eHumanista/Cervantes* 5 (2016) (reprinted in *Cervantes' Persiles and the Travails of Romance*, ed. Marina Brownlee [Toronto: University of Toronto Press, 2019]); David Castillo and Bradley Nelson, "Introduction: The Poetics and Politics of Apocalyptic Discourses," in *Writing in the End Times: Apocalyptic Imagination in the Hispanic World*, ed. David Castillo and Bradley Nelson, *Hispanic Issues On Line* 23 (2019); William Egginton, "The Art of Fiction and Political Lies," *Baltimore Sun*, 26 January 2016; William Egginton, "There's No Such Thing as

Reality (and It's a Good Thing Too!)," LA *Review of Books*, 10 November 2016; and William Egginton, "The Revenge of the Middle Class," *Arcade: Literature, the Humanities & the World*, 13 January 2012.

WHAT WOULD CERVANTES DO?

PROLOGUE

The Deadly Devolution of Language

In 2015, then American presidential candidate Donald Trump explained how he felt about his words in the midst of a campaign rally in South Carolina: "I know words; I have the best words."[1] On 11 January 2018, then president Trump seemingly added a pair of shiny best words to his hall-of-fame vocabulary: "shithole countries."[2] As reported by the *Washington Post*, Trump was referring specifically to immigrants from Haiti, El Salvador, and the African continent when he blurted out, in the presence of lawmakers from both parties, "Why are we having all these people from shithole countries come here?"[3] Reportedly, he went on to offer that "the United States should instead bring more people from countries such as Norway," while insisting that Haitian immigrants must be left out of any deal on immigration policy: "Why do we need more Haitians? ... Take them out."[4] Initially, the White House did not deny Trump's word choice, pointing out instead that, for all the outrage that his tough words had sparked in Washington circles, they would play well with his base, which had apparently grown anxious about the prospect of a presidential endorsement of a Deferred Action for Childhood Arrivals (DACA) deal. As if to confirm this notion, conservative author Ann Coulter, who had loudly criticized any sign of "weakness" in the president's hardline immigration stance, wasted no time before tweeting "he's trying to win me back."[5]

Predictably, the morning after, Trump and the White House were busy working on half-hearted denials and smokescreens, as in the following presidential tweet: "The language used by me at the DACA meeting was tough, but this was not the language used. What was tough was the outlandish proposal made – a big setback for DACA!"[6]

Just as predictably, the talking heads of Fox News defended Trump's remarks, found reasons to attack Democrats, and suggested that Trump's words didn't matter as much as his deeds and that Americans needed to judge the president's actions over a four-year period rather than fixating on his word choice on a given day. Never mind that, earlier in the week, the Trump administration had announced its decision to end temporary protected status for people from El Salvador, one of the countries included in Trump's shithole category, potentially forcing the departure of 200,000 Salvadorans who had made their lives in this country. As for whether his words matter, it was also reported that the Office of the United Nations High Commissioner for Human Rights had called the president's language "shocking," "shameful," and "racist," while "Haiti's foreign minister summoned the U.S. Chargé d'Affaires Robin Diallo for clarification."[7] By the week's end, the African Union was demanding "a retraction of the comment as well as an apology, not only to Africans but to all people of African descent around the world."[8]

Without even departing from the news cycle of that very same day, we may also recall a CNN article authored by the network's senior medical correspondent Elizabeth Cohen, "The Truth about Those 7 Words 'Banned' at the CDC." The piece suggested that reports of outright Orwellian censorship at the Centers for Disease Control and Prevention (CDC) may have been "overstated."[9] At least according to officials from the Department of Health and Human Services, there was no explicit ban or prohibition, but rather a suggestion to avoid the words "vulnerable, diversity, entitlement, transgender, fetus, evidence-based and science-based" because they might "cause someone to jump to a conclusion."[10] The CNN article points out that such a strategy of word avoidance and substitution was not uncommon, even in previous administrations. As Dr Thomas Farley, Philadelphia's health commissioner, explained, "you phrase your request to match the political bent and world view of the people who will make decisions about your budget."[11] Yet, these same officials warned that there was something "deeply troubling" about the Trump administration guidance.[12] Emily Rothman, former Massachusetts public health official makes the point that the advice to avoid such words as "vulnerable," "transgender," and "diversity" shows who the administration cared about and who it was willing to discard: "It doesn't matter if you ban these words or subtly suggest that you don't use them. People will connect the dots and see who they're hoping to leave by the wayside."[13]

Interestingly, the article's author notes that "some of the response from scientists was likely colored by recent news that references to climate change have been removed from several pages on the Environmental Protection Agency's website."[14] Perhaps even more disturbing, CDC employees were encouraged to come up with creative phrasings to get around such language as "evidence-based" and "science-based," and the example provided is revealing: "CDC bases its recommendations on science in consideration with community standards and wishes."[15] In the current political context, consideration of "community standards and wishes" can easily slide into the familiar logic of denialism deployed by the powerful lobbyists who have declared war on climate change science.

It doesn't take a rocket scientist (or a health scientist, or a climate scientist …) to understand that the battle over *words to avoid* and *better* or *best words* is ultimately about power – the power to censor, edit, and control reality – but it sure helps to have read George Orwell. This type of power is ultimately what Orwellian Newspeak is for: to erase all traces of the inconvenient truths that stand in the way of those community standards and wishes recognized and guarded by the Party. James Clapper, director of national intelligence under Barack Obama, directly referenced Orwell's novel in talking about Trump's "flexibility" in the treatment of facts, where "up is down, black is white, war is peace."[16] Clearly, what Clapper had in mind is lines like these: "There is need for an unwearying, moment-to-moment flexibility in the treatment of facts … And if the facts say otherwise, then the facts must be altered."[17]

The anti-science rhetoric of the Trump administration and its aggressive reversal of environmental regulations suggests that we just got much closer to the Orwellian nightmare, in which truth is the exclusive prerogative of the Party: "You must get rid of those nineteenth-century ideas about the laws of nature. We make the laws of nature … We can shut them out of existence."[18] Indeed, there is no need to worry about climate change when we can simply erase the term from our vocabulary. Since the evidence-based findings of climate change science run afoul of "community standards and wishes" (America First values), they must obviously represent foreign interests adopted as part of the radical anti-America liberal agenda, which is why it would be best to kill (character assassinate) the messenger and defund the science. It's no wonder that *1984* topped the best-seller lists in January 2017, some sixty-eight years after it was published.[19]

If we could jump back just one more twenty-four-hour news cycle to Wednesday, 10 January 2018, we would see the White House engaging in just this kind of erasure of inconvenient words/facts in its own transcript of the DACA meeting that had taken place earlier in the week. It seems that the line in which President Trump agreed with Democratic senator Diane Feinstein over the need for a clean DACA bill did not play well with his base, so it needed to be expunged from the record in the name of the same alternative reality in which the White House asserted that millions of illegal immigrants had voted against Trump while it resized the presidential inauguration crowds to his standards of greatness. Where have we come across this kind of thing before? You guessed it! "Who controls the past ... controls the future: who controls the present controls the past ... Reality control."[20]

With Fox News talking heads continually resorting to their last-ditch line of defence (Trump's words don't matter, his actions do), it is important for us to remember the Orwellian lesson and insist that, when it comes to the language of power, the distinction is itself part of the smokescreen: Trump's words were and still are, in effect, actions. His words have real consequences and damage real people and threaten real institutions when he calls the free press "the enemy of the people" and labels the products of their reporting "fake news";[21] when he complains that the system is rigged and millions of illegal immigrants were allowed to vote against him; when he refers to Mexicans as rapists and Muslims as terrorists, and suggests that Haitian, Salvadoran, and African immigrants debase or downgrade America; when he claims that the 2020 election was "rigged" and that he actually won it, "by a lot"; when he traffics in denialism, misrepresentation, "alternative facts," and disinformation.

It is no accident that, since Trump's election – and, more recently, his failure to win re-election – journalists have been facing an unprecedented level of animosity. Something is very wrong when death threats directed against news organizations and their employees include presidential language, as in the widely reported phone call received at the CNN Atlanta headquarters on 9 January 2018: "Fake news. I am coming to gun you all down."[22] This after months of such tweets as:

> @FoxNews is MUCH more important in the United States than CNN, but outside of the U.S., CNN International is still a major

source of (Fake) news, and they represent our Nation to the WORLD very poorly. The outside world does not see the truth from them![23]

We should have a contest as to which of the Networks, plus CNN and not including Fox, is the most dishonest, corrupt and/or distorted in its political coverage of your favorite President (me). They are all bad. Winner to receive the FAKE NEWS TROPHY![24]

CNN'S slogan is CNN, THE MOST TRUSTED NAME IN NEWS. Everyone knows this is not true, that this could, in fact, be a fraud on the American Public. There are many outlets that are far more trusted than Fake News CNN. Their slogan should be CNN, THE LEAST TRUSTED NAME IN NEWS![25]

In January 2018, two GOP lawmakers, Senators Jeff Flake and Bob Corker, broke ranks with their complicit colleagues in response to Trump's Fake News Trophy circus to sound the alarm. As Flake lamented,

> It is a testament to the condition of our democracy that our president uses words infamously used by Josef Stalin to describe his enemies ... When a figure in power reflexively calls any press that doesn't suit him "fake news," it is that person who should be the figure of suspicion, not the press ... Not only has the past year seen an American president borrow despotic language to refer to the free press, but it seems he has in turn inspired dictators and authoritarians with his own language ... As Orwell warned: "The further a society drifts from the truth, the more it will hate those who speak it."[26]

Indeed, Orwell's landmark novel taught us something about the power of words as the building blocks of reality, which explains why the original act of resistance in *1984* is a language crime, as the protagonist resolves to begin recording in writing his thoughts, memories, and emotions. Word control is an integral component of the machinery of power that – as Erich Fromm reminds us in the novel's afterword – "creates reality."[27] In the words of Orwell's own appendix, the "purpose of Newspeak was not only to provide a medium of expression for the world-view and mental habits proper to the devotees of Ingsoc [the fictional English Socialist Party], but to make all other modes of thought impossible."[28] Isn't it time to recognize Trump's collection of "best words" as a grotesque form of Newspeak meant to reframe reality to fit his alt-factual world and impose it on the rest of us? Trump's tweets give us a diminished reality when it comes to inconvenient facts and people ("all bad," "fake news," "Russia hoax," "good old Global Warming," "Liddle Bob Corker," "stop the steal" ...) and an augmented reality when it comes to all things Trump ("greatest assets," "powerful button," "really smart," "very stable genius," "VERY successful," "favorite President" ...).

While it could be said that Orwell's *1984* is nothing more than a work of fiction and not a description of the present, the Orwellian accents of much of the contemporary political environment are at best unsetting and at worst outright terrifying, especially within the echo chambers of conservative media circles. When Stephen Colbert joked in his famous appearance at the 2006 White House Correspondent's Dinner that "reality has a well-known liberal bias,"[29] he was identifying the very essence of the kind of media manipulation that conservative pundits were mastering and that Donald Trump would ride to victory ten years later. In our 2016 study *Medialogies*, we cited an aide to President George W. Bush who, in the summer of 2002, lectured journalist Ron Suskind on how the new (political) world works.[30] According to Suskind, the aide (later identified as Karl Rove) explained "that guys like me were 'in what we call the reality-based community,' which he defined as people who 'believe that solutions emerge from your judicious study of discernible reality.'"[31] While our citation in the book ended there, Suskind's quotation went on: "'That's not the way the world really works anymore,' [Rove] continued. 'We're an empire now, and when we act, we create our reality. And while you're studying that reality – judiciously, as you will – we'll act again, creating other new realities, which you can study too, and that's how things will sort out. We're history's actors ... and you, all of you, will be left to study what we do.'"[32] The question then is, how surprised should we really be to see Trump attempting to create reality, one tweet at a time, or Conway, Spicer, Sanders, and, finally, McEnany, consistently doubling down on "alternative facts"?[33]

In his afterword to *1984*, Erich Fromm notes that it would be "most unfortunate" if the reader interpreted Orwell's dystopian novel as simply "another description of Stalinist barbarism, and if [the reader] does not see that it means us too."[34] He builds on Alan Harrington's notion of the "mobile truth" in corporate America:[35]

> If I work for a big corporation which claims that its product is better than that of all competitors, the question whether this claim is justified or not in terms of ascertainable reality becomes irrelevant. What matters is that as long as I serve this particular corporation, this claim becomes "my" truth, and I decline to examine whether it is an objectively valid truth. In fact, if I change my job and move over to the corporation which was until now "my" competitor, I shall accept the new truth, that its product is the best … It is one of the most characteristic and destructive developments of our own society that man, becoming more and more of an instrument, transforms reality more and more into something relative to his own interests and functions.[36]

From this perspective, the Trump presidency would appear to be just one more step in the *corporatization of truth*. Hadn't candidate Trump promised he would run the United States government like he ran his businesses? This kind of promise has been around for decades, at least since Ross Perot's presidential campaign back in the 1990s, but, with Trump, we finally got to experience the naked "mobile truth" described by Harrington in *Life in the Crystal Palace* as it spread from the White House in spectacular fashion.

A few years ago, Michael Sandel noted that our society has evolved into what he called a "market society," which he crucially distinguished from a market economy. As he succinctly put it in an interview about his landmark book *What Money Can't Buy: The Moral Limits of Markets* (2012), a "market economy is a tool; it's a valuable and effective tool for organizing productive activity. A market society is different. A market society is a … way of life where market relations and market incentives and market values come to dominate all aspects of life … Without quite realizing it, over the past three decades, we have drifted from having a market economy to becoming a market society, a society where just about everything is up for sale."[37] We appear to be on track for a full-on corporatization of all things American, from politics and government to news media and education, to reality itself. This is what we can call *market fundamentalism*.

Against the radical alienation and dehumanization described in Harrington's book and Orwell's dystopia, Erich Fromm calls for "a renaissance of the spirit of humanism and dignity."[38] While the Trump presidency was both a result and a symptom of our medialogy, if there is to be a renaissance of the kind Fromm was urging in his commentary on *1984*, the humanistic resistance must be directed not just against Trumpism but against the underlying market fundamentalism that is threatening to colonize every aspect of our lives. We could start by asking if "market relations and market incentives and market values" should indeed dictate matters of public policy, drive the conversation on climate change, and be adopted by educational institutions. Is it really in our best interest when governments and universities operate like corporations?

While references to Orwell's landmark novel have multiplied in cultural and political circles since the beginning of the Trump presidency – even leading, on 4 April 2017, to synchronized screenings across the country of Michael Radford's decades-old adaptation of the novel – the public interest in other classic dystopias is on the rise as well. Margaret Atwood's nightmarish vision of a future totalitarian theocracy in *The Handmaid's Tale* (1986) has seen a number of new printings. The Hulu TV series by the same name, which closely follows the original novel, became wildly popular, leading to major recognition and a number of awards. Atwood's MaddAddam trilogy achieved best-selling status too. In those books, the beginning of the end of humanity is signalled by the decline of the liberal arts under the weight of STEM (science, technology, engineering, and mathematics) fields controlled by corporations in a planet ravaged by environmental devastation.

And what about Aldous Huxley's dystopian vision in *A Brave New World* (1931)? In some ways, Huxley's nightmare seems to provide the most unnerving parallels to our age of inflationary media. In *Amusing Ourselves to Death* (1985), Neil Postman argues that, while we were fixated on the Orwellian nightmare of a totalitarian state built on the active suppression of information, omnipresent vigilance, physical punishment, and psychological torture, the second half of the twentieth century was bringing us much closer to Huxley's vision of a society built on the promise of unlimited and instant gratification in which humanity would drown in trivializing, stupefying, and addictive media-technologies. As he explains,

What Orwell feared were those who would ban books. What Huxley feared was that there would be no reason to ban a book, for there would be no one who wanted to read one. Orwell feared those who would deprive us of information. Huxley feared those who would give us so much that we would be reduced to passivity and egoism. Orwell feared that the truth would be concealed from us. Huxley feared that the truth would be drowned in a sea of irrelevance. Orwell feared we would become a captive culture. Huxley feared we would become a trivial culture.[39]

A number of recent news-media pieces make the case that the Trump phenomenon proves Neil Postman right – that we are indeed living in Huxley's nightmarish *technopoly*. In a *Forbes* article titled "Amusing Ourselves to Death with Donald Trump," Chris Teare expressed this notion most explicitly in the context of the 2016 election year:

As Donald Trump moves toward the Republican nomination, a book may help explain the otherwise inexplicable. Neil Postman's *Amusing Ourselves to Death: Public Discourse in the Age of Show Business* first made an impression on me 30 years ago when I was a television anchorman. The author's argument, and the fact than none of the newscast's viewers seemed to be learning anything other than whether they liked my smile or voice, led me to leave TV and return to education. That a Reality TV star running for the highest office is being taken seriously by millions of Americans would not surprise Postman.[40]

More recently, Andrew Postman (Neil Postman's son) reflected on his father's legacy in the age of social media and twenty-four-hour news. He emphasizes the trivialization and fragmentation of public discourse and the conversion of the news media into a spectacle and a form of entertainment. He believes that his father predicted the arrival of the autocratic reality TV president as a logical outcome of our stupefying technopoly:

How engaged can any populace be when the most we're asked to do is to like or not like a particular post, or "sign" an online petition? How seriously should anyone take us, or should we take ourselves, when the "optics" of an address or campaign speech – raucousness, maybe actual violence, childishly attention-craving gestures or facial expressions – rather than the content of the speech determines how much "airtime" it gets, and how often people watch, share and favorite it? ... So, yes, my dad nailed it. Did he also predict that the leader we would pick for such an age, when we had become perhaps terminally enamored of our technologies and amusements, would almost certainly possess fascistic tendencies? I believe he called this, too.[41]

Indeed, Huxley's vision of a totalitarian technopoly that keeps its citizens drowned in all-consuming, addictive, and trivializing media technologies provides as good a parallel for our age of inflationary media as Orwell's "doublethink" and "Newspeak."[42] While neither Huxley nor the author of *Amusing Ourselves to Death* can be said to have offered many reasons for hope, and they certainly do not provide actionable suggestions on how to avoid the arrival of their prophesied technopoly, Andrew Postman's assessment of his father's warning comes with urgent recommendations to reclaim an active role as responsible citizens in understanding our media condition and teaching our children to become "aware of our information environments, which in many instances have become our entertainment environments ... Check sources. Consider what wasn't said. Ask questions. Understand that every storyteller has a bias – and so does every platform."[43] And this brings us to the core argument of the present book. We believe that the humanities have a crucial role to play in human survival. We must reinvest, as individuals and as communities, in the politics of responsible citizenship, the art of reality literacy, and the spirit of humanism and dignity.

But the humanities is a wide-ranging set of disciplines, and many would be forgiven for saying, "Okay, I get that philosophy or history could be important, but literature?" Or, to up the ante, literature written in a foreign language? This is where our book comes in. We are both literature professors whose main area of interest is the literature of early modern Spain, and who also happen to direct humanities institutes at our respective universities. We have a keen sense of the importance of humanities education for nourishing and sustaining a democratic citizenry; but we also feel that specific humanistic fields, even one as apparently arcane as early modern Spanish literature, can and should be researched and taught in a way that benefits this educational mission. In this book, we try to show how this might be done – first, by opening up some questions more broadly broached by philosophical, literary, and cultural studies, and, then, by engaging with some of the classic literary texts we often find ourselves writing about and teaching in our college courses. Throughout, we are driven by the conviction that these classic works can and should be read and discussed with an eye toward our present problems and concerns.

In a March 2018 speech delivered at SUNY Buffalo as part of the event series "Humanities to the Rescue," Margaret Atwood encouraged the audience to reflect on the crucial role of the humanities today. Her words resonate powerfully in our current media environment:

> Here is a question that is at the core of the humanities ... Where and how do we want to live? Is it in a society that strives to right ancient wrongs, to search for balance and equality, and to respect truth and fairness, or do we want to live in some other place in some other way? It will be up to you younger people to decide that, to question values, to explore the nature of truth and fairness. It will be up to you to understand the stories and to create better ones.[44]

We believe the humanities offer innumerable fields in which to do just that, not least of which the study of a particularly rich period of literary and cultural production that flourished under the watchful and even paranoid eye of an overstretched and crumbling empire almost half a millennium ago.

PART ONE

True Lies and Other Rules of Engagement

I

Reality Entitlement

Several years ago, as we began exchanging notes and drafting sections of what would eventually become *Medialogies: Reading Reality in the Age of Inflationary Media*, neither of us really noticed that our examples tended to return with disproportionate frequency to a single buffoonish reality TV star. Now we think that the 2016 election of Donald Trump, on the back of his use of the "fake news" epithet to undermine any reporting that didn't serve his purposes, and his alt-right, alt-facts presidency, up to and including his promulgation of the "big lie" following his 2020 defeat, ought to make us even more aware of the fact that, without *reality literacy* and some recourse to a notion of *truth* (situational as this notion might be), American democracy is in imminent danger.

As Santiago Zabala has recently written,

> The wall on the Mexican border, the ban on Muslims, and Trump's hostility toward the facts of climate change are not meant to create a "state of emergency." They are meant to create a condition without emergencies – where nothing can emerge from the overwhelming order and difference, change, and predefined others must be avoided or overwhelmed lest they disrupt the safety that order is supposed to represent. If this order reveals itself every day as more authoritarian by reducing civil liberties, it does so because it holds itself to be in possession of the essence of reality, defining truth for all human beings.[1]

In possession of the essence of reality – this more than any other aspect of Trump's character (in the theatrical sense of the word) powers his ability to manipulate the media as effectively as he has. This is the central paradox of reality in the age of Trumpism: Trump's alt-factual world is not the expression of too little reality, but a symptom of *reality entitlement*, which is actually a key promise of the market society: the right to our own portable, ineffable reality.

To clarify: if we are claiming that Trump is a symptom of today's medialogy, it is also clear that the medialogy is vast and long, and Trump, despite his claims to the contrary, is small and short(-fingered). The medialogy does not explain Trump; Trump illustrates the medialogy to the extent that he navigates it so well.

As Benjy Sarlin has noted in yet another journalistic "study of discernible reality," "the combination of a president with his own facts who also never backs down has created a feedback loop in which dubious statements raise new questions which then generate false responses which foster even more questions."[2] Those mainstream journalists who insist on inhabiting what Karl Rove defined as the anachronistic "reality-based community" are still displaying their dismay and calling for the truth in defence of democracy. As Dan Rather put it in a 4 March 2017 Facebook post, "we cannot afford for our democratic institutions to be consumed by a bonfire of lies, innuendos, and conspiracy theories … We want the truth. We demand the truth. We can handle the truth."[3]

For many of these journalists, searching for the truth would be a matter of finding information from "sources that can be trusted," as Chris Anderson wrote in his online piece "Combatting Misinformation in a World of Alternative Facts."[4] But the "trusted sources" argument is not without potential pitfalls. This same argument was used by public officials in imperial Spain to secure its version of the truth of the world via recourse to the authority of the Roman Catholic Church. Cervantes pokes fun at this kind of "authorized truth" with relentless frequency. He takes a different route in his fictional approach to the question of truth and reality, a route that could serve as an ethical guide in the midst of our own medialogy.

It is vital to point out here that we do not argue that a fundamental alignment exists between the medialogies of the first and second age of inflationary media; rather, we posit an inverted structure, in which the second frames the "reality concept" originally created by the first. In our formulation, the medialogy of the sixteenth and seventeenth century was characterized by things (printed words, bodies on a stage) being treated as copies of absent things; in the current age of inflationary media, those copies themselves are treated as things, ultimate bits of reality with no further referential value. Modern societies are not a revolution, but an evolution from the first medialogy. Once the subject (*Untertan*) has been conceived as citizen, in the formulation of Étienne Balibar, the stage is set for republicanism, but the citizen's body still represents an ideal, equal, yet absent citizen.[5] Fundamentalisms of the kinds that have blossomed around the world today are symptoms of the inversion of that medialogical framing. Bodies cease to refer to ideal/absent units of democratic exchange and instead solidify as non-referring substantial things, each supported entirely by its own private fundamentalism.

Trumpism seen as a symptom of the second medialogy acquires its power precisely as a reflection of how bodies no longer accrue value as indices of a universal and abstract citizenry, but only as instances of a particular ethnic, religious, racial substance. Trump, more than any other figure, rose to power because he tapped into what the medialogy was implicitly saying about republicanism – that it is a sham. This is the point of Richard Rorty's now famous "something will crack" passage from his 1998 book *Achieving Our Country*:

> At that point, something will crack. The nonsuburban electorate will decide that the system has failed and start looking around for a strongman to vote for – someone willing to assure them that, once he is elected, the smug bureaucrats, tricky lawyers, overpaid bond salesmen, and postmodernist professors will no longer be calling the shots … One thing that is very likely to happen is that the gains made in the past forty years by black and brown Americans, and by homosexuals, will be wiped out. Jocular contempt for women will come back into fashion … All the resentment which badly educated Americans feel about having their manners dictated to them by college graduates will find an outlet.[6]

The strongman in the second age calls the bluffs of the first: what counts is power; money is coterminous with the wealth it performs; women are reduced to vessels for a powerful man's desire, requiring no autonomous desire of their own, just as artifice can be intelligent precisely because intelligence is a pure quantity without reference – "I have a very good brain."[7] – rather than a point of ineluctable opacity. What is needed now, more than ever before, is a public trained in methods of reading-creation and the kind of discernment that is, at the same time, a fundamental exercise in self- and community formation. Such practices are, we feel, the only defence against the wholesale transformation of reality into a product-of-consumption that has given us our current political catastrophe.

This continuity between reading and creation is thus a call to educators, artists, intellectuals, and activists to come, to the best of their ability, out of the (frame)woodwork. Hence the WWCD motto (What Would Cervantes Do?) that we first proposed in *Medialogies*.[8] Having now witnessed years of the reality-transforming power of Trumpism, we insist it is time to double down on this ethical call. A vital pivot for understanding how Cervantinism, a philosophy we draw from the literature of Miguel de Cervantes, can be an answer to Trumpism – and yes, how humanists and literary scholars can come out of the (frame)woodwork, and how reading (interpreting) is also creating – is the one between lies and fiction. To read-create requires not distinguishing lies from facts, or even facts from alternative facts, but distinguishing lies from fiction, which is another word for the ability to read literature.

A lie is a false statement that the speaker knows is false, and with which he or she intends to deceive the receiver. Fiction, in contrast, is made of false statements that the receiver knows are false but listens to or reads anyway for the sake of entertainment. But fiction is also much more than that. For us to be satisfied and moved by fiction, we expect it to engage our emotions in ways that feel real without being real. We need to believe in the characters we are encountering at the same time that we know what we are experiencing is not happening, at least not now, and at least not to us.

When politicians lie – for instance, by asserting that one of the most closely monitored elections in history was "stolen," or that it would be beneficial, feasible, or constitutional to stop Muslims from entering the United States, or that the United States runs a trade deficit with Canada – they are empowering their lies with some of the belief that makes fiction so effective, but without nuancing them with the knowledge of their falsity that protects us from fiction's allures.

Cervantes wrote fiction at a time when institutions like the Hapsburg monarchy and the Inquisition were propagating beliefs that helped buttress the crumbling foundations of their power. These institutions fed an overtaxed peasantry the belief that their "old Christian blood" made them superior to neighbours of Jewish descent. Neighbours with Muslim origins were eventually exiled en masse in an act of almost apocalyptic scapegoating for Spain's financial and political woes.

Weaned from his own beliefs by personal disappointment, Cervantes put these sorts of big, public lies into his books, along with characters who believed in them and then suffered the consequences. The result was an imaginary world populated by characters who feel more real to us because they share our blindness and perplexity. But that world also helped train a slowly growing reading public in the subtle art of believing something while knowing it not to be true. By making characters his readers could believe in, he created an art form that helps clarify not what readers should believe but what they have been asked to believe and how their own desires are invested in the required show of belief.

Today's political class benefits from a public that has unlearned that art. Their lies have all the appeal of fiction, all the thrall of religious belief, without the clarifying knowledge of their falsity. Citizens treat politicians like beloved characters from a novel: Donald Trump is "real" because "he says what everyone is thinking"; he's "authentic."[9] In other words, Trump is a well-wrought fictional character that his public has forgotten, or simply no longer cares, is fictional. This is the most treacherous and effective kind of lie.

In *Medialogies*, we quoted the philosopher and mathematician Gottfried Leibniz's assertion that, if someone "reads more imaginative novels and listens to more strange stories, then he can be said to have more knowledge than the other, even if there is not a word of truth in all that he has seen and heard ... provided that he takes nothing in these stories and pictures to be true which really is not so."[10] Leibniz was writing from a vantage built on the lessons of Cervantes's fiction. Our point is that fiction, art, philosophy, and history have the power to inoculate our beliefs with the self-knowledge that keeps us from being enthralled, and with the self-difference that deflates the power of a rhetoric predicated on collapsing artifice and thing.

Thus, what we could call a kind of "fictional awareness" lies at the heart of our approach to media and is key to understanding how deploying what we call the "minor strategy" is essential for liberation politics.[11] Let's take the problem of the so-called bubble filter and its effect on contemporary political discourse. Given that social media sites and search engines are built on algorithms that mathematically reproduce and reinforce well-documented selection biases and sociodemographic sorting, how do we ensure some modicum of objective knowledge about the world?

Our answer lies in the importance that we grant to certain artistic and literary practices – specifically, in the ability of artists and writers (and, in some cases, philosophers, historians – in other words, humanists) to inculcate fictional awareness. Fictional awareness, a reading skill honed by engaging in representations that reframe and problematize how the media frame and position reality, primes us to be critical receptors of media in general, and to be attuned to how our own identities and desires are implicated in mediatic representations. The research indicates that, while enthralment to highly biased information sources is a trans-political phenomenon, today its incidence is notably higher on the right wing of the spectrum. While there is no doubt that left fundamentalism is real, our thesis is that it is mitigated by a closer alignment between left politics and the inculcation of the fictional awareness we are describing.

To put it more clearly, irony is somewhat more abundant across the left spectrum, even in commercially popular and available forms. Let's take the example of *Saturday Night Live*, clearly both an openly anti-Trump platform and a commercially successful, mainstream media presence. In its first episode after the 2016 election, following the famous cold open in which Kate McKinnon in character as Hillary Clinton sat at a piano and sang the recently deceased Leonard Cohen's ballad "Hallelujah," the team presented a sketch skewering Brooklyn's liberal bubble. "The Bubble is a planned community of like-minded free thinkers. And no one else," as one liberal says in the skit.[12] "We don't see color here. But we celebrate it," another happily spouts, as his Black counterpart looks on sceptically.[13] We don't claim it is easy to burst the bubble; but maintaining a balancing and relativizing awareness of how one's own take on the world is actively influenced by the media's framing function has considerable liberating potential.

One way of summarizing our argument on this point is that, in today's inflationary media age, the main danger is how our desires can be ensnared by discourses of authenticity, with the caveat that the craving for authenticity was itself already a dominant feature of our culture since the age of Romanticism. The difference we see between Romantic authenticity and our version in the second age of inflationary media is best captured by the contrast between two literary images. The hero of Goethe's 1774 international best-seller, *The Sorrows of*

Young Werther, is credited with being one of the key inspirational texts of the German Romantic movement that started to surge in the decades after that book's appearance. The suicide of the title character when faced with the impossibility of fulfilling his desire was seen as the acme of an authentic commitment to one's self, which paradoxically led to a rash of copycat suicides and the book's subsequent banishing in several European states.

We can contrast Goethe's young character with that of Almodóvar's brilliant transgender character La Agrado in his sublime *Todo sobre mi madre* (*All about My Mother*), who claims, in an impromptu monologue on stage, that a woman "es más auténtica cuanto más se parece a lo que ha soñado de sí misma" ("is more authentic the more she resembles what she has dreamed for herself").[14] By putting these words in the mouth of a trans woman, Almodóvar is, in essence, redefining authenticity for the second inflationary age. Very much in line with Judith Butler's theory of gender performativity, he sees the authentic self not as a buried essence to be searched for but as a self built over time, iterations, and countless citations.

To illustrate this point further, let us turn back to the argument of one of our last chapters in *Medialogies*, "Empire of Solitude."[15] There, we used the sociologist Mark Granovetter's theories about how individuals perform acts in groups that they would never do alone to point out that network relationships established in the virtual sphere may similarly lower thresholds when it comes to committing violent acts. Paradoxically, however, our argument is not that digital relationships themselves lower the threshold for committing violent acts, but that living online has contributed to a kind of widespread digital isolation, an empire of solitude, out of which islands of fundamentalist doctrine more easily emerge. Fundamentalism has the effect of lowering the threshold for violence because, once you experience yourself as having access to a singular, unmitigated truth that the majority of those around you deny, you are less likely to hold their lives as having the same value as your beliefs. Concomitantly, the empire of solitude is, we believe, a major contributor to the extraordinary rise of suicides, especially among teenage girls, since the emergence of social media in the United States, which many commentators have attributed at least in part to the decimation of traditional forms and feelings of community in the digital age.

In the current medialogy, as in the prior one, the media themselves can function both in a regulatory way, helping organize society hierarchically, and in a deterritorializing way, undermining hierarchical structures by allowing for horizontal connectivity and resistance. What is important to note, however, is that horizontal connectivity isn't necessarily or automatically beneficial or liberating. What counts in the new medialogy is the strategy. Fundamentalist islands of identity, like fake news sites and their support for an alt-fact politics, all depend on the major strategy: they posit the ultimate, unshakeable reality of their worldview. The minor strategy, which stays focused on the media themselves and not the reality behind them, is always self-reflexive and self-ironizing and is, hence, a defence both against top-down or "vertical" deployments of media as well as against the kind of internecine violence that is sustained and encouraged by digital isolation.

Today, digital technologies raise the stakes when they promise us our own personal alt-reality: the world the way we want it. We can take total editing control of our reality by erasing objects from our field of vision (diminished reality) or by adding desired elements (augmented reality). The self-identified "worldwide first real-time *Diminished Reality* system" ends its promotional video with the words "your imagination is the limit": "change your world the way *you* want," "now in real-time."[16] As Evgeny Morozov writes, "last year the futurist Ayesha Khanna even described smart contact lenses that could make homeless people disappear from view, 'enhancing our basic sense' and, undoubtedly, making our lives so much more enjoyable. In a way, this does solve the problem of homelessness – unless, of course, you happen to be a homeless person. In that case, Silicon Valley could hand you a pair of overpriced glasses that would make the streets feel like home."[17] To quote an ad for Samsung's fancy TV sets, "Reality. What a letdown.'"

Unfortunately, contact lenses that could make the homeless disappear would be redundant, strictly speaking, insofar as homeless people are already largely invisible in our media-framed reality – excepting in cases like that of San Francisco or Los Angeles, where their overwhelming numbers produce a political crisis that requires the attention of politicians and the public – as are so many other "unpleasant" or "inconvenient" realities. As for examples of augmented reality, we could cite Sean Spicer's presidential inauguration crowds or Kellyanne Conway's alternative facts, but we could also recall the selfie of the Syrian refugee that was pasted all over Facebook as the face of the perpetrator of multiple terrorist attacks. The refugee in question – his name is Anas Modamani – has literally (and tragically) become an alternative fact.[18]

So where would Cervantes go today in search for truth in our age of inflationary media and reality entitlement? If his prescient *Stage of Wonders* (*El retablo de las maravillas*) is any indication, he would surely tell us that the truth is to be found among the victims of our own stages of wonders: among the pieces of the world that are routinely removed from view by those diminished versions of reality that shield us from what we don't want to see – say, the homeless – and also, among the victims of our augmented reality – say, the Syrian refugee who has become an alternative fact solely to justify our own fears and to allow us to double down on our chosen reality.

2

The Imagination of the Possible

The very concept of reality seems to be at risk today; but if we look to the great Italian philosopher Gianni Vattimo, this may not be such a bad thing. While his book *Of Reality: The Purposes of Philosophy*, like much of his thought, is an extended interpretation and advocacy of the philosophy of Martin Heidegger, the philosophical leitmotif comes from Friedrich Nietzsche's dictum, "Against the positivist ... 'There are only facts' – I would say: no, facts are just what there aren't, there are only interpretations ... But that itself is an *interpretation*."[1]

This embrace of interpretation over facts would seem to play into popular characterizations of continental, "postmodern" philosophers. In a typically trenchant and funny moment in her recent review of Michael P. Lynch's book *The Internet of Us: Knowing More and Understanding Less in the Age of Big Data,* Harvard historian and *New Yorker* staff writer Jill Lepore cites an unidentified voice striving to be heard above the melee in one of the 2016 Republican presidential debates: "I tell the truth, I tell the truth."[2] To which Lepore dryly intones, "Eat your heart out, Samuel Beckett."[3]

Lepore's overall point in the review is to historicize Lynch's philosophical argument about the decline of standards of truth in the age of the Internet, by claiming, essentially, that a modern culture of basing truth claims on demonstrable evidence – namely, empiricism – arose out of a medieval culture of trial by ordeal, into which it is now showing every sign of having devolved once again. As she puts it, "for the length of the eighteenth century and much of the nineteenth, truth seemed more knowable, but after that it got murkier. Somewhere in the middle of the twentieth century, fundamentalism and postmodernism, the religious right and the academic left, met up: either the only truth is the truth of the divine or there is no truth; for both, empiricism is an error."[4]

Our admiration for Lepore's wit and writing skills notwithstanding, here we find she is rehearsing what has become an all-too-common misunderstanding in recent years: that an academic left under the moniker of postmodernism has given up on truth, and thus on any legitimate means of resisting or criticizing the "fact-free zone" of a resurgent, fundamentalist right wing. But the rampant rise of what Stephen Colbert deliciously called "truthiness" is not a result of too much academic postmodernism;[5] rather, it is an effect of the growth of fundamentalisms of all kinds. And it is emphatically not the case that the former somehow leads to the latter. On the contrary, there is and can be no epistemological equivalence between postmodernism and fundamentalism. The latter is a growth industry spurred on by the social fragmentation of modern life; the former (at least those proponents with whom we find ourselves most often in agreement) is a coherent philosophical position born of a thoroughgoing confrontation with the conditions of knowledge-production over time. The continued demonization of this term by a secular, educated public is largely due to a failure to grasp the nuances of what is, admittedly, a set of positions decidedly difficult to articulate, but that do not, it bears repeating, boil down to "anything goes."

At first glance, of course, Vattimo's evocation of Nietzsche is exactly the kind of assertion that would seem to support Lepore's and so many others' characterization of the academic left's denial of truth – let's face it, it sounds a lot like an embrace of Trumpian alternative facts! But this is only, as Vattimo argues, because we approach the problem from a pre-interpretation position based on a metaphysical model – namely, the presumption of what we call reality as external, independent of observation and interpretation. Only on the basis of this assumption (reality is something that exists independent of any and all interpretations of it) can Nietzsche's assertion become evidence of a denial of truth in the sense of "anything goes," for only on the basis of that assumption can truth be understood unproblematically in Thomas Aquinas's formulation as *adaequatio intellectus et rei*,[6] where "the things" stand in for that pristine state of independence of observation we are calling reality.[7]

One problem with this assumption, however, is that it can quite easily be shown to be a highly specific and historical interpretation. Different cultures and ages have had very different notions of such a reality. In Western culture, Plato's reality of ideal forms was already significantly modified by his student Aristotle, whose thought on the matter was transformed by Arabic translators and their Christian interpreters in the Middle Ages. Our own modern version of the notion of reality dates from only the beginning of the seventeenth century, when the concept entered the majority of vernacular European languages, and was eventually canonized when Descartes threw up the wall separating the thinking thing that he was from the extended world that he could come to know only through his senses.

As dominant conceptualizations of reality shifted over time, so too did the dominant mode of producing and consuming representations of these realities, following a trajectory that Jean Baudrillard traces from the purely self-evident approximation between representation and reality characteristic of pre-modernity, to the near identical replication of industrial modernity that "masks the *absence* of a profound reality," and to the postmodern, post-truth representation that now determines the reality that attends it ("it has no relation to any reality whatsoever").[8] These autonomous, xenocidal representations Baudrillard defines as simulacra and the form of truth that arises from them must be understood entirely as the result of communicative choices, choices handled effectively, though without even much art, by L. Ron Hubbard, Trump, and other simulators-in-chief.

Indeed, Baudrillard has been anointed "Prophet of Fake News" for his prescience in understanding the potential of mass media to create artificial realities that perpetuate themselves through reader internalization and relay, experiences categorized by social media technicians as "engagement."[9] As we engage more and more with media that appear to satisfy our own understanding of the reality they had already generated for us, the haptic pings of media events delivered by "friends," "followers" and "content creators," now thirty years after Baudrillard's arguments, incontrovertibly engage us into performing our own derivative simulacra "IRL." At no point in modern US history was this any clearer than during the weeks-long explosive multiplatform production of an undulating simulacrum – the "big lie" that Trump won the 2020 US election, through a byzantine conspiracy of voter fraud never documented outside the conspiracy[10] – leading a cult of insurrectionists to break into the Capitol, acting on their belief in Trump's manufactured reality, even when Trump had forewarned them of this very manufacture weeks before voting began.

So, while it is indeed common sense to assume that there is such a thing as reality and that it exists independently of our interpretations, that is, in fact, all it is: a common *sense*, namely, meaning, or interpretation, shared uncritically by most of us, but one that is neither necessary nor, it turns out, particularly useful to anyone but those who have a vested interest in *not* thinking critically, in *not* changing how things are.

Let's call the mode of thinking and talking about the world that assumes an interpretation-independent reality "reality-talk." Coming back to Lepore's appraisal of the current messy state of "truth" in political discourse, we can find an almost constant chatter today in the mode of reality-talk, even – and often – from those who would like to advocate change, and those who believe they are staving off the advance of fundamentalisms that are demonstrably noxious for individual and collective freedoms.

Lepore tries to tease out what might or might not be new about the current slipperiness of truth in politics: "also newish is the rhetoric of unreality, the insistence, chiefly by Democrats, that some politicians are incapable of perceiving the truth because they have an epistemological deficit: they no longer believe in evidence, or even in objective reality."[11] As she goes on to show, this stance became part of candidate Hillary Clinton's campaign in the form of an ad titled "Stand for Reality."[12]

It's possible that the smoking gun for the (relative) left in American politics was the 2004 Ron Suskind interview with Karl Rove cited above, in which Rove ridiculed Suskind for belonging to the "reality-based community," whose members "believe that solutions emerge from the judicious study of discernible reality," whereas he and other members of the Bush administration were always a step ahead, defining what that reality looked like. While the (relative) left has embraced this moniker and identity, however, it is questionable if reality-talk gives them any advantage. Quite possibly, Rove was right in his assessment: discernable reality is rather easy to manufacture, which is why it is far from a safe ground on which to build one's political message.

In brief, reality-talk isn't politically useful for those motivated to alter a political situation, because it just plays into the hands of the fundamentalists. Today, everyone always claims their views are reality-based. But not only is reality-talk not politically useful for critical discourse, it also actively supports the status quo and its fundamentalist avatars, and it does so by creating an implicit moral equivalency between political positions that reflects, effectively, the very kind of relativism that reality-talk seems to think it is opposing.

To make this point clear, let us take the example of an opinion piece one of us published in the *New York Times* that managed to incite the wrath both of liberals and the anti-immigrant right. The piece discussed a minor legal case in Austria in which a female schoolteacher was suing a Muslim man for refusing to shake her hand. Some commentators, believing that this piece was a defence of the man's actions (it was not, but reading for nuance is a lost art these days) lambasted the author for inconsistency in expecting Westerners to adapt to Muslim cultural norms when in a Muslim country, and yet supporting Muslims' right to flout Western cultural norms when in a non-Muslim country. What these critics fail to realize is that it is precisely their position that depends on a kind of moral equivalency that we are condemning here. If we were to adhere to fundamentalist norms while visiting a fundamentalist country, we might do so out of fear of bodily harm, but we would never claim or believe that our liberal, ethical commitments – to the equality of women, the inalienable nature of basic human rights, the freedom of political expression – are in any way interchangeable with a culture that refuses or actively represses those rights.

The argument to expand rather than contract the sphere of tolerance around certain behaviours, even if they are offensive to Western liberal commitments, is based on the passionately held belief that the "toleration" inherent in the liberal philosophical tradition is not simply one among many positions from which one can choose, but is, rather, *better* than its fundamentalist alternatives. This position is fully ethnocentric in Richard Rorty's sense – namely, that one's beliefs are unavoidably ethnocentric, and one can either be aware of that or ignore it, but to do the latter can blind individuals to the effects of their ethnocentrism on the world. Our argument to be tolerant of the visitors' expression of their belief system is thus not based on an each-to-their-own-reality, or an anything-goes mentality, but rather on an ethical commitment to the notions of freedom that underlie our own political and philosophical tradition. In contrast, when we criticize societies that try to defend the liberal tradition by limiting the expression of illiberal beliefs, we are targeting a blind ethnocentrism in which we import into our model of liberal freedoms a very specific ethnic model of what those freedoms look like.

This position is a solid illustration of why Gianni Vattimo's consistent adherence to Nietzsche's dictum that "there are no facts, only interpretations, ... and this too is an interpretation" is not only *not* a statement of anything-goes relativism, but a critique of the relativism that currently goes under the name of realism.[13] To live by this motto requires that we renounce the crutch of objective reality when justifying our arguments and political positions. Instead, it forces us to examine the place of enunciation of our positions, and those of our opponents. Vattimo's "nihilism," which has accepted fully the consequences of "and this too is an interpretation," thus corresponds to the position that the French psychoanalyst Jacques Lacan called the "not-all" – namely, the position from which no totalizing statements of truth can be made, but which also does not insist on surreptitiously excepting itself from the truth judgments that it does make. As Lacan once playfully insisted, "I always speak the truth. Not the whole truth, because there's no way, to say it all. Saying it all is literally impossible."[14]

Lepore ends her piece by delimiting two options for "people who care about civil society": "find some epistemic principles other than empiricism on which everyone can agree or else find some method other than reason with which to defend empiricism."[15] Agreeing with Lynch that the former is likely impossible, she paraphrases his argument that the "best defense of reason is a common practical and ethical commitment," which she interprets as popular sovereignty.[16]

As Vattimo shows us, though, this defence of reason is already inherent in the hermeneutic model that Lepore and others associate with postmodernism. The academic left was never really at odds with empiricism, and certainly not in the way the academic middle has tended to characterize it. A good chunk of Vattimo's *Of Reality* is dedicated to demonstrating that empiricism and the scientific method – the way in which they are in fact practised, as opposed to theorized – are in no way opposed to Vattimo's "weak thought" and in many ways are illustrative of it.[17] Indeed, to a certain extent, hermeneutics, at least a thoroughgoing hermeneutics of the sort advocated and practised by Vattimo, is nothing other than a highly self-aware empiricism.

Indeed, just as reality-talk is strikingly useless for political progress and, indeed, is a useful tool only for those seeking to slow or stop such progress, reality-talk also has no conceivable use for science, whose interest is, or should be, advancing knowledge and articulating the evidence with which to make factually supported claims, not defending some overarching and vague entity called *reality*. The very notion of reality can get in the way of science's drive to solve problems, to answer tricky questions. As the famous quantum physicist John Wheeler once put it, "Useful as it is under everyday circumstances to say that the world exists 'out there' independent of us, that view can no longer be upheld."[18]

Vattimo's point, of course, is that reality-talk is not useful, at least not for him or anyone else who is committed to a philosophy that strives to improve the world and its social relations, in contrast to those who simply support the world in its present form. To reinforce this point, let us turn to a concept Vattimo again draws from Heidegger, which has been at the core of both his and Santiago Zabala's recent interventions: *Notlosigkeit* (lack of emergency).[19]

According to Vattimo, the lack of emergency is as much a condition of our current times as is the hermeneutic *koiné*, as he calls it, whereby everyone is entitled to their own reality, a common sense that emerges from a failure to grasp the essentially historical nature of how each and every one of us is projected into a given culture and tradition – that is, how we find ourselves thrown into space and time and caught up in the project that is our life, the contours of which are understandable only within a tradition, the set of values, expectations, and meanings that a given community brings to bear at a given moment in time. Lacking or rejecting this insight is what generates the elision between the academic left and the fundamentalist right, the illusion that we are all awash in the same epistemic quandary. Indeed, the fragmentation of worldviews by the media and the diminution of any sense of common ground have fuelled the rise of fundamentalism; the philosophical positions often labelled as postmodernist are not a symptom of this, but rather a tool to combat it.

Opposing these positions are a flattened and flattening hermeneutic *koiné* and the reality-talk that promotes moral equivalencies between an individual's ethical commitments and noxious strains of fundamentalism; and both contribute to the implicit quietism of *the lack of emergency*. As Vattimo argues, it's not that we lack events. The world is full of events. Indeed, our twenty-four-hour news cycle perpetuates a near constant vigilance with respect to the next event, crisis, emergency. As aware as we like to think we are of the world, we are put to shame by our children's immediate knowledge of the most recent event in world politics, clued in as they are by their smartphones' instant and always urgent updates concerning the state of the world. But this constant stream of updates masks a profound "resignation ..., one that remains undisturbed even when there is an economic crisis like the one we are experiencing."[20]

Here is Vattimo:

> The absence of emergency is perhaps the most complete form of the forgetting of Being that belongs to metaphysics. That today nothing might happen seems difficult to believe. And yet even the big crises that we have lived through and that we continue to live through do not give rise to a "paradigmatic" novelty in the sociopolitical sense. September 11? It only gave the United States more reason to intensify its various forms of control, but it did not give the country reasons for any transformation of "regime."[21]

If fidelity to reality offers nothing to progress, nothing to scientific knowledge, nothing to the political improvement of our world, but instead acts only as a force for quietism, for repressing or discouraging an active participation in the world, then perhaps its time is up. Could it be, as Vattimo claims, that the real calling of philosophy, like that of science (and we would add fiction – at least in its Cervantine variety), is not the depiction or representation of reality but its dissolution? Shouldn't philosophy, fiction, and cultural criticism, like science, like politics, strive for something other than what presents itself as already the case? Should they not be driven by the imagination of the possible instead of the assumption of the real?

3

The Art of the Real

On 9 January 2017, God TV aired a documentary titled *Apocalypse and the End Times*, in which host Paul McGuire interviewed author, radio personality, and public speaker Bill Salus, from the Prophecy Depot Ministries, about his 2016 book *The Now Prophecies: Disaster in Iran, Destruction of Damascus, Decline of America, the Final Arab-Israeli War*. During the course of the interview, Salus repeatedly claimed that the biblical prophecies associated with the Apocalypse are fast converging in our own time. His conclusion is that all the signs point to the fact that we are living "in the end times."[1] The homepage of the Prophecy Depot Ministries from around the same time showed that Salus was far from done trumpeting (and profiting from) the imminent end of the world:

> ALERT: the APOCALYPSE has ARRIVED! NOW AVAILABLE: Apocalypse Road, Revelation for the Final Generation. Enjoy a thrilling Novel and a Bible commentary at the same time. If you enjoyed the Left Behind books, you will appreciate the biblical explanations provided in *Apocalypse Road* ...
> Millions of Christians disappeared, apparitions of the Virgin Mary have reappeared, and meanwhile the Antichrist begins his beastly career ...
> ARE YOU AND YOUR FAMILY PREPARED FOR THE APOCALYPSE? CLICK HERE FOR MORE INFORMATION.[2]

Whether we consider the religious media markets (Christian and otherwise), or the secular zombie mythology that fills an endless stream of best-selling novels, survival manuals, blockbuster films, and wildly popular television shows like *The Walking Dead*, there is no doubt that the Apocalypse is big business today. But the 2016 presidential election in the United States suggests that the Apocalypse is also big politics. As noted by a wide cross-section of national and international news-media commentators, the Donald Trump presidential campaign fed on and contributed to the normalization of a form of paranoid speech of apocalyptic overtones that used to be thought of as fringe politics attributable to the radical right in Europe and the United States. Indeed, the Trump phenomenon may be described most accurately as the political coming out and the converging of fringe and mainstream cultural and ideological apocalypticisms.

Referring to the highly publicized speech of then nominee Trump at the Republican National Convention in Cleveland in 2016, the editorial board of the *Washington Post* published an opinion piece aptly titled "Donald Trump: The Candidate of the Apocalypse," stating that Trump exploited the public's fears and anxieties as he "took real challenges and recast them in terms that were not only exaggerated but also apocalyptic."[3] While the *Post* editorial reflected the reaction of much of the mainstream media to Trump's shocking (yet largely predictable) speech, progressive news outlets were even more attuned to his apocalyptic rhetoric. A good example would be the article "Trump's Apocalyptic Message: Biblical Prophecy, Survivalist Ideologue and Racist Conspiracies in One Package," published by John Feffer in the online news service AlterNet:

> The world according to Donald Trump is very dark indeed. The American economy has tanked. Mexico has sent a horde of criminals over the border to steal jobs and rape women. The Islamic State, cofounded by Barack Obama and Hillary Clinton, is taking over the globe. "Our country is going to hell," he declared during the Republican primaries. It's "like medieval times," he suggested during the second presidential debate. "We haven't seen anything like this, the carnage all over the world." For Trump, it's not morning in America, it's just a few seconds before midnight on the doomsday clock.[4]

He took this view straight into the presidency, trumpeting it for the world to hear in one of the darkest, most fear-mongering inaugural addresses ever given. For many in this country and around the world, that speech will be remembered for the line "this American carnage stops right here!"[5]

Whether or not "medieval times" might offer a fair historical parallel to our own troubled present in terms of the "carnage all over the world," what we can say is that, in the context of Trump's political rhetoric, the allusion to "medieval times" was meant to evoke images of widespread instability, violence, and chaos, a hellish present-future for the United States, and indeed the whole world, from which only his presidency could save us. This is, of course, a familiar rhetorical trick. As specialists of the early modern period, we can think of rhetorical parallels in the political culture of Habsburg Spain, none more fitting perhaps than the baroque writings of seventeenth-century royal theologian Cristóbal Lozano (1609–67). His dramatic description of the fall of Christian Spain (the medieval Visigoth kingdom) to hordes of Muslim barbarians in the year 711 is just as rich in apocalyptic imagery: "quedó España perdida, despobladas sus ciudades, cautivos sus hijos, saqueadas sus riquezas, ... la fe cristiana extinguida, muertos sus ministros, deshechos sus santuarios, derribadas sus iglesias ... ¡La pluma tropieza en tanto cuerpo difunto como puebla la campaña!" ("Spain was lost, its cities depopulated, its children captive, its riches looted, ... the Christian faith extinguished, its ministers dead, its sanctuaries destroyed, its churches in ruins ... The pen stumbles upon the countless corpses left on the battlefield!").[6]

In Lozano's version of history, the supposed darkness of medieval times would have plagued Spain well beyond the Christian conquest of Granada of 1492 – which had marked the culmination of the Spanish Reconquista – stretching into the early seventeenth century, when Phillip III decreed the expulsion of the Moriscos. But even the mass deportation of hundreds of thousands of *cristianos nuevos* (every man, woman, and child suspected of Muslim ancestry) that took place between 1609 and 1614 would have to be followed by the proper cultural cleansing needed to ensure the nation's safety. As one of us noted previously in *Baroque Horrors*, even the remnants of the un-Christian past needed to be locked away behind impenetrable walls to prevent the advent of a new Dark Age. This is ultimately the point of Lozano's baroque updating of the legends of the cave of Toledo in *The Cave of Hercules* (*La cueva de Hércules*) and other stories included in *The New Monarchs of Toledo* and *David Persecuted* (available today in the collection *Historias y leyendas*).

Lozano's creative mixture of spiced-up storytelling, dire warnings, apocalypticism, and biblical commentary may be said to have anticipated the rhetorical flair of Bill Salus and other popular Christian writers, radio hosts, and televangelists, particularly in their familiar recycling of Old Testament motifs. Thus, when Jerry Falwell and Pat Robertson reworked the Old Testament logic of divine punishment in *The 700 Club*, the flagship television program of the Christian Broadcasting Network, to explain the tragedy of 9/11 as America's punishment for its many sins – among them the nation's tolerance of abortionists, homosexuals, feminists, and liberals – these present-day leaders of the Christian right were inadvertently taking a page from Lozano's dramatic account of the destruction of Spain at the hands of Muslim terrorists as a punishment for the moral failings of the Visigoths: "Con mil estragos de religión y costumbres se hallaba el imperio gótico, cerca de los años de setecientos y once ...: esto fué la causa que España se perdiese" ("The Visigoth Empire was plagued by the corruption of religious values and behaviour in the years preceding 711 ...: this is what caused the loss of Spain").[7]

Similarly, we can't help but hear echoes of the political rhetoric that justified the Habsburgs' campaigns of racial cleansing in Trump's calls for mass deportations, anti-Muslim immigration laws, Muslim-American registries, and his (largely unfulfilled) promise to build a massive wall along the US southern border to prevent Mexicans from stealing "our" jobs, raping "our" women, and destroying "our" way of life (where the "our" clearly indicates that his implicit audience is largely white and male). At least at the rhetorical level, Trump's calls for (and commitment to) an effort of national resurgence, "Make America Great Again," share in the logic of religious and cultural fundamentalism that drove the monarchical cause of national restitution in imperial Spain. As Robert Tate noted in his seminal article "Mythology in the Spanish Historiography of the Middle Ages and the Renaissance," the recovery of Spain, which royal chroniclers proclaimed with the phrase *Hispania tota sibi restituta est* (All Spain is restored to herself), was entangled in an ideology of national purification coded as a defence against external encroachments.[8]

On the other hand, those who have read *Trump: The Art of the Deal* might be inclined to believe that the real estate mogul and reality TV star was simply trafficking in fear, anti-immigrant sentiments, and racially tinged fantasies of national superiority in the same way that his business persona admittedly traded in misrepresentation and hyperbole in playing to the fantasies of potential clients. As he asserts in chapter 2 of *The Art of the Deal*, aptly titled "Trump Cards: The Elements of the Deal," "I play to people's fantasies. People may not always think big themselves, but they can still get very excited about those who do. That's why a little hyperbole never hurts. People want to believe that something is the biggest and the greatest and the most spectacular. I call it truthful hyperbole. It's an innocent form of exaggeration – and a very effective form of promotion."[9]

Indeed, based on his frequent use of hyperbole and misrepresentation, it would seem that Trump recycled his businessman's "Trump cards" for his political campaign; and he did not cease trying to use them as president or, ultimately, as losing presidential candidate either, no matter how much they flew in the face of reported facts. Of course, in the political arena, this form of self-serving hyperbole and the manipulation of perceptions that plays to people's fantasies and prejudices have a long and distinguished history of tragic success. The politicians and public figures who are known to have employed such techniques are commonly referred to as demagogues, a term defined by the *Oxford English Dictionary* as a "leader of a popular faction, or of the mob; a political agitator who appeals to the passions and prejudices of the mob in order to obtain power or further his own interests; an unprincipled or factious popular orator."[10]

One of the key arts of the present-day demagogue is the manipulation of the press. Here's Trump again, this time discussing his handling of the press:

> One thing I've learned about the press is that they're always hungry for a good story, and the more sensational the better. It's in the nature of the job, and I understand that. The point is that if you are a little different, or a little outrageous, or if you do things that are bold or controversial, the press is going to write about you. I've always done things a little differently, I don't mind controversy, and ... got a lot of attention, and that alone creates value.[11]

Trump's self-promoting confessions read as a how-to manual for today's business leaders in the same way that such works as Baldassarre Castiglione's *Book of the Courtier* (*Libro del Cortegiano*) (1528) and Baltasar Gracián's *Pocket Oracle and Art of Prudence* (*Oráculo manual y arte de prudencia*) (1647) were meant to serve as practical guides for the power elites of their age. The baroque lessons in worldly wisdom that fill the pages of Gracián's books, especially his best-known work *Pocket Oracle and Art of Prudence*, are at times virtually indistinguishable from Trump's own recommendations in *The Art of the Deal*. The self-promoting businessman and the Jesuit moralist draw similar conclusions as they take stock of the crucial importance of the public's perception, although Gracián's thinking is much more subtle and his style eminently more sophisticated than that of the capitalist self-promoter. They both focus on the need to embellish reality and manipulate appearances to serve one's self-interest and bend the will of others. This is what Gracián calls the crown jewel of practical wisdom, "el Saber coronado."[12] He even makes the case that obeying one's self-interest, or *conveniencia*, is a virtue, and that it is a sin to go against it.[13]

Both Trump and Gracián see the world as public theatre and man's life as a game of thrones. In talking about his life-long pursuit of success, Trump makes an interesting confession: "money was never a big motivation for me, except as a way to keep score. The real excitement is playing the game."[14] Here, we are reminded of the confessions of the fictional president played by Kevin Spacey in the Netflix series *House of Cards*, when he tells his audience in one of his characteristic asides that he has no respect for those who are motivated simply by money: the real prize of the game is power. This is also the end goal of the practical wisdom that Gracián was offering to the elites of his time, power over hearts: "Es gran victoria coger los corazones ..., nacida del genio superior y ayudada de los méritos" ("it is a great victory, that of capturing hearts ..., born of the superior genius with the assistance of his merits").[15] And again: "Poco es conquistar el entendimiento si no se gana la voluntad ... Conseguir esta gracia universal, algo tiene de estrella; lo más, de diligencia propia" ("Conquering minds has little value if wills are not subjugated ... This universal grace can be achieved through good fortune, but most of all through personal diligence").[16]

Regarding the subject of apocalypticism, Gracián's view of the present state of the world is just as dark as Trump's. He draws on the traditional baroque motif of the topsy-turvy world, *el mundo trabucado*, to paint his doomsday picture of the "estado del siglo" ("state of the century"), a scene of irredeemable chaos, with hordes of hyenas standing atop deserted dunghills and all manner of beasts invading the cities.[17] Like many other baroque writers, Gracián attributes the sorry state of Spain to the erosion of traditional social barriers and the shuffling of estates: "barajados los estados, metiéndose los del uno en el otro, saltando cada uno de su coro y hablando todos de lo que menos entienden" ("shuffled social stations, infringing those of one estate into the other, [people] exceeding the limits of their stations and speaking of what they do not understand").[18] But Gracián does not seem interested in proposing political solutions, unlike the aspiring reformers known as *arbitristas*, or even reactionary writers such as Francisco de Quevedo, who celebrated the old glories of Spain while lamenting the ruins of the present, as in his well-known verses: "Miré los muros de la patria mía,/si un tiempo fuertes, ya desmoronados,/de la carrera de la edad cansados,/por quien caduca ya su valentía" ("I looked upon the walls of my fatherland,/strong in their time, now in ruins,/eroded by the passing of time,/their bravery expired").[19] In fact, Gracián detests the *arbitristas* and political reformers; he refers to them as "vulgo en corrillos" ("huddling rubble"). His recommendation for the man of substance is not to attempt to change the world, no matter its present estate of devastation and decay, but to retool and adapt in order to thrive in it, making judicious use of the political arts of concealment, dissimulation, deception, and manipulation.[20]

While the Jesuit used the familiar motifs of the world upside-down and the age of decay to set the stage for his defence of cynical reason, other theologians struggled with what they saw as unmistakable signs of moral bankruptcy and impending doom: rampant corruption, widespread violence and devastation, the absence of charitable souls and basic human empathy, and the deepening crisis of the Christian faith. Even the once idealistic missionaries in the Americas who had been intent on (re)building the Christian utopia in the New World would be overcome by a tragic sense of disillusion as a result of witnessing "the destruction of the Indies," as Bartolomé de Las Casas had candidly called it in the title of his well-known denunciation of colonial devastation in the Americas.[21]

As Fernando Rodríguez de la Flor explains in his landmark article "Sacrificial Politics in the Spanish Colonies," the Jesuits had supplied "the court, as well as the military and administrative establishment of the colonies, with the necessary justification for the 'politics of dissimulation' embraced by the discourse of power" but, "once the possibility of 'historical intervention' has failed, revealing the demoniacal face of colonization[,] ... the monstrous political body created by the imperial power ... begins to be visualized – dreadfully so – as a land 'uninhabited by God.'"[22] De la Flor also notes that, in the context of the Americas, the scandal of colonial slavery would come be seen as the ultimate failure of the Christian ethos and the final proof of the moral bankruptcy of the Spanish Empire. These tragic revelations will be "sublimated, in missionary discourse, in a type of sinister allegorical story about a 'fallen' world devoid of the possibility of redemption in which a humanity deprived of utopias and ideals of self-fulfillment simply awaits the end of all suffering."[23]

In the eyes of such disillusioned missionaries as Jerónimo de Mendieta, the Americas had become a valley of tears and a new devastated Jerusalem. As he writes in his *Historia eclesiástica indiana*:

> Más como yo ... haya visto los adversos fines en que todo esto ha venido a parar, ... no solo no puedo ofrecerle cántico de alabanza por fin de mi Historia, más antes (si para componer endechas tuviera gracia) me venía muy a pelo asentarme con Jeremías sobre nuestra Indiana iglesia, y con lágrimas, sospiros y voces que llegaran al cielo (como él hacía sobre la destruida ciudad de Jerusalem), lamentarla y plañirla, recontando su miserable caída y gran desventura.
>
> (And yet, since I, having enjoyed – thanks to the divine grace – a good portion of these prosperous beginnings, have seen the adverse ending to which everything has come, not only can I not offer a song of praise at the end of my story but would much rather – had I the grace to compose a lament – sit down with Jeremiah, mourning our Indian Church with tears, sighs, and screams so as to reach the Heavens – as he did over the destroyed city of Jerusalem – recounting its miserable fall and great misfortune.)[24]

The apocalyptic accents of Mendieta's *Historia* and the confessional writings of other disillusioned missionaries such as Gregorio de Matos, known as the first eremite in the Americas, have little or nothing to do with the rhetorical apocalypticism of royal theologian Cristóbal Lozano and the Jesuit moralist Baltasar Gracián, or the end-times talk of Christian leaders such as Bill Salus, Jerry Falwell, and Pat Robertson in our times. The apocalyptic imagery that we see in the writings of de Matos and Mendieta springs from their painful coming to terms with the contradictions of evangelical reason and their first-hand experience of colonial devastation. Unlike the type of doomsday rhetoric that blames racial, religious, cultural, or social others for the decline of the nation and/or the imminent end of the world, their apocalypticism may be considered a redemptive *mea culpa* as much as a way of speaking truth to power, a last-resort denunciation of colonial violence. Their tragic voices urge us today, just as they did in their own age, to look in the mirror as we search for the lurking horsemen of the Apocalypse.

4

The Apocalypse Will Not Be Televised!

While we may speculate about the reasons behind the cultural obsession with the Apocalypse in different time periods, including the baroque age of disillusionment at the dawn of modernity and our own age of the "post" (postmodern, post-human, post-truth), what the literature suggests – then as well as now – is that apocalypticism is a *rhetoric of warning* and *a call to action*, to get busy averting the impending disaster or preparing for its aftermath. But as we have seen, those warnings and urgent calls diverge vastly, even in the relatively stifling ideological environment of imperial Spain. The signs may point to an outside threat, which is why we would need to strengthen our borders and beef up our military, even engage in pre-emptive war; or they may shine a light on the moral failings of our neighbours, the sins of our fathers, or the consequences of our own lifestyle. Conversely, the horsemen of the Apocalypse may look like alien invaders, Muslim terrorists, biblical plagues, radiation leaks, planetary chemical saturation, or genetic modifications; they might even look like President Obama or President Trump, depending on which side of the political spectrum you find yourself.

To help us make this point, readers might run a couple of Internet searches pairing terms like "apocalypse" or "end-times" with the word "genetic," for example, or the name "Trump." For our part, on the subject of genetics, we quickly found three short pieces making diametrically opposed claims. The first draws on biblical thought: "the Bible describes Noah as being perfect in his generations, and that his was the only family saved indicates that Noah's bloodline hadn't been contaminated by the genetic tinkering and that his was perhaps the only pure human strain left from which a Redeemer could come."[1]

The second piece, from a Christian blog called *The End Time*, entitled "Genetic Modification and Dinosaurs," concludes:

> Having failed to corrupt man through the direct tactic of genetic manipulation from marriages of themselves to daughters of men, … they now pollute the food we eat, embarking on an indirect method to corrupt us. Have you ever wondered why we are experiencing the ever-earlier onset of puberty? … Or why we're all huge? … Or why suddenly, celiac disease has sprouted up …? Or why food has to be genetically modified in the first place?[2]

The next quote is from a piece published on the website KQED *Science Quest*, with the title "Explosive Hypothesis about Humans' Lack of Genetic Diversity":

> Genetically, we're all pretty much the same. A massive volcanic eruption 75,000 years ago may be why. Last blog I talked about how East Africans are genetically more diverse than Asians. Who are generally more diverse than Native Americans … Species are in danger long after they go through a bottleneck. They have a pretty limited gene pool which means they may not be particularly healthy and are in danger of being wiped out by, for example, a single disease.[3]

Clearly the authors of the items quoted above hold very different assumptions about the kinds of potentially catastrophic genetic dangers that we are (and have been) facing. While the first two pieces warn against genetic contamination attributable to diabolical forces, the third makes the point that the danger of mass extinction lies in our lack of genetic diversity. The author of the first piece would seem to advocate for the preservation of our genealogical and genetic integrity so we can be as pure as Noah's generation; by contrast, the author of the third suggests that we should strive to diversify and muddle our genetic pool, to be more like our East African neighbours. We could certainly imagine very distinct – possibly opposing – ideological projects that might be conceived as a response to such apocalyptic warnings.

As for the pairing of Trump with the keyword "apocalypse" in a Google search, we came across a good number of entries referencing

Trump's tough talk (some call it honest) about the sorry state of the Union and the need for a full-on campaign of national restoration, as well as journalistic articles dealing with Trump's apocalyptic rhetoric; but we also landed in a progressive Trump Apocalypse Watch site, which kept track of his controversial would-be cabinet appointees.[4] Moreover, we found several pieces, from both legitimate journalists and known disinformation engines, that pointed to Donald Trump himself as the ultimate sign of the impending doom and the primary agent of the Apocalypse, citing, for instance, the frequency of the appearance of the number 666 in relation to Trump.[5]

So what should we do with (and about) the seemingly unprecedented spike in apocalyptic rhetoric and the wave of demagoguery that accompanies it? In *Medialogies*, we argue that apocalypticism is in part a result of the kind of disinformation overload that plagues our media culture, as it did that of the baroque. As noted in chapter 1, we refer to both these historical periods as ages of inflationary media, which is why we look at the Spanish baroque in search of ways of dealing with the practical consequences of living in the end-times. Our takeaway is that we need to relearn, not so much the art of the deal, but the art of the real – that is, the art of "reading reality" – for, in the context of our vast misinformation overload, "reality literacy" may prove to be the true art of worldly wisdom. We look back to the fictional work of Cervantes, and forward to the comedic craft of Colbert, both of whom we consider supremely versed in the art of reality literacy.

There are others, of course. The video for rapper Kendrick Lamar's "Humble" has rightfully drawn a great deal of critical praise. In it, he raps, "I'm so fuckin' sick and tired of the Photoshop/Show me somethin' natural like afro on Richard Pryor/Show me somethin' natural like ass with some stretchmarks," against images of a woman's buttocks, a model, and his own face being shown in a split screen with and without photoshopping.[6] The theme continues throughout the video, with camera movements that alternately conceal and reveal the framing strategies that permit "reality" to be perceived or constructed in certain ways. Shots of Lamar teeing off with a golf club quickly change perspective to show him standing on the wreck of a car in the dystopic setting of LA's giant run-off canals.

The take of such a video is that of what we call a defender-of-being's approach to reading reality. Defenders of being recognize that what is at stake in reading reality is clarifying or revealing the multiple and embedded interpretations within which reality always appears. It means focusing on the *cui bono* of those interpretations instead of claiming to present reality as unadulterated. Such an approach to apocalyptic themes in general can be formulated as "the Apocalypse will not be televised," in a riff on the 1970 spoken-word classic by Gil Scott-Heron, "The Revolution Will Not Be Televised." That song begins with the famous lines:

> You will not be able to stay home, brother.
> You will not be able to plug in, turn on and cop out.
> You will not be able to lose yourself on scag and
> skip out for beer during commercials because
> The revolution will not be televised.[7]

Scott-Heron's song is primarily a call to arms against Black oppression coupled with a cautionary alert that the media's "culture industry" is constantly working to sap attention from the proper focus of political struggle. As he goes on to recite,

> The revolution will not give your mouth sex appeal.
> The revolution will not get rid of the nubs.
> The revolution will not make you look five pounds thinner.
> The revolution will not be televised, brother.[8]

The lyrics suggest that "the revolution" is to be equated with all that underlies the distractions of the televised, media world. Especially important for our current medialogical climate, however, is a later line that states "There will be no pictures of pigs shooting down brothers/on the instant replay," since, of course, something like this – namely, cellphone videos recording the repeated slaughter of young Black men by police officers – is exactly what has permitted the rise of such revolutionary social justice movements as Black Lives Matter.[9]

By nature of the very flexibility built into today's medialogy, our contemporary manifestation of the media framing that Scott-Heron depicts in his lyrics thus wraps itself around and incorporates such protest. If the new technologies allow for the "televisation" of what could not be seen before, the medialogy must find a way to render that invisible as well – or, if not invisible, then irrelevant. This it does by cultivating a general apocalyptic sensibility according to which Western civilization is under siege by the forces of chaos – terrorists,

Black protesters, refugees. "Our" reality is white, smooth, clean, and well-mannered. "They" – dirty, mostly Black or brown, speaking incomprehensible languages and undermining our civic institutions – threaten that reality with destruction.

The Apocalypse is, in this way, a made-for-television fantasy, and a verifiable and ultimately containable threat. It is personified by the brown/Black zombie hordes living outside the walled-off, hypergentrified urban centre in George Romero's *Land of the Dead*, seen not through that slyly subversive film, but rather through the walled-off and well-heeled citizens of a very real hypergentrified Manhattan today, where crime is at a historic low precisely because poverty – along with graffiti, broken windows, and a whole lot of Black and brown people – has been photoshopped and/or stop-and-frisked right out of the picture.

In other words, what this fantasy version of the Apocalypse elides is precisely the apocalypse that won't be televised, the one that the very policies supported and enacted by many of today's establishment politicians hasten along. The Trump administration turned out to be the *ad absurdum* of the externalizing logic of today's medialogy, by which the coherence of the fantasy depends on the exclusion of disruptive matter, whose exclusion in turn exacerbates the very conditions that lead people to cling in fear to the fictions holding that fantasy together. Just take the example of coal: surrounded by beaming coal miners, Trump happily rolled back Obama-era executive orders intended to reduce American reliance on coal. This rollback would have no effect on coal-mining jobs, which already accounted for fewer than 5 per cent of West Virginia jobs prior to the regulations because of innovations in the industry and competition from other fossil fuels and renewable energies. But the rollback, along with the general policy of non-compliance toward and abandonment of US support of international climate treaties, threatened to exacerbate global warming trends. This, in turn, will increase demand around the world for renewable energy sources, which will further undermine the very livelihood those smiling faces are hoping to retrieve.

While the real Apocalypse is not being televised, the medialogical disconnect between framed and real apocalypses is being registered in another subgenre of television, one that resonates closely with the fake-news plague of the past several years. In a wide range of shows such as *Legion*, *Westworld*, and *Mr. Robot*, the inability to tell the difference between framed reality and some external, possibly real, world is the entire point of the show. As the *New York Times*'s television critic James Poniewozik writes in a review of these shows, "there is undoubtedly something timely about stories in which there's no stable baseline of agreed-on reality."[10] Poniewozik goes on to mention "a pair of spectacles that allow [a character from *Legion*] to see through a mental projection created by the show's villain." He points out that this is "a nod to John Carpenter's 'They Live,'" before adding that "there may not be a better metaphor for the way our own mediating devices – electronic, social, political – come between what happens in the physical world and the perceptions our brains relay."[11]

Programs like these show us that, if the Apocalypse will not be televised, its failure to be televised can itself become television. This, in a nutshell, is what reality literacy entails: a hypersensitivity, trained by art and fiction, to the strategies deployed by today's medialogy that render invisible the exclusions and externalizations that lend reality its fantasy of coherence. The reason "all lives matter" is an absurd and even racist rejoinder to "Black lives matter" is that "Black lives matter" doesn't signify as a declarative description of reality. Rather, it is an exercise in reality literacy, a reminder that the coherence of the frame in which, precisely, all lives *seem* to matter has depended on a violent reality in which some lives very clearly matter less than others – not merely because Blacks are stopped, arrested, and imprisoned at up to four times the rates of whites, but because these statistics are in many ways the result of a historical pattern of systematic oppression beginning with slavery, spanning through Jim Crow, continuing during the civil rights era in the form of housing and education discrimination, and leading up to the bevy of new legislation aimed at voter suppression in response to the GOP's losses in the 2020 elections.

As we argued in *Medialogies*, the apocalypticism in the first age of inflationary media was oriented toward an ultimate but deferred reality behind the veil of appearances, some real and stable thing undergirding a world of copies. In contrast, our current medialogy eclipses and engulfs that model, making those copies – the bodies that refer to souls, the subjects that refer to citizens, or even the paper money that refers to a nation's wealth – into unanchored floating things, independent of any grounding commons. For us today, the world appears to consist of *resources* that individuals, corporations, and states use and manage. When the entire world is conceived as an ultimately expendable resource, the concept of sustainability comes into play. In other words, the truth of sustainability as a concept or ideology is the unconscious or implicit belief that the world, which before was the ineffable common ground of all appearances, has become just a greater resource among equals.

And in an analogous way, the logic of today's medialogy is that of the disintegration of the commons, of a feeling of community underlying the multiple expressions of individual and group claims for recognition. Hence, the desperate cry that "Black lives matter" reveals the truth that all lives don't in fact matter, that "mine" and those of "my" clan matter, and that "I" base their mattering on "my" blindness toward "your" people's plight, whether "you" be historically underprivileged groups in the United States or the ever-growing waves of refugees seeking succor from the clash of violent states we have supported and the fanatic movements our actions and inactions have helped foster.

This, then, is the challenge in the age of Trumpism: not to see in one pitiful man some ultimate agent of the Apocalypse, but rather to see in our apocalyptic fantasies the truth of our own complicity. The Apocalypse will not be televised; it's sitting on your couch watching TV.

5

From Breaking Bad to Breaking Worse

The call comes in the middle of the night, but the groggy hotel guest quickly acquiesces to come down to the hotel lobby for a drink. Despite the late hour, the bar will be open for them, the caller assures him. Over cognac with a sticker price of $175 a glass, as the man quickly recognizes, they talk business. The man is an accountant. He has ethics. He knows his host deals in drugs and wants him to launder his money for him. He knows he would do a good job at it, but he tells him he has principles, lines he isn't willing to cross. His host nods understandingly. He is empathetic but starts pushing at those lines. Would he work for big tobacco, for J.P. Morgan? Can he be so sure that his lines are the right ones? "What are your ethics? The one thing that trumps all the others?" he asks him. The man doesn't pause. "To protect and provide for my family." "Exactly," the drug lord pounces. "You will be able to earn enough to afford your great-great-grandkids' tuition."[1]

The accountant, Marty Byrd, played by Jason Bateman, has weakened. After overcoming paltry resistance from his wife, he announces the next morning to Del, the drug lord, that they have a deal. Delighted, Del shakes his hand and then promptly orders the gruesome execution of his current money launderer in front of Marty's aghast eyes. The dead man's eyes, in contrast, are removed by the killers, and plopped into a glass of whisky, for "a rainy day," as Del puts it.[2] The rainy day will come years later, when Del is pressuring Marty to come up with $8 million under a tight deadline. This episode of the series *Ozark* closes with Marty and his wife greeting their kids after returning from the vacation during which he agreed to Del's proposition. Bateman's face in close-up tells us all. Marty has learned the hard way that he crossed that line.

Several years before *Ozark* premiered, TV critic Eric Deggans identified a new trend: shows – like *Hell on Wheels*, *Sons of Anarchy*, *Dexter*, and *Breaking Bad* – that featured "characters the audience likes and wants to see succeed, even though they act an awful lot like villains."[3] *Ozark*'s most famous predecessor, *Breaking Bad*, tells the story of Walter White, a high school chemistry teacher who has to work in a car wash to support his cashed-strapped family as they expect a second child. His daily humiliation includes kneeling at the tires of a sports car while its owner, the same high school jock who mouths off in his class, orders him to wipe off another speck. The uninsured Walter eventually hits the wall when he is diagnosed with lung cancer. Realizing the illness will bankrupt his family while leaving him dead, he joins forces with a former student and starts to cook and sell crystal meth. By the end of the second season, Walter has murdered at least three people and taken on New Mexico's biggest drug lord, and we are rooting him on.

Dexter Morgan, the hero of the Showtime hit *Dexter*, is, if anything, cut of even less ambiguously evil cloth. He is, of course, a serial killer. Even though he is charming, specializes in killing other serial killers, and has a soft spot for kids, his voiceover repeatedly acknowledges that the real motivation for his killings is his "urges," which he sometimes refers to as his "dark passenger."[4]

In the movie *Limitless*, a Bradley Cooper vehicle also starring Robert De Niro, Eddie, a bright but underachieving writer, takes a pill that unlocks his brain's full potential. By the end of the film, Eddie has made millions, killed an innocent woman in a drug-induced haze, slaughtered a Russian mobster and his henchman in a blood-soaked rampage, and is on the verge of winning a seat in the US Senate. The presidency is around the corner, and Eddie has even managed to use his hyper-intelligence to refine away the drug's more unfortunate side effects of addiction and death – a move redolent of the always-outlawed first wish that we all know we'd present to the genie of the lamp, the one for unlimited wishes. Deggans calls the characters we've just described "a statement on our times" because, "in a world filled with war, recession and cynicism, straight-up heroes feel fake as a three-dollar bill. So the confused guy who does bad things for the right reasons just might be the best reflection of where we are today."[5]

While it is debatable the extent to which these characters are motivated by "the right reasons," we agree that the shows and films are a sign of the times. Specifically, they are the manifestation of an unconscious or not so unconscious revenge fantasy, one we could call the "revenge of the middle class." To begin with, all of these characters are decidedly middle class, if not already members of the underclass. This is in marked contrast to their creators, who, by virtue of being successful Hollywood writers and showrunners, are (at least by now) comfortably ensconced among the 1 per cent. The shows also usually feature a member of the 1 per cent or 0.1 per cent as a foil, nemesis, or object of envy. In *Limitless*, this character, portrayed by De Niro, is a top hedge-fund manager; in *Breaking Bad*, it is a sympathetic former partner who founded a successful company; and in *Dexter*, normally devoid of non-middle-class characters, the fifth season featured a mega-rich self-help guru as its super villain.

When we are confronted on a daily basis with real-life stories of billionaires routing the economy and getting tax-payer-subsidized bonuses as their punishment, who wouldn't be tempted to identify with a fictional common man who breaks all the rules to get his own, especially if a few billionaires get their comeuppance in the process? No doubt this much is true, and no doubt it accounts in part for the appeal of these types of shows and films, as well as for the audiences' willingness to root for characters who in better times would have been maligned for their poor choices and weak moral character. But if the revenge fantasy of the middle class is an effective explanation for this trend, that fact alone provokes a second, more penetrating question of the adequacy of this fantasy and its cultural expression as a political response. How, in other words, do we evaluate such fantasy scenarios in light of the emergence of real political movements, from the Tea Party to the Occupy movement to Trumpism, or as compared to other possible or real responses?

Let us return to Deggans's claim that these characters do "bad things for the right reasons," and that we feel justified in rooting for them because other characters are just that much more repugnant. This statement suggests that the shows are presenting us with an ethical argument. As a matter of fact, the philosopher Immanuel Kant argued that an action could be considered ethical even if it produced bad results, as long as it was done for the right reason. The drug lord Gustavo in *Breaking Bad* enunciates an apparent ethical maxim along these lines when he tells Walter, previewing Del's wooing of Marty, that "a man provides for his family."[6] But justifying murder and mayhem, cheating and lying, the selling of dangerous and addictive substances, on the implicit claim that others are doing it and that the character has a good reason for it, can signify only the breakdown of ethics, not an actual ethical choice. While it is certainly good to provide for one's family, Gustavo's real motivation is for Walter to cook his heavenly meth.

Kant argued that true ethical action requires the agent to evacuate all personal interest; indeed, for Kant, the only trustworthy indicator of whether an action is ethical would be if the agent were acting against his or her own interests. He wrote, for instance, that while many of us would bear false witness in order to save our own necks, we would all at least pause to consider what we were doing.[7] This pause was evidence for Kant of that aspect of our being that inspired in him the greatest awe: the moral law within. His point was that self-interest is not the most fundamental motivator of human action; that etched into our deepest being is a freedom from the tyranny of both conformity and self-interest.

There is, despite implicit and at times explicit claims to the contrary, no ethical basis for the middle-class revenge fantasies portrayed in these shows and films. While eminently enjoyable, ultimately they constitute a self-indulgent response by the gilded class to an economic reality that continues to benefit them. The fantasy is, in fact, unethical because it passes the buck on personal responsibility. Its message is, "you in the 99 per cent would be doing this too, if only you could." And to the extent that we identify with these characters, we should probably grant that, at some level, that message contains some truth. A part of our nature, and not its better angels, would like to flout law and convention in the service of our own enrichment.

So what might an ethical politics of resistance to the dominance of entrenched elites look like? The field becomes much more restricted, of course, since perfectly adequate responses could be in conformity with an ethical position while still being self-interested, and hence merely neutral in ethical terms. A Wall Street Occupier who is unemployed would, from a Kantian perspective, be entirely justified in taking action without deserving the awe that accompanies a truly ethical motivation, whereas a gainfully employed member of the 1 per cent who left their job in protest would be. What about other cases of action in apparent violation of self-interest? What about Thomas Frank's famous argument, from *What's the Matter with Kansas?*, that the Republican Party manipulates voters with wedge issues to vote against their economic self-interest? To paraphrase his memorable formulation, "values voters" were so enraged at seeing Madonna French kiss Britney Spears that they voted to give both of them a huge tax cut.

It would appear that Frank got this one right. Middle- and lower-class whites, in particular men, who vote overwhelmingly Republican, are not doing so because they want to bequeath the 1 per cent a better lifestyle. To establish that kind of altruism, one would have to ask those voters if it is their express intent to make wealthy people wealthier, even if their own quality of life may decrease as a result. Our guess is they would say no. In contrast, Warren Buffett went to some effort to draw attention to the tax laws that benefit him and his billionaire friends and tried to get them changed to his economic detriment.

We will see below how the nascent baroque theatre cultivated commoner revenge fantasies against powerful aristocratic abusers. These dramatic fantasies projected a sense of moral autonomy anchored in a new concept of honour as the unalienable patrimony of the soul (*patrimonio del alma*) – not only the noble soul – in imperial Spain.[8] Far from advancing progressive or liberating ideals, this early modern version of honour as the potential "democratic" and "universal" (albeit Christian) patrimony of the soul served the vital purpose of strengthening the bonds between the empire's monarchist-seignorial power structure and all the monarch's subjects, by means of the creation of an illusory private sphere.

While the mechanisms of reproduction, naturalization, and justification of the structure of political authority inherent to the functioning of any given society depend on the constant articulation of certain packages of values, the Spanish baroque theatre invested greatly in the value of honour, which was in turn tied to other epochal notions, such as the relative value of appearance over interiority, the metaphor of life as theatre, the centrality of the monarchy to everyday life, and the divine right of kings. In this cultural context, honour functioned as a primary signifier or "quilting point" that served to anchor Counter-Reformation and imperial ideology.[9] As with any such symbolic anchor, honour was invoked as the fundamental basis of an entire constellation of meaning, even when it was itself devoid of any specific content independent of the totality of that symbolic system.

In the most popular format of the *Comedia Nueva*, the honour play (*drama de honor*), conflicts of honour inform both the plays' moral themes and their treatment of those themes throughout. Hence, the profiles of the characters are in a constant process of self-definition and redefinition according to the pervasive presence of the value of honour: there are characters with honour, without honour, defenders of honour, physicians of honour, mirrors of honour, those who destroy their own honour or that of others ... Honour is the leitmotif, the driving force of history and of individual life-stories within these plays. This theatrical version of honour transcends the traditional nobiliary barriers in connection with a nascent sense of individual autonomy and an ethics of personal responsibility. As Pedro Crespo famously put it in Calderón's *El alcalde de Zalamea* (*The Mayor of Zalamea*): "el honor/es patrimonio del alma/y el alma sólo es de Dios" ("honour/is the patrimony of the soul/and the soul belongs only to God").[10]

As wealthy commoners, such legendary characters as Pedro Crespo and Peribáñez, among many others, feel justified in defending their honour against any violations, even if they come from noble hands. In his classic study *Teatro y literatura en la sociedad barroca*, José Antonio Maravall suggests that the abundance of characters and situations of this ilk in baroque theatre can be explained by the growing economic and demographic role played by wealthy peasants in sustaining the Spanish monarchy.[11] According to this view, the *Comedia*'s proffering of honour to a traditionally non-privileged class would have resulted, at least in part, from an historical necessity that demanded the incorporation of that class's economic prowess without a return investment of real political power. To continue with the example of *El alcalde de Zalamea*, Crespo has no problem conceding that, while his honour is the patrimony of his soul, his estate and belongings are the king's.

Going beyond Maravall's economic focus, we would argue that this extension of honour to the non-noble estates works as a symbolic call that names all the king's subjects (all those worthy of *the call*), while projecting an illusory private sphere, which is modelled on the official notion of sovereignty. Hence, in their attempts to assert their domestic autonomy as *honorable subjects*, wealthy peasants resort to royal metaphors, referring to themselves as kings within their private domain.[12] Clearly, this use of political and monarchist terminology cannot refer to any real political power. As we see in *El alcalde de Zalamea*, the proudly "honorable" Pedro Crespo is powerless to prevent the army from commandeering his property, or the monarchy from taxing his estate. This perception then, refers to the estate of honour, which, for any man who adheres to the code, resides in part in the sexual purity of his wife and daughters. Thus, if, on the one hand, honour is a thing of the soul, on the other, it is entirely contingent upon social relations in the real world, including opinions, suspicions, and insinuations.[13] This is the fundamental contradiction that we wish to underscore here: how honour can be the patrimony of the soul – the absolute criterion of domestic privacy and moral autonomy, differentiating the individual from society and the ambit of political authority – and, simultaneously, be contingent on the public sphere in which political authority holds sway. Again, insofar as this potentially "democratic" notion of honour is ultimately contingent on the public realm, the private sphere claimed by such honorable characters as Pedro Crespo is purely illusory.

While this analysis shows how political investments that seem "altruistic" in their advancement of "democratizing" goals can be dependent on ideologically supported illusions (or delusions) of self-interest, this is not to say that real movements of social, economic, and political resistance cannot or should not be *self-interested*. Where would the gay rights, feminist, civil rights, or workers movements be without the passion, eloquence, and perseverance of LGBT people, women, African Americans, and workers who have made profound sacrifices *in their own and others'* interests? But for change to solidify, for a racist or homophobic society to come to a point where a majority of its citizens no longer believe that whites are superior or gays are sick, that requires real "turncoats" – people who turn on their group or tradition in order to embrace the future, to embrace a better idea of what it means to be human. Finding discourses that help bring about that change is a natural goal for activists. To this end, slogans like "We are the 99 per cent" or "Black lives matter" can have a mobilizing impact.[14] In a truth-neutral media landscape like that in the United States, so can slogans like "Keep your government hands off my Medicare" or "Stop the steal."[15]

This could be the true "democratic" legacy of Crespo's dramatic claim that honour is the inviolable domain of the soul: *Keep your government off my honour!* To be sure, the claim of moral autonomy on which *El alcalde de Zalamea* (among countless commoner-revenge dramas) is built may remind us today of how far we still need to go, even if we ultimately recognize that, in the context of imperial Spain, this rhetorical claim was nothing more than a theatrical illusion (or self-delusion) similar to the middle-class revenge fantasies of our time.

Today, the entertainment industry, with its awesome reach, has the power to do real harm but also some good. Entertainment programming from Fox News (yes, it's entertainment, not news) to *24* (the CIA procedural widely seen as justifying torture in the name of antiterrorism) to the majority of reality TV shows preys on ignorance, fears, and prejudices to breed more of the same. Some programming fights back in a media-critical vein, be it in overt forms (as in *The Daily Show* and the discontinued *Colbert Report*) or in more subtle ways. As an example of the latter, we would cite HBO's *True Blood* as a metaphor for the anxiety provoked by the normalization of gay life in America, or *Big Love* for its at times disturbing explorations of the nexus between politics and family values. As for the new antihero revenge fantasies? No question about it, they are a lot of fun, but of course fantasizing only gets us so far.

6

Playing the Game

In his rural *entremeses* (interludes), Cervantes does not follow the norm in his representation of the paradigmatic wealthy commoner, which would be to associate him with the *caballero/galán* archetype. Rather, he ridicules this familiar typology, and the values implicit therein, by targeting a barrage of signs, including language, cultural level, leisurely activities – signs that traditionally distinguish estates from one another – in order to dismantle the image propagated by the honour plays of his day.

The parodic characterization of the peasants begins with their very names; there is no attempt to dignify them with names like García, Peribáñez, or Crespo. Rather, they are gifted with such absurdities as Panduro (Crusty), Humillos (Puff), Rana (Frog), Pesuña (Hoof), Algarroba (Stringbean), Pedro Estornudo (Peter Sneeze), Benito Repollo (Ben Cabbagehead), Juan Castrado (John Gelding); the mockery extends to their daughters, Juana Castrada (Joan Gelding) and Teresa Repolla (Theresa Cabbagehead). These names have a more or less explicit relation to the characters' personality and language and, what's more, give the impression that their wearers are mere country bumpkins. The second sign to hit the reader is the way most of these characters speak – their register is distinctly "vulgar," with frequent errors of grammar and diction as well as malapropisms, while they attempt to imitate a more exalted level of speech (and fail miserably). Here is an illustration from the *entremés La elección de los alcaldes de Daganzo* (*The Election of the Magistrates of Daganzo*):

> PANDURO: Aviso es que podrá servir de arbitrio
> Para su Jamestad; que, como en corte
> Hay potra-médicos, haya potra-alcaldes.

(CRUSTY: This idea could well be recommended/To His McMajesty; just as the Court is filled/With impotent doctors, let us fill our town/With impotent magistrates).[1]

We can safely say that the words *Jamestad*, *potra-médicos*, and *potra-alcaldes* have never appeared in any Spanish dictionary. Beyond a simple marker of Panduro's lack of education, Cervantes is taking the opportunity to make a play on words around the different referents of *caballo* (horse), accentuating both the mockery and the speaker's rustic origins. Another example of Cervantes's playing with the cultural level of his characters is their frequent random and spurious references to Greek or Roman figures. Jarrete (Knuckleknees), trying to defend his legitimate claim to the mayorship, enumerates his talents, among which he counts his abilities as an archer, saying "tiro con un arco como un Tulio" ("[I'm] handy with a bow as any Roman").[2] To our knowledge, Marcus Tulius Cicero was not best-known for his skills as an archer. Again, Cervantes's strategy works at two levels; first, enriching the reader's experience of humour and, second, ridiculing the speaker for trying to appear more educated than he really is.

One traditional attribute of the *caballero/galán* archetype in the *Comedia* is his meticulous attention to questions of manners and behaviour. The character Berrocal (Clod), once again a candidate for mayor, manifests a complete disregard for any such standards, when, through his customary wine-drenched haze, he attempts to inflate his image, honouring such a jurist as Bártulo by graciously offering to use his writings as toilet paper.[3] A good number of those signs by which characters are distinguished socially have to do with activities that for the *caballero/galán* character type would invariably be of a leisurely kind, such as hunting and riding, duelling for the sake of preserving one's honour, pursuing women for the sake of damaging others' honour, and socializing in general. But even when they devote themselves to these kinds of leisurely pursuits, the Cervantine wealthy peasants show a distinct ineptitude. When the local authorities charged with electing the mayor consider the abilities of each candidate, they speak somewhat ambiguously of Jarrete's skill as an archer. As the character Algarroba puts it, "Es de manera,/Que, si no fuese porque los más tiros/Se da en la mano izquierda, no habría pájaro/En todo este contorno" ("[His aim is] so good, indeed,/That if more of his shots managed to land/On their mark and not in his other hand,/No birds would be heard in this neighbourhood").[4]

In his edition of the *Entremeses*, Nicholas Spadaccini clarifies that "un arco de bodoques" is a bow that shoots pellets of mud or metal instead of arrows, hardly a weapon for a gentleman.[5] Let us imagine, for a moment, the hilarious picture drawn by Algarroba. The context is an official gathering to elect the highest authority in town, in which the candidates are being considered on the basis of the skills they can bring to the office. Now, this fellow is introduced as having the singular talent of being a marvellous shot, which might indeed elevate the character somewhat above the average commoner. However, the weapon he uses is not the most dignified, being, rather than a bow with arrows, something more akin to a sling shot, using such varied ammunition as hunks of clay and scraps of metal. On top of that, we are told, so gifted is his sight that there would not be a bird left in town were it not for his eccentric habit of shooting himself in the left hand. Surely, Jarrete would have had better luck imitating the nobility had he been written by Lope rather than by Cervantes.

Along similar lines, Berrocal is further convinced that his abilities as a connoisseur of wines have well prepared him for the job of governing Daganzo:

> BACHILLER: ¿Qué sabe Berrocal?
> BERROCAL: Tengo en la lengua
> Toda mi habilidad, y en la garganta;
> No hay mojón en el mundo que me llegue:
> Sesenta y seis sabores estampados
> Tengo en el paladar, todos vináticos.
> ALGARROBA: Y ¿quiere ser alcalde?
> BERROCAL: Y lo requiero;
> Pues cuando estoy armado a lo de Baco,
> Así se me aderezan los sentidos,
> Que me parece a mí que en aquel punto
> Podría prestar leyes a Licurgo
> Y limpiarme con Bártulo.

> (BACHELOR HOOF: Let's continue.
> What can Clod do?
> CLOD: All my skills and talents
> Lie in my tongue as well as in my throat:
> You'll never meet a better judge of wine.
> Sixty-six flavours are stamped on my palate,

And every one is vinicultural!
STRINGBEAN: You want to be a magistrate?
CLOD: Most surely.
For when I've sacrificed at Bacchus' shrine
My senses seem to sharpen and I dream
Lycurgus asks me what is what in law
And then I wipe my arse with legal texts.)[6]

In other words, the inhabitants of Daganzo would be safe so long as its highest official is under the influence.

Cervantes's mockery is not limited to the characterization of his rural protagonists but resonates throughout the humorous piece, from the authorities' bickering at the beginning to the Gypsies' insulting jingles at the end. The very title of the interlude, *The Election of the Magistrates of Daganzo*, is a joke, because the election never takes place. In fact, the only events that occur have little or nothing to do with the electoral process, such as the customary tossing of the *sacristán* in a blanket (one of Cervantes's contributions to the genre of the *entremés* in the wake of church prohibitions on the unflattering portrayal of church officials). If in the absence of an elected (or electable) mayor, Cervantes limits his attack to mayoral candidates in *La elección de los alcaldes de Daganzo,* he has no such difficulties in *El retablo de las maravillas*. Here, the town's mayor, Benito Repollo, confronted with the Latin expression *ante omnia*, used by the con woman Chirinos (Trifles) in reference to the company's stipend, responds, "Señora Autora, aquí no os ha de pagar ninguna Antona ni ningún Antoño; el señor regidor … os pagará más que honradamente, y si no, el Concejo. ¡Bien conocéis el lugar, por cierto! Aquí, hermana, no aguardamos a que ninguna Antona pague por nosotros" ("Mistress Manager, no Antónia – or, for that matter, no Antony – among us is going to pay you anything. Alderman … will see to it that you get a good wage, and then some. And if not, the Town Council will see to it. It's clear you don't know us very well. In this town, young woman, we don't expect any of our Antónias to pay for us"), plainly showing that he has no idea what the Latin words really mean.[7]

If there were no significant feminine roles in *La elección de los alcaldes de Daganzo,* this is not the case for *El retablo de las maravillas*. Aside from Chirinos, who is the play's co-producer, we have the daughters of Benito and his subordinate Juan Castrado, Teresa Repolla and Juana Castrada. The characterization of these ladies differs radically from the dainty and prudish *dama* archetype we are accustomed to seeing in other baroque Spanish works. After an initial scare from illusory mice, the girls seem quite excited at the prospect of being chased by lions and bears. Furthermore, as Michael Gerli notes:

> The dialogue between Teresa Repolla and Juana Castrada is a burlesque of the *de rigueur* female declarations of happiness, honor, modesty and chastity which saturate the *comedias villanescas*. Indeed, their exchange recalls similar feminine dialogues in works like *Fuenteovejuna* (Act i, Laurencia and Pascuala) and *Peribáñez* (Act i, Casilda and Inés), though here, rather than make affirmative protestations of womanly virtue in the context of the rustic life, Teresa and Juana admonish each other about commonly shared sexual and genealogical secrets, hence highlighting the need to guard against carelessness during the production.[8]

The critique of character types is a strident element in Cervantes's rural *entremeses*; however, his commentary must be understood in a wider context. These *entremeses* are involved in a much more profound examination of the conventions of the *Comedia Nueva*, particularly the genre or subgenre of the honour play, in relation to the theatre as an institution and the functioning of that institution in society.

As others have noted, there seems to be a satirical connection between the character of Chanfalla and his *retablo* and Lope's towering presence as the author of blockbuster plays and the primary theoretician of the *Comedia Nueva* in *El arte nuevo de hacer comedias en este tiempo* (*The New Art of Writing Plays in This Time*). Following Gerli's lead beyond the mere association with Lope, we find in Chanfalla, the ultimate showman and manipulator, an ideal metaphor for a type of showbusiness that creates illusory and manipulative images of society. As Chanfalla, Chirinos, and their musician, Rabelín, arrive at the village, Chanfalla advises Chirinos: "date un filo a la lengua en la piedra de la adulación" ("sharpen your tongue on the whetstone of flattery").[9] The essential component of this advised adulation has to do with the treatment of principal commoners as honourable men, which should remind us at once of the portrayal of the wealthy peasants in such Lopean plays as *Fuenteovejuna* and *Peribáñez y el comendador de Ocaña*: "CHIRINOS: Honrados días viva vuestra merced, que así nos honra. En fin, la encina da bellotas; el pero, peras; la parra, uvas, y el honrado, honra, sin poder hacer otra cosa" ("[TRIFLES:] May you be long honored, sir, for honoring us this way. Naturally, the oak bears acorns, the pear tree pears, the vineyard grapes, and the honorable man honor, for they can't do otherwise").[10]

How can one fail to notice the immediate association between the use of honour and the act of manipulation? Furthermore, Chanfalla's very first speech juxtaposes his adulatory use of honour with a mocking description of the governor ensconced in double-edged adjectives, such as "anchurosa" (ample) - suggesting both greatness and obesity - and "peripatética" (peripatetic), calling him an ambulant philosopher while stressing the fact that he is no *caballero*.[11] Indeed, such characterizations work to undermine the *galán/caballero* archetype, while at the same time linking the figure of Chanfalla with those institutions responsible for propagating manipulative images of the countryside and its principal inhabitants.

Honour serves two purposes here: first, as pure adulation, as a means of attracting prospective clients; and second, preconditioning those clients, or victims, to the acceptance of the rules, or conventions, of the game to come (the "nuevo embuste"). We must emphasize the effect of this beginning on a reader familiarized with the context of the familiar honour play and its obsessive treatment of *honor/honra*. These somewhat simple commoners are "honoured," not once, not even twice, but rather three or four times in one short speech, in which Chirinos implies (using agricultural metaphors to ensure the governor's comprehension) that the governor himself is a virtual fountain of honour.

What is, then, the nature of the game to which these men are being lured? It is, precisely, a theatrical spectacle; and the rules the participants are expected to accept are an exact parallel to those conventions governing the understanding of the familiar honour play. Chanfalla announces the stipulations by which his *retablo* may be seen in the following manner:

Por las maravillosas cosas que en él se enseñan y muestran, viene a ser llamado Retablo de las Maravillas; el cual fabricó y compuso el sabio Tontonelo debajo de tales paralelos, rumbos, astros y estrellas, con tales puntos, caracteres y observaciones, que ninguno puede ver las cosas que en él se muestran, que tenga

alguna raza de confeso, o no sea habido y procreado de sus
padres de legítimo matrimonio; y el que fuere contagiado destas
dos tan usadas enfermedades, despídase de ver las cosas, jamás
vistas ni oídas, de mi retablo.

(Because of all the marvelous things it reveals and teaches,
it came to be known as the Wonder Show. It was Tomfool the
Learned who originally contrived and composed it according to
such reckonings, parallaxes, stars, and constellations, modified
by such axioms, rhumbs, and Zodiac characters that nobody
can see what is going on in the show who is not a pureblood
Christian and who was not engendered and procreated in lawful
wedlock. So that anyone tainted by these two rather common
maladies must abandon all hope of witnessing the marvels,
never seen nor heard before, of my Wonder Show.)[12]

Not surprisingly, the conventions of Chanfalla's theatre coincide with some of the key conventions by which the whole social system is cemented, stratified by the markers of blood, lineage, and legitimacy. If the semiological system of the *Comedia* is built upon a social code of conventions, the brilliance of Chanfalla as a metaphor is that, in his set of rules, the two codes are one and the same. In Chanfalla's *retablo*, theatrical conventions are social conventions.

Chanfalla offers the commoners an illusory spectacle built on principles that they already accept, at least implicitly, as a basis of their integration into society. These principles are rooted in the essential differences between kinds of people. By not accepting the rules of the theatrical game, the *aldeanos* would be questioning the validity of those differences and hence the one modicum of self-worth that is left to them in the estatist system. This explains why, when the villagers buy into the spectacle, the actual content of what they are about to "see" is, to a certain extent, unimportant; it is the fact that *they will see* or *will have to see* that is foremost in their minds.

CHANFALLA: Vamos, y no se les pase de las mientes las calidades que han de tener los que se atrevieren a mirar el maravilloso Retablo.
BENITO: A mi cargo queda eso, y séle decir que, por mi parte, puedo ir seguro a juicio, pues tengo el padre alcalde; cuatro

dedos de enjundia de cristiano viejo rancioso tengo sobre los cuatro costados de mi linaje: ¡miren si veré el tal Retablo!
CAPACHO: Todos le pensamos ver, señor Benito Repollo.

(CHANFALLA: We'll go, but now don't forget the qualifications you need to have if you would dare gaze upon the Wonder Show.
BEN: It's just made for somebody like me. For my part, I'll tell you I've no reason to be afraid. I'm the son of a mayor with four solid trunks of old Christian stock supporting me on all four sides of my family tree. Don't worry about me seeing that show!
SACK: We expect to see it too, Master Ben Cabbagehead.)[13]

The words of Pedro Capacho (Peter Sack) are most telling of the peasants' attitude toward the *retablo*, not simply "we will see it," but rather "we expect to see it," which, in this context, implies intent, as in *we are most definitely planning on seeing it.* The same attitude informs the conversation between Teresa Repolla and Juana Castrada several pages later, the daughters of, respectively, or irrespectively, the mayor and his *regidor*, as Juana warns her cousin "y pues sabes las condiciones que han de tener los miradores del Retablo, no te descuides, que sería una gran desgracia" ("now you know about the high qualities one must have to see this show, so be very careful. Otherwise it would be a terrible disgrace").[14]

As Stanislov Zimic, among others, has noted, there is extensive textual evidence that the characters are not suffering from any sort of delusion, but are, rather, consciously denying the truth of what they all fail to see.[15] One of those moments noted by Zimic occurs when Benito Repollo, inexplicably enraged by the presence of Rabelín, threatens to throw a bench at him if he doesn't get behind the blanket. In this moment, Repollo unconsciously violates the code, since, according to Chanfalla's instructions, what he identified as a simple blanket was to be seen as a richly ornamented curtain (*repostero*).

Recall Chanfalla's justification for the inclusion of Rabelín in the confidence game at the outset of the play, in which he states that there must be music to fill in the spaces while the audience awaits the figures of the *retablo*. This is a doubly ironic statement, for, not only is the entire play a hiatus between dramatic sequences, but also, as Benito frequently observes in his outbursts against Rabelín, the poor musician has no instrument on which to play: "¡Válgate el diablo por músico aduendado, y qué hace de menudear sin cítola y sin son!" ("The devil take you – you're no musician but a spook; you sit there strumming without a zither and no sound out of you!").[16] Benito once more betrays the code to which all have adhered, which would, naturally, include the belief that Rabelín, for better or for worse, was actually playing something. Perhaps we can come to a greater understanding of Benito's seemingly irrational rage toward Rabelín if we picture this fellow of slight stature sitting in front of an old blanket where he is supposedly playing his music, without an instrument, making no sound other than his occasional retorts to Benito. Surely, the contradictions are too striking for Benito, already beleaguered by doubts about the activity in which he has involved himself. Taking into account the descriptions we have of Rabelín's less than imposing appearance, it must be a terrible mental strain for Benito to be aware that he's being taken in by this guy.

Cervantes brings his work to a close with the introduction of a furrier, who arrives in town to request lodging for a group of travelling soldiers. What follows is again a wonderful parody of a familiar theme in such honour plays as *El alcalde de Zalamea*, in which, instead of showing their respect for the king's troops by welcoming them into their homes, the local authorities try to take advantage of the situation to avoid their traditional responsibility. To this end, Castrado actually calls upon Chanfalla to reopen the *retablo*, and continue the previously truncated dance of Herodías, in hopes of bribing the furrier: "Por vida del Autor, que haga salir otra vez a la doncella Herodías, porque vea este señor lo que nunca ha visto; quizá con esto le cohecharemos para que se vaya presto del lugar" ("Come on, Manager, bring out that Herodias girl again, and let this gentleman see what he's never seen before. Maybe then we can bribe him to get right out of town").[17]

When the newcomer fails to see the above-mentioned young lady, the villagers join in chorus, accusing him of lacking pure Christian blood, to which he naturally responds by starting a brawl. Interestingly, it is precisely he who is accused of being impure who causes the others to flee, especially if we consider the traditional association of old Christian blood with valour and convert blood with cowardice. As Américo Castro put it, "la valentía ocupaba inmediato y prominente lugar en la escala de las valoraciones populares, de lo estimado por la 'opinión,' simplemente porque desde hacía siglos se daba por supuesto que el judío y sus descendientes eran cobardes, aunque fuesen cristianos desde hacía varias generaciones" ("bravery occupied a prominent place at the top of the value scale of the populace, singularly esteemed by public opinion, in part due to the long-standing belief that the Jews and their descendants were cowards, even if they had been Christians for generations").[18]

Again, the spectators are not hypnotized, or suffering from communal delusions of any kind; rather, they are voluntarily invested in the hypocrisy required by Chanfalla's game. Chanfalla presents the spectators with rules they are already implicitly accepting. In this sense, the "nuevo embuste," the new or novel lie, is not *nuevo* by any means; it is, rather, a rearticulation of previously held beliefs based on irrational and intangible but essential differences. Indeed, the only new thing about Chanfalla's game is the particular manner in which those differences are expressed, explicitly and precisely as theatrical conventions. If we accept the metaphor of Chanfalla as a representative of the *Comedia Nueva*, *El retablo de las maravillas* goes far beyond a mere anecdote about a trickster profiting from a group of fools, and instead becomes a resounding critique of the manipulative and co-optive function of the new theatre – at least in its most popular Lopean version – in legitimizing and naturalizing the values upon which social divisions rest. If the conventions Chanfalla enumerates deal exclusively with the purity of one's lineage (if one is a *cristiano viejo* or not), and one's legitimacy at birth, then clearly the element in common is the quality of one's blood.

Is the case, then, as many have claimed, that Cervantes is issuing with this *entremés* a critique of his society's anti-Semitism and obsession with legitimacy? We would agree that this is indeed the case. But we also argue that he does something more. Consider the governor's aside, "Basta; que todos ven lo que yo no veo; pero al fin habré de decir que lo veo, por la negra honrilla" ("This is too much. They all see something I don't see. Still, to save face, I'll have to say I saw it").[19] Honour, as expressed in these significant lines, presents itself as an essential command to participate in the social game and accept as *real* what one neither sees nor understands. Obviously, the referent of the sentence is the governor's status as a legitimate and established Christian, but this cannot exhaust the wealth of the statement's meaning. To realize the full impact of this scene, we must go beyond the context of this one *entremés*, and the nature of its dialogue with theatrical conventions, and seek instead its referents within the broader historical context of the ideological games that distort their social reality.

Cervantes's behind-the-curtain look reveals how the dramatic format of the honour play is built on a manipulative image of the countryside as inhabited by commoners who are in possession of something called "honour," which they have the right to defend with blood against aristocratic abusers. This expansive version of honour would, in turn, be contingent on their identity as *cristianos viejos*, suggesting a form of differentiating power and privilege that is distinct from that of the historical system of aristocratic privilege.

Maravall has written extensively on this subject and concludes that there was at no time what could be called a parallel system of privileges:

> No hay dos mecanismos oligopódicos: el exclusivismo de la limpieza y el exclusivismo de la nobleza. No hay más que un sistema de participar en la exclusividad de la clase distinguida: el de la nobleza. No hay un segundo sistema parecido a éste que sea el de la limpieza. Ni lo hay, colocado paralelamente, ni se confunden, ni cubren el mismo campo. Lo que sucede es que se utilizó la «limpieza» como una difícil barrera más a vencer para penetrar en el sistema de exclusión o, mejor, de reserva.
>
> (There are not two separate systems of privilege: the exclusivism of blood purity and the exclusivism of nobility. There is only one system of participation in the exclusivity of the privileged class: nobility. There is no second or equivalent system of blood purity, either parallel to it, blended with it or covering the same terrain. Rather, blood purity was utilized as one more hurdle that needed to be cleared in order to participate in the system of exclusion or social reserve.)[20]

The purity-of-blood factor – descent from old Christian stock – served largely as an official precondition for buying one's way into the nobiliary ranks; yet, those who already enjoyed the privileges of the nobility had, in fact, little to fear from lack of sufficiently Christian heritage, even as the blood factor could be used as a weapon in the struggle for "positioning" within the ranks of the nobility.[21] Moreover, historical evidence shows that, outside the baroque stage, commoners did not succeed in their attempts to wield their blood purity and personal honour against aristocrats.[22]

Thus, *El retablo de las maravillas* does several things beyond calling attention to the business aspect of the new theatre: it criticizes the empty values of caste differentiation; it indicts the fanciful portrayal of the countryside and its inhabitants as an ideological ploy; and, most importantly, it recognizes the function of the theatre in propagating this ideology and exposes its very mechanism, the empty exchange value of honour, the sublime keystone that holds the system together.[23] Cervantes shows, through the metaphor of Chanfalla, how the honour plays that commanded the baroque stage offered the commoners escapist illusions, much like our own middle-class fantasies of revenge against the powerful.

Chanfalla offers the town leaders honour, and, in exchange, they will lie, assert difference where there is none, and voluntarily claim to see what is not there to be seen. The brilliance of Cervantes's satire truly shines in the end, when the villagers try to use the myths of religious purity they have swallowed for real social change, challenging the arbitrary humiliation it is their lot to bear – clearly the furrier couldn't care less about their old Christian blood when it comes to challenging his right to enter their homes. This is when their illusory bubble breaks. Faced with the state's repressive force, they have neither the valour to withstand it nor the legal right to avoid it, and they find that their honour never meant anything at all.

PART TWO

He Said, She Said

7

Not Your Father's Classroom

Words, images, and stories are the building blocks of reality. They literally make sense of our world, shaping our nightmares as much as our dreams. They define the relations of kinship within which we learn to recognize who we are and what we want (or should want) to become, in reference to certain norms and expectations. If our aim is to understand our reality, we must be willing to critically examine those key words, images, and stories that frame what we know or think we know about ourselves and others. In patriarchal societies, understanding reality requires looking into the ways in which gender roles are constructed and transmitted over time. The literature and culture classroom can be a rich laboratory for the critical examination of representations of gender in different historical contexts against the familiar images of our own cultural environment.

In terms of our disciplinary specialty, albeit from a much earlier period than most of our examples in this book, we could start with "Exemplo XXXV" of Don Juan Manuel's *Libro de los ejemplos del conde Lucanor y de Patronio* (*Tales of Count Lucanor*) (1335), the short medieval "example" that served as the basis for Shakespeare's play *The Taming of the Shrew* (1590–92). Don Juan Manuel's story describes how an ambitious and canny young groom poses as a murderous madman in order to terrify his wealthy and notoriously rebellious bride into abject compliance. The young man's violent performance (he slaughters and dismembers his dog, his cat, and his horse, and threatens his wife's life on their wedding night) is celebrated in the text as an example of judicious behaviour that set the gender roles straight, that being a necessary precondition of a good marriage: "cuando todo esto oyeron, fueron mucho maravillados, et desque sopieron cómo passaron en uno, preciaron mucho el mancebo porque assí sopiera fazer lo quel' cumplía et castigar tan bien su casa. Et daquel día adelante, fué aquella su muger muy bien mandada et hobieron muy buena vida" ("upon hearing this [i.e., about the husband's behaviour], they esteemed the young man very highly for he had figured out how to command his house right from the start. From that day forward, his wife was exceedingly obedient and they lived in peace for the rest of their days").[1]

But when the bride's own father follows the example of his son-in-law, sacrificing a rooster in an attempt to frighten his wife into submission, we witness a very different outcome. As his wife wryly informs him, "A la fe, don [F]ulano, tarde vos acordastes, ca ya non vos valdría nada si matássedes cient caballos, que ante lo hobiérades a començar, ca ya bien nos conoscemos" ("truth be told, Don Fulano, it is much too late for you, and you will gain nothing from slaughtering a hundred horses; indeed, you should have started on this path long ago, for we know each other too well").[2] This final scene turns out to be central to the practical lesson provided at the conclusion of the story: "Si al comienço non muestras qui eres,/nunca podrás después cuando quisieres" ("if you don't show who you are from the beginning, you will not be able to do it when you are willing").[3] This is an interesting way to distil the story's meaning and its teachings; for one thing, the violent actions of the young groom and his father-in-law stand in stark contrast with the men's actual temperate personalities. Far from an expression of who they are, theirs is a self-reflective performance of (violent) masculinity aimed at establishing the "proper" gender hierarchy in the context of marriage.

As we look at the products of our own popular culture today, we might resort to the lyrics of Luis Miguel's ballads to help us unpack the story's central lesson about the performative nature of gender relations. Their romantic content notwithstanding, such verses as "amarte como yo lo haría/como un hombre a una mujer" ("to love you as I would, as a man would love a woman") reveal a certain (unavoidable) gap between the speaking "I" that would love "you" and the gender type "man" that would love the gender type "woman."[4] Such is the nature of the relation of similitude introduced by the grammatical marker *como*: To love you *as* I would, *as* a man loves a woman. There's a certain impersonation involved here, a form of role play, where "man" is invoked as a behavioural model that frames/conditions how "I would love you." We can now return to the seemingly paradoxical lesson of Don Juan Manuel's didactic example about the need to show your wife *who you are from the beginning* (of marriage). We can see that, in the context of Patronio's exemplum, "showing who you are" refers to the culturally determined expectation/obligation to inhabit the symbolic placeholder *man/ husband*: in this case, head of the household whose authority and dominion ought to be unquestioned.

Fast-forward roughly three centuries to the visual and mass-oriented culture of the baroque. The historical dramas and honour plays authored by Lope de Vega, Calderón de la Barca, and others for the stage of the *Comedia Nueva* treat their heterogeneous audiences to action-packed spectacles built on similar models of violent masculinity. Within the honour play, a woman's honour is typically linked to her sexual virtue and her willingness to bend unquestioningly to the will of her father, husband, or brother; for a man, by contrast, honour takes the form of a mandate to protect and control their dependants (especially his wife and daughters) and to perform violent acts of retribution in defence of his family name. Hence, we can say that the honour code works as a gendered form of ideological interpellation (in the Althusserian sense) and a constant reminder of differential social obligations, a "religión de la obediencia" ("religion of obedience") as José Antonio Maravall aptly called it.[5] In this context, the masculine act of self-affirmation that's encapsulated in the honour mandate *yo soy quien soy* (I am who I am) is a call to arms in defence of the family's reputation, as in the popular gangster movies and TV shows of our own age, from the award-winning *Godfather* saga of the late twentieth century to the recent BBC series *Peaky Blinders*. Indeed, in these and other gangster flicks, it is not difficult to find displays of violent masculinity that closely parallel climactic scenes in such classic plays as *Peribáñez y el comendador de Ocaña* and *El alcalde de Zalamea*, to mention but two of the most canonical works of the baroque period. As a matter of fact, the archetypal characters that populate these and many other honour dramas would also seem familiar to fans of the action-hero genre, going back to the classic westerns of the 1950s and 1960s and forward to the typical Steven Seagal movies of the 2000s and the recent screen adaptations of the Jack Reacher novels authored by Lee Child. With relatively minor variations, these popular forms of entertainment reproduce, reify, and capitalize on spectacular images of "protective" masculinity that glorify violence.

These protective models of masculinity are but the flip side of a more sinister and baldly abusive masculinity, as the plots beloved of the baroque theatre demonstrate again and again. A recurrent theme in the *dramas de honor* is that of the fragility of woman's honour, and consequently that of man's. And while that honour can be protected by shielding a woman from exposure to the outside, once it has been stained, the honour code demands a blood sacrifice. This is the fundamental structural element, the thematic basis for suspension and resolution, that makes for a successful plot in the mould popularized by Lope de Vega.[6]

Calderón's *El médico de su honra* (*The Surgeon of His Honour*) offers an extreme version of this sacrificial dimension of honour, as Don Gutierre arranges for the killing of his wife, Doña Mencía, at the hands of a medical surgeon, who is himself threatened into compliance. The innocent woman is methodically bled in a sacrificial ritual meant to repair Don Gutierre's honour (which he wrongly believes has been damaged). Not only is the perpetrator not punished for his honour killing; he is actually rewarded with a new bride (his former lover, Doña Leonor) by none other than the king himself, who expresses admiration for the judicious way in which his noble subject has set about privately and discreetly mending his honour. The play concludes with Don Gutierre's chilling reflection that honour's stains must be cleansed with blood – "que el honor/con sangre, señor, se lava" – and his ominous warning to Doña Leonor: "Mira que médico he sido/de mi honra: no está olvidada/la ciencia" ("Be advised that I have been surgeon of my honour and have not forgot the science").[7]

In another play, *La Estrella de Sevilla*, which some critics have attributed to Lope de Vega, when the king enters Estrella's house without the consent of either Estrella or her brother Busto, the latter immediately accuses her of having stained his honour. Although she convincingly assures her brother that she was not aware of the king's actions, and furthermore had not offered him the slightest encouragement, this does nothing to lessen the stain against Busto's honour. In Francisco de Rojas Zorilla's *Del rey abajo ninguno* (*None Beneath the King*), the mere fact of having seen a man enter his house, although he is perfectly aware of his wife's innocence, is enough to drive the husband to try to kill her.

While honour is – as we have seen – the essential value by which the archetypal characters of the *Comedia Nueva* measure themselves and their actions, its symbolic weight is by no means uncontested in baroque culture. One of the most interesting responses came from María de Zayas, whose second collection of exemplary novellas, *Desengaños amorosos (The Disenchantments of Love)* (1647), is explicitly framed as a feminine exposé of masculine violence and a denunciation of marriage and the honour code as death traps for women. Her third *desengaño, El verdugo de su esposa (His Wife's Executioner)* reproduces much of the familiar plot of Calderón's *El médico de su honra* while foregrounding the victim's innocence and the calculating cruelty of her husband, who uses the honour code as a cover for his crime. Here, the focus in not on the tragic dilemma of the honour-bound husband, as in the Calderonian model, but on the monstrous nature of the aristocratic system that feeds on the blood of innocent women.

Each of Zayas's *desengaños* is designed to serve as an example of masculine hypocrisy, cruelty, and deceit, and as a warning for women to avoid the prison-house of marriage. There is probably no better and more graphic illustration of the oppressive and confining "architecture ... of patriarchy" than the image of an innocent wife imprisoned inside a house wall in Zayas's fifth *desengaño, La inocencia castigada (Innocence Punished)*.[8] Having learned of his wife's rape, and despite her legal exoneration, Don Alonso conspires with her brother and sister-in-law to punish her for her involuntary desecration of the family honour. They bury her inside a wall, where she is kept alive for six years. The narrator's graphic description of her decaying flesh is the literal embodiment of the putrid honour system, as Zayas sees it:

> En primer lugar, aunque tenía los ojos claros, estaba ciega ... Sus hermosos cabellos, que cuando entró allí eran como hebras de oro, blancos como la misma nieve, enredados y llenos de animalejos ...; el color, de la color de la muerte; tan flaca y consumida, que se le señalaban los huesos, como si el pellejo que estaba encima fuera un delgado cendal; ... los vestidos hechos ceniza, que se le veían las más partes de su cuerpo; descalza de pie y pierna, que de los excrementos de su cuerpo ... no sólo se habían consumido, mas la propia carne comida hasta los muslos de llagas y gusanos, de que estaba lleno el hediondo lugar.
>
> (In the first place, although her eyes were clear, she was blind ... Her lovely tresses, which when she entered were strands of gold,

white as the very snow, tangled and full of little animals …; her colour, the colour of death, so thin and emaciated that her bones showed as if the skin that covered them were but a thin veil; … her clothes turned to ashes, so that most parts of her body were visible; her feet and legs bare, because the excrement from her body … had not only eaten into them, but her very flesh was eaten up to the thighs with wounds and worms, which filled the stinking place.)[9]

In the dark domestic world of *Desengaños amorosos*, the house itself works as "an instrument of torture employed against women," even as a murder weapon.[10] Thus, in the next *desengaño*, *Amar sólo por vencer* (*Love for the Sake of Conquest*), we witness Don Bernardo's cold-blooded killing of his unmarried daughter whose honour had been "stained" by a deceitful lover. A wall of the house is once again the patriarch's weapon of choice. The narrator's description of the young woman's death provides a powerful illustration of the asphyxiating architecture of patriarchy: "la pared la había abierto la cabeza, y con la tierra se acabó de ahogar" ("the wall had split her head open and she died of asphyxiation amidst the rubble").[11] As one of us has argued elsewhere, the monsters come with the house in Zayas's baroque tales of domestic terror:

> At the end of the last *desengaño*, *Estragos que causa el vicio* (Ravages Caused by Vice), we are left with nothing but dead bodies and ruins everywhere. This is an implosion of the aristocratic house not unlike Poe's vision of decay and destruction in "The Fall of the House of Usher" … If, indeed, the code of honor may be seen as a "fortification" in service of the aristocratic dream of self-containment, then the *Desengaños*' nightmarish parade of tortured and suffocating bodies and mangled corpses is a shocking reminder of the code's monstrous face.[12]

Zayas's femicidal house is a powerful representation of the oppressive and violent "architecture of patriarchy," which can be linked to familiar tales of gothic terror, from the works of Anne Radcliffe and Edgar Allan Poe to Stieg Larsson's Millennium Series, including *The Girl with the Dragon Tattoo*, *The Girl Who Played with Fire*, and *The Girl Who Kicked the Hornet's Nest*. As Diana Russell notes, while "femicide" refers to "the killing of women by men *because* they are women," it is only "on the extreme end of a continuum of antifemale terror."[13] Notably, in her landmark study *Reclaiming the Body*, Lisa Vollendorf resorted to the work of Russell and other scholars on femicide to support her interpretation of *Desengaños amorosos* as a work of early modern feminism. More recently, Bradley Nelson has built on Vollendorf's insights and the scholarship of Russell and her collaborators in a provocative essay that uses Larsson's Millennium Series as the frame story for a close analysis of Zayas's *El traidor contra su sangre* (*Traitor of His Own Blood*), Nelson argues that, in the male-dominated societies described by both Zayas and Larsson, violence against women is not an aberration but "a logical and necessary component of a patriarchal social, economic, political, and, yes, aesthetic order [that] depends on the cultivation and (violent) maintenance of a (*gender*) *politics of inequality*."[14]

In Larsson's series, protagonist Lisbet Salander's personal history of abuse and torture at the hands of representatives of state institutions reveals the structural feedback loops that provide cover to perpetrators who pose as protectors and benefactors. As the narrator explains in the first novel of the series, "This was the natural order of things. As a girl, she was legal prey, especially if she dressed in a worn black leather jacket and had pierced eyebrows, tattoos, and zero social status."[15] It is worth noting that the literal translation of the original Swedish title of the novel is not *The Girl with the Dragon Tattoo*, but *Men Who Hate Women*. As Nelson observes, Salander's personal history effects the "unveiling of the absolute inequality and violence of gender roles in Swedish law enforcement, correctional, judicial, and even medical institutions. As a consequence, men who violently and perversely exercise their power on female victims are not reformed ... because the cause of their perverse and often psychotic behavior is their absolute hatred of women, a hatred Larsson finds firmly rooted in all of the previously mentioned modern institutions."[16] Analogously, the tales of domestic terror included in Zayas's collection of *desengaños* are explicitly framed as personal histories of female victimization meant to unmask the wolves in shepherds' clothing and to expose the misogynist social and cultural institutions that enable the perpetrators and offer them cover.

While Salander will eventually figure out how to use her marginal status and her brilliant hacking and camouflaging skills to exert a kind of vigilante justice over her abusers (outside of, and often against, the legal system), the female victims that populate the pages of the

Desengaños cannot escape the terrors that come with the house. They are the sacrificial victims of the "protective" architecture of patriarchy. Their tragic destiny is prefigured right from the beginning of the *Desengaños* (both within the overarching narrative frame and in each individual novella), as martyrs in the waiting: *mártir, corderilla, inocente palomilla, inocente victima...*

8

The Poison of Purity

A political cartoon from the 1990s in response to the Clarence Thomas/Anita Hill scandal – now all the more trenchant in light of today's #MeToo movement – portrayed two workers, a woman and a man, sitting side by side and facing out toward the reader. As if on the spur of the moment, the woman turns to the man and asks something to the effect of, "How would you like it if I suddenly started telling you lewd jokes, describing pornographic movies I had seen, and propositioning you to join me in illicit sexual acts?" To which the man, after pausing for a frame, answers, with a desperately hopeful expression on his face, "Oh would you, please?"

That cartoon, and the event, reactions, and cultural anxiety that inspired it, still reflects some of the dilemmas and tensions around gender relations abounding in a nation that propagates its own image as the apex of Western cultural and historical development, the true intellectual child of the Enlightenment, espousing human rights and proclaiming the equality of all human beings, even while electing to its highest office a man who revelled in relating his sexual assaults on women over whom he wielded power. Clearly even the least critically minded observer of American society knows of the gross disparities between everyday life and the "American dream," but nevertheless it is surprising the extent to which, at a time when gender inequality has been the focus of acute criticism and political action for several decades, the most basic assumptions about who we are and what we are supposed to desire, consistently belie hopes for reconciliation – or at least understanding – while continuing to determine our daily behaviour and attitudes toward one another.

Analysis of how sexual difference was theorized in late eighteenth-century works of political philosophy reveals characterizations quite similar to those satirized by that cartoon, which suggests an epistemological congruity in terms of sexuality but does not begin to explain the origins of otherwise arbitrary gender distinctions. Furthermore, reading pre-Enlightenment texts, one may be struck once again by the similarity between the articulation of gender roles found there and those of contemporary Western society, suggesting, in fact, that the latter may have their roots in social and political changes occurring as early as in the fifteenth century.

At the end of the eighteenth century, the beginning of what Foucault called the "modern *episteme*," one finds many attempts to rationalize traditional marital behaviour in terms of the powerful new ideas that were coming to characterize the age of Enlightenment.[1] Johann Gottlieb Fichte, renowned as the father of German Idealism, published at this time his *Science of Rights*, in which he attempts to derive from their respective natures the relationship between men and women that he sees, not only in his own culture, but repeated *ad infinitum* since time immemorial. In doing so, he made a curious claim about female nature: that woman's only drive in life is to love, and to be loved in return, and, what is more, that the object of her love is stable, and is a man, the one man whom she should choose to marry. Fichte bases his argument about the natural roles of men and women on the presumed radical opposition between the sexes in terms of activity and passivity. Having established the male as the active sex and the female as the passive, Fichte then evokes a definition of reason as "absolute self-activity" in order to argue that the satisfaction of the male sexual impulse, being an active one, is completely in accord with Reason, "but it is absolutely against reason that the other sex should propose to itself the satisfaction of its sexual impulse as an end, because in that case it would make a pure passivity its end ... Such an end and rationality utterly cancel each other out in that sex."[2] According to Fichte's argument, since all humans are creatures of reason, women's sexual impulse must be a thing very different from men's, something that would allow them – indeed, demand of them – to render themselves as a means for the satisfaction of another, without making their own, passive drives an end in themselves. Fichte's solution to this problem, and the groundwork for his whole theory of sexual rights and responsibilities, merits quoting at length:

Since she can give herself up only in obedience to an impulse, this impulse must assume in woman the character of an impulse to satisfy the man. Woman becomes, in this act, the means for the end of another, because she cannot be her own end without renouncing her ultimate end – the dignity of reason! This dignity she maintains, although she becomes means, because she voluntarily makes herself means in virtue of a noble natural impulse – *love*! Love, therefore, is the form in which the sexual impulse appears to woman.[3]

Such an authoritative statement creates certain problems for Fichte – namely, what to make of all those women who are plainly using their bodies for other ends than the satisfaction of their men and the eventual production of children. Although he does admit of their existence, he categorizes them all as being, in one way or another, in contradiction with reason, and therefore not an integral part of the rational society and state; while concubines are to receive no protection or recognition from the state, prostitutes are actually to be considered insane, and for this reason may be expelled from the realm.[4]

Thus, we find in the Enlightenment a move to formalize the difference between the sexes under the rubric of their relation to sexual desire. Men are understood to have roving, highly active sexual appetites, with no particular need to choose or stay with a given woman, while women become the stabilizing factor in the coupling; their "natural" faculty to love one man and to give themselves completely to that man will, in turn, provoke a reaction of generosity on the part of the man, who will then learn to love, as the woman does naturally. Women who allow their desire to assume a more "brute" form are acting neither in accordance with their own natures nor within the dictates of reason, and thus they are marginalized.

These passages complement nicely the familiar rhetoric of sexuality that still works as the quiet standard in contemporary Western societies and, in doing so, add credence to the idea of a model of patriarchal normativity that spans from the late eighteenth century to the present. However, this exemplary theory of gender roles is not an invention of the Enlightenment; rather it is, as we have indicated, a formalization of identities, and only the licit ones, that had been actively propagated for the previous centuries. The question was not one of an origin, as if one could assume a time of sexual equilibrium that, for some reason, or as a result of some economic or political cause, became unbalanced; rather, it was the articulation of a new tension, the emergence of a pole, specifically a model of feminine ideality, that, in turn, implied a negation, an illicit sexual other. The sexual struggle of early modern mentalities was one between obsession with and erasure of female desire. With the emergence of new forms of social organization and identification required by political absolutism, the latter trend was championed at an official, or public, level, and, by the time of the eighteenth-century theorization of the modern nation-state, came to define the licit subjective norm for all women.

At the end of the fifteenth and beginning of the sixteenth century, parts of Europe were entering what Maravall called a crisis of expansion. New economic classes were forming; people were finding a new mobility, both vertical and horizontal; and what would become the first nation-state and empire of the post-medieval age christened itself with a powerful political union and subsequent "reconquest" of the capital of Iberian Islam, Granada. Maravall characterizes the profundity of these changes as follows:

> El mundo se presentaba al hombre medieval, cualesquiera que fuesen las apariencias adversas que le surgieran al paso, como la perfecta unidad de un orden. Esa unidad se traducía en la unidad de Dios, en la del universo, en la unidad de una ordenación moral, en la unidad de un sistema social. Orden y jerarquía fundaban esa unidad. Pues bien, esa unidad es la que queda fundamentalmente trastrocada: se desorganiza la unidad del orden y se viene abajo la jerarquía entre cosas divinas y humanas, entre los valores morales, entre las clases y los individuos en la sociedad, tal y como tradicionalmente venían entendiéndose.
>
> (The world appeared to the medieval man, regardless of any evidence to the contrary he might have encountered, as the perfect unity of an order encompassing the unity of God, the universe, and the moral and social orders. Order and hierarchy grounded that unity. That unity is fundamentally upset: the unity of this order is eroded and the hierarchy encompassing divine and human affairs, moral values, social classes and individuals, as they were traditionally understood, comes crashing down.)[5]

While the epistemological slate was certainly not wiped clean, the tremendous disruption of traditional modes of understanding that Maravall describes would create the space for new forms of political power and social organization. Instead of a world whose different elements and strata were regarded as mere variations on a fundamental unity, one finds a world where diversity and multiplicity were quickly becoming the norm. At the same time, there occurs a globalization of political vision, particularly in conjunction with the discovery of the New World – or, as it was already known in the sixteenth century, the "invención" of America – that has as its goal the agglomeration of people and territory, and the accumulation of capital on an enormous scale.[6]

Such a dramatic change in the material and political dimensions of the continent demanded a correlative transformation of subjectivity at its most basic level. Elsewhere we have argued that this shift may be gleaned from changing practices of visual and spatial representation, from painting, to theatrical spectacle, to mapping techniques.[7] The change, simply stated, is between an image of self as engaged in bipolar relationships of power – for example, serf and lord, lord and king – that involve personal contact, and one in which the individual is one subject among others, whose connection to these others is mediated by the figure of political authority, personified in the monarch. This last configuration, the basic matrix of the modern state, involves an ability to grasp power as *symbolic*, rather than as always present to the senses. The subject may owe allegiance to the state, through the person of the monarch, but will only ever come in contact with a representative of the monarch, a carrier of some signifier of legitimacy, such as the royal seal.[8] This recognition at the same time implies the existence and the reciprocal recognition of other subjects, whose perceived desire to "subject" themselves to the representation of royalty perpetuates and redoubles its legitimacy. This is a form of social control that depends more on representation and desire than it does on brute force, and, in turn, it encourages the development of subjectivities that are themselves more complex, desiring to partake in symbolic power and to advance socially through the garnering of recognition.

While the emergence of symbolic power and its correlative subjective form enabled the construction of vast state bureaucracies amidst the potentially chaotic diversity of shifting fortunes, elites, and desires, it also required the rethinking of some of the most basic, microcosmic relations of the social fabric – those between men and women and, more generally, between women and the social body as a whole. Accordingly, furious debates arose in the sixteenth century around the inherent nature of women, their sexual desires, and the role they ought to play in society and in marriage (usually one and the same in the writings of moralists). The predominant tension that appears in the texts about this "woman question," or *querelle des femmes*, as it was known in the French context,[9] is between the reality of male dominance and the worrisome impression that, in sexual and reproductive matters, women hold the upper hand. Constance Jordan shows how this uncertainty is portrayed in terms of a rhetoric of sexuality in which the woman is by nature more voluptuously inclined and, by means of her strength and enormous desires, drains her husband by demanding too much sex from him. The author of *Les quinze joies de mariage* (*The Fifteen Joys of Marriage*) (c. 1425) sees in this imbalance of desires the cause of marital strife – and, one could perhaps extrapolate, civil instability:

> If his wife ... is as desirous as she was at first, and [if] the husband's ardor continues to diminish, the pleasures, the delights, the lovely pastimes that they used to have together in youth and when the husband was potent turn to quarreling and contention, and also as his ardor diminishes, they begin to fight. And when her husband's ardor no longer is sufficient for the wife, even though she may be a good wife and wish to do no wrong, she believes that her husband is less potent [than other men] and that she has a good reason to believe it, since she has tried him and he doesn't satisfy her [*il ne lui suffist pas*].[10]

The passage ends by invoking the authority of God and the church in order to argue that the preceding state of affairs is somehow wrong, even if the author has portrayed it as occurring both naturally and frequently, in that, if one man were truly not enough for one woman, these powers "would have ordered that a woman could have two husbands or as many as would satisfy her."[11]

The rhetoric moves from merely troubled musings on family stability to paranoid couplings of feminine desire with death. *Nef des dames vertueuses* (*The Ship of Virtuous Ladies*), a text by Symphorien Champier from 1515, presents itself as a defence of women, but, as

Jordan demonstrates, the text also reveals many of the aggravated anxieties underlying the *querelle*. In particular, there is the pervasive idea that too much sex is dangerous to one's – that is, to a man's – health, "for [sex] *dissipates and kills* [the person through the excesses of the body] because appetite often exceeds power and you see often that men who take beautiful women die young and often suddenly. For their superficial pleasures a person is wickedly murdered by his own knife."[12]

If female sexuality was unnerving enough for the patriarchy, the possibility of same-sex relations among women was almost too much to bear. Patricia Parker begins her article "Fantasies of 'Race' and 'Gender'" by quoting several of the French surgeon Ambroise Paré's descriptions of the physical monstrosity of the female genitals, descriptions intermingled with a distinct fear and loathing of their possible use in lesbian enjoyment: "Now that these women, who by means of these caruncles or nimphes, abuse one another is a thing as true as it is *monstrous and hard to believe*."[13] She also quotes Paré's advice to remove the clitoris from women on whom it has grown to an unnatural size – that is when it begins to resemble a phallus that can "grow erect like the male rod" and can thus be employed for sex with other women.[14] What is at stake in these passages is a fear of an economy of pleasure between women that thereby excludes men – which, in itself, perhaps implies the spectre of a self-enclosed, reproductively autonomous society of women, the extreme foreclosure of the very function that justifies male existence. What is *abusive* about the unnatural acts that are perpetrated between these women is the appropriation of a power that is not meant to be theirs; the power of the phallus to grant pleasure to a woman is a guarantee of the symbolic power, associated with patriarchal rule, of being the formal link – and proper name – in a reproductive chain.

Such fears, omnipresent throughout the sixteenth century, are brought into striking relief in Rabelais's books, specifically with Panurge's vacillations on the subject of marriage in the *Tiers livre* (*The Third Book*). According to Lawrence Kritzman, Panurge's desire to "settle" is offset by his fear of being a cuckold;[15] but why this is a fear at all is a more interesting question. As Kritzman argues, the descriptions of women in the Rabelais's works place great importance on the ineffability of their desire, which is, in effect, mapped onto women's bodies in an elusive search for some explanatory physical trace, some X to mark the spot, or "locus" of satisfaction: "Nature leurs a dedans le corps posé en lieu secret et intestin un animal, un membre, lequel n'est es hommes" ("Nature has placed in a secret and interior place in their bodies an animal, an organ that is not present in men").[16] There is, in such descriptions, an implicit insecurity, a fear of finding a fundamental incompatibility between the sexes that would leave man forever incapable of satisfying female desire. This is, as Kritzman also notes, evocatively close to Lacan's placing of woman outside the limits of language, and thus unattainable to man, "discursively, or in any other manner."[17] As in some of the texts cited above, this inability to satisfy the animal, labyrinthine desire of woman has as its correlate a perceived threat to man's power or, more specifically, his potency, which must be fortified by the constant use of his genitals: "Si continuellement ne exercez ta mentule, elle perdra son laict, et ne te servira que de pissotiere" ("If you don't give your john-thomas continuous exercise, it'll lose its milk and only be good for a pisser").[18] This insecurity again speaks of man's doubtful place in the reproductive order, and can thus be seen as "a 'hysterical' male reaction to an epistemological anxiety about the ideals of male hegemony and paternity."[19]

If, as these critics have argued, both fictional and polemic texts from early sixteenth-century France bear witness to a popular explosion of male insecurities about female sexual desire, a tendency toward the suppression of that desire can be seen even earlier south of the Pyrenees. Fernando de Rojas's *La Celestina*, considered by many to be one of the most important and influential pieces of literature in the Spanish canon, was written just before the beginning of the sixteenth century. Although its canonical status alone would not justify privileging it as a unique window into early modern mentalities, its exploration of the limits of social norms and moral values may help us understand the flux of ideas at this crucial historical juncture. As Maravall argues, "*La Celestina* nos presenta el drama de la crisis y transmutación de los valores sociales y morales que se desarrolla en la fase de crecimiento de la economía, de la cultura y de la vida entera, en la sociedad del siglo XV" ("*Celestina* shows the crisis of social and moral values and the dramatic transformation of the culture and the entire social life that takes place in this phase of expanding economy in the society of the fifteenth century").[20] Indeed, *La Celestina* provides a rich picture of the changing sensibilities and values of a society in crisis. Maravall does not hesitate to identify in the work a distinct moral position: "Hay en la obra – y tal es su propósito final – una reprobación de la sociedad que pinta, por lo menos en algunos de sus aspectos principales. De ahí, su carácter de 'moralidad' o de 'sátira' ... Pero, al mismo tiempo ..., hay una aceptación de la sociedad misma que se critica" ("The work incorporates – and this is ultimately its objective – a rejection of the society that's depicted in it, at least some of its central aspects. Hence, its moral and satirical dimensions ... Yet, ... there's also an acceptance of the very same society that's criticized").[21]

While we would certainly question whether or not it is so easy to decide the attitude of a work toward its social context of production, we must agree with Maravall that the play has a decidedly moral character, in that it is steeped, from start to finish, in the discourse of illicit love, by definition one of the focal points of all questions of morality. From here, it is only a simple step to the idea that the moral positions taken up by characters in the play, as satirical or hyperbolic as they may be, would form a comprehensible constellation of values for an audience or readership of the time.

Rojas recalls in his prologue Heraclitus's notion that all things are in constant struggle as the basis of a theory of existence. The struggle between the living permeates every aspect of the natural world, right down to copulation, conception, and the moment of birth:

La víbora, reptilia o serpiente enconada, al tiempo del concebir, por la boca de la hembra metida la cabeza del macho, y ella con el gran dulzor apriétale tanto que le mata, y, quedando preñada, el primer hijo rompe los ijares de la madre, por do todos salen y ella queda muerta y él cuasi como vengador de la paterna muerte. ¿Qué mayor lid, qué mayor conquista ni guerra que engendrar en su cuerpo quien coma sus entrañas?

(The viper, that forbidding reptile, conceives and bears its young in this manner: the male places his head in the female's mouth and she, delighted with its sweet taste, presses down so hard upon it that he dies; and then, while she is pregnant, her first future offspring bursts through her side, followed by its brothers and sisters. The first-born thus is more or less the avenger of its father's death. What greater struggle or contention can there be than to have engendered in one's own body the child that will eventually devour one's very entrails?)[22]

Two elements of this narrative deserve immediate comment. First, at a very general level, the author's insistence on the primacy of struggle at all levels of existence would appear to corroborate Maravall's description of a broad epistemological shift from the certain unity of the medieval world to a more pluralistic, and hence contentious, view of social relations.[23] Second, the author's example is clearly one of sexual aggression, which exhibits the same sort of anxiety about female sexuality as the previously mentioned texts. The sexual act culminates in the killing of the male by the female serpent at the very moment of conception. The offspring of this encounter enter the fray of life with a debt to recover. Birth is thus represented as a murderous act of revenge for the father's death.

Mary Gossy situates the fear of sexuality in *La Celestina* in the context of its literary tradition in order to show that this anxiety – the violence that will be associated with untamed desires – is something new. Beginning with the *Libro de buen amor (The Book of Good Love)*, this literary tradition features many of *La Celestina*'s central elements, including the figure of the go-between (*alcahueta*) and the concept of a transgressive sexual passion, *amor loco*. *La Celestina*, however, does not treat this subject with as much moral indifference as earlier works. As Gossy writes, "Rojas takes the established didactic tradition and gives it a decidedly inquisitorial bent; *loco amor*, here, becomes a public sin, heresy, instead of something to be dealt with privately, in confession. As such it is explicitly a threat to the interdependent order of society, not just to an individual soul."[24] If this is an accurate characterization, then one aspect of the broader transition Maravall discusses must be a growing need, from the perspective of the agents of social order, to see sex and marriage as fundamentally linked. Nevertheless, at this particular moment, the open representation of sexual desire, on the part of women and of men, is clearly not outside the limits of the fictionally licit. Indeed, as Michael Gerli has noted in his illuminating study *Celestina and the Ends of Desire*, "the stirrings of desire in Celestina can be discovered at every turn in the text."[25] *La Celestina*'s subject matter and treatment of it do not fall short of the more permissive standards set by previous traditions. Yet, beyond merely explicit descriptions of sexual acts and sexual speech, the text engages in a remarkably frank discussion of the social value of chastity and honour.

In an important scene, Celestina, the go-between and the play's principal character, explains to Sempronio how she intends to interest the chaste and beautiful Melibea in Calisto's amorous intents: "Cosquillosicas son todas; mas después que una vez consienten la silla en el envés del lomo, nunca querrían holgar. Por ellas queda el campo: muertas sí, cansadas no ... Y aun así, vieja como soy, sabe Dios mi buen deseo. ¡Cuánto más éstas que hierven sin fuego!" ("Young girls are all skittish, you know. But I can tell you that once they allow a saddle to be put upon their backs they nevermore wish to be unburdened. The field is theirs. You can kill them, but they never tire ... And even though I am now an old, old thing, God knows how great my longings are. Oh, they begin to boil even before the fire is lit").[26]

There can be no doubt that just talking about the deed is stoking Calisto's desire. As Gerli remarks, "Calisto's pleasure multiplies with the proliferation of discourse, to the point where, as we have seen, he insists on amplifying his desire by continuing to talk about it with Celestina."[27] This is precisely the kind of scene that scandalized the moralist Juan Luis Vives, with whom we will deal more in depth shortly. In his *De institutione feminae christianae* (*The Education of a Christian Woman*), Vives condemns the immoral character of Rojas's play, listing it among those works that Christian women should not be permitted to read. Years later, however, Vives will praise it in *De causis corruptarum artium* (1531) for its central moral lesson that illicit passions lead to violent ends.[28] There need be no contradiction between these two opinions if one takes into account the intended readers of the first piece: young women who could not be expected to grasp the play's moral lesson but would dwell instead in its scandalous actions, which, in the case of *La Celestina*, must have been too much like those "foolish pastimes that tempt the fickle minds of girls."[29]

Despite its purported condemnation of the commerce in illicit sex, the play nevertheless allows certain characters to express cynical attitudes toward the value of female chastity and even to encourage extramarital sex. These characters question the distinction between prostitutes and virtuous women. As Celestina explains, Calisto's reticence and his tardiness in attaining Melibea's assent is due to a misconception about what it means to be a lady, beyond the social enforcing of chastity:

> Y si así no fuese, ninguna diferencia habría entre las públicas que aman, a las escondidas doncellas, si todas dijesen sí a la entrada de su primer requerimiento, en viendo que de alguno eran amadas. Las cuales, aunque están abrasadas y encendidas de vivos fuegos de amor, por su honestidad muestran un frío exterior, un sosegado vulto, un apacible desvío, un constante ánimo y casto propósito.

(There would really be little difference between public prostitutes and close-sheltered girls ..., if when they're aware that they are loved they all said "Yes" at the very first possible moment. No. Your gentle ladies, though burned and devoured by love's fierce flame, exhibit a cold visage, composed countenance, calculated coldness, evenness of temper, and chaste bearing.)[30]

The erasure of the line that separates the lady from the virtueless woman leads to the blurring of another border, that between the virgin and the sexually initiated, which is of course a mainstay of Celestina's profession. Furthermore, this passage, and many others like it, intimate close parallels between marriage and prostitution as social practices of commerce in women, separated only by a question of legality, and, as Celestina will make clear, agency. For Celestina, desire has a use value, the delights of the flesh, as well as an exchange value. A woman can and should capitalize on the charms of her sex, seeking multiple lovers: "¿Y tú temes que con dos que tengas, que las tablas de la cama lo han de descobrir? ¿De una sola gotera te mantienes? ¡No te sobrarán muchos manjares! ... Nunca uno me agradó, nunca en uno puse toda mi afición. Más pueden dos, y más cuatro, y más dan y más tienen, y más hay en qué escoger" ("Do you think the bed slats would reveal your having two friends? Is your tank supplied by only one pipe? Then there won't be any leftovers at your table ... One man was never sufficient for *me*; never did I give all my affection to a single one. Two are better; four – better still. The more there are, the more there are to choose from, and the more you'll get out of them").[31] Needless to say, any notion of honour falls by the wayside here: "Honra sin provecho no es sino como anillo en el dedo. Y pues entrambos no caben en un saco, acoge la ganancia" ("Honour without profit is like a ring on the finger ... And since honor and profit don't sit too well together in the same sack – choose the profit").[32]

Thus, *La Celestina* discusses ideas that will become harder to express in later centuries. At the same time, when we situate the work historically in light of its literary antecedents, we can see a new focus on the question of licit versus illicit sexual activity, which will become the basis for a redefinition of femininity and of a woman's proper role in society. In effect, in the next few decades, moral treatises would place severe limits on women sexuality as part of a repositioning of femininity in the structural economy of everyday life. Mary Elizabeth Perry argues that the increased concern over chastity was a function of the renewed religious orthodoxy of the Counter-Reformation: "In the peculiar mathematics of Counter-Reformation moralists, the female who lost her chastity acquired in exchange a frightening license to break every other taboo. The unchaste woman, in this view, posed not only a threat to the social order, but a real danger to the salvation of men's souls."[33]

Perry gathers a wealth of historical evidence that shows a significant increase in restrictions on the prostitution trade throughout Catholic Europe in the aftermath of the Council of Trent, as the Crown intervened to encourage municipalities to "play a greater role in enforcing prostitution laws."[34] She also shows that medical regulations of prostitutes intensified in the aftermath of the notorious syphilis outbreaks of the mid-1500s.

Perry's research is undoubtedly very helpful, but we would question whether it is necessary to establish a direct causal nexus with the Council of Trent. Indeed, some of the changes in legal restrictions on prostitution that Perry describes occurred either during the eighteen-year duration of the council (1545–63) or so soon after that it is difficult to imagine the council having played a direct role.[35] It is interesting to note, in this light, the striking similarity between the words with which Perry describes the "official" view of the unchaste woman in Counter-Reformation Spain – "not only a threat to the social order, but a real danger to the salvation of men's souls" – and those with which Gossy refers to the dangers of *loco amor* in *La Celestina*: "explicitly a threat to the interdependent order of society, not just to an individual soul."[36] Even if we do not assume a clear-cut moral condemnation of sexual deviancy in *La Celestina*, we would argue that its plot and character development reveal emerging epochal anxieties about female sexuality and a woman's place in society. By the time of Juan Luis Vives's writing, we can see that these issues have become a state matter.

In her article "The Exclusion of the Feminine in the Cultural Discourse of the Golden Age: Juan Luis Vives and Fray Luis de Léon," Emilie Bergmann identifies a trend in sixteenth-century Spanish didactic prose that corroborates the changes we are describing. In her view, the span of the sixteenth century marks a process of the virtual disappearance of "the feminine" from literary discourse.[37] Whether we think of it in terms of a "disappearance" or a symbolic reworking of the feminine, we witness crucial changes in the moralistic writings of the time, including in the treatment of motherhood. As Bergmann writes, "the role of mothers in initiating children in language and culture virtually disappears from didactic prose by the seventeenth century: mothers disappear almost completely from literary representations of the family, or they actively reject their children, as in the picaresque novel."[38]

Indeed, this de-emphasizing of the maternal role is one of the key tropes of the early modern rearticulation of femininity. Bergmann connects this phenomenon with important changes in cultural institutions and social mores. She argues that such didactic texts as Vives's *De institutione feminae christianae* constitute a concerted effort toward the "exile of women from cultural discourse and from the responsibility for educating children, an exile that will be established more clearly after the Council of Trent and further development of educational institutions."[39] One possible explanation for this trend, and one at which Bergmann also hints, is that the state had acquired a vested interest in a more radical separation of the domains of the sexes. In this context, the mothering of male children could represent a risk to their masculinity. The exclusion of the mother would thus be meant to guarantee the radical gender division that was rapidly becoming the centrepiece of state ideology.

Vives defines the female sex in terms of two key qualities: chastity and love for her husband. The first ought to govern a woman's years prior to marriage; the latter, her married life. The supreme importance of chastity is unequivocal in Vives's view: "In a woman, no one requires eloquence or talent or wisdom or professional skills or administration of the republic or justice or generosity; no one asks anything of her but chastity. If that one thing is missing, it is as if all were lacking to a man."[40] As Bergmann notes, this is to define a woman by a mere absence as opposed to any positive quality she may possess.[41] Vives transforms this "negative" quality into a forceful social responsibility, linking the woman's chastity to the role of the church in defending the truth of Christ – her husband – against the would-be adulterers, both inside (like baptized heretics) and outside (like Turks and Jews) the doors of His home.

The two womanly qualities of which Vives writes will merge into one, insofar as love for one's husband means nothing more than a continuation of the idea of chastity. According to this view, the woman's body ceases to be the property of her father, only to become her husband's property. Within this moral paradigm, the woman's chastity/fidelity is the keystone that holds the social field together. If you commit adultery, Vives tells his female reader, "you will have dissolved the greatest of bonds, *broken the holiest association that exists in human affairs*: trust, which many have given even to an armed enemy and kept it, although it meant their own certain destruction."[42]

In accordance with this view, the role of women, or more properly speaking, of their chastity or self-negation, is that of a mediating agent between men. Her negation of her own will (described in terms of the utter subjection of her body) is the fundamental guarantor of social cohesion. Thus, the entire social field of symbolic exchange is grounded in her promise of renunciation of her sexual desire. By evacuating her desire, woman becomes the vessel of a man's honour and the unit of exchange for his subjection to the state.

Above we argued that the theatrical phenomenon known as the *Comedia Nueva* that emerged at the end of the sixteenth century propagated an illusion of moral autonomy within the private or domestic sphere, organized around the "quilting point," or "ideologeme," of honour.[43] As we showed, this purported moral autonomy of man (every man worthy of the honour call) turned out to be little more than the right – and deadly obligation – to preserve and defend the sexual purity of all women pertaining to him (although the truth was most likely quite different from the theatrical portrayal).

The flip side of this idea, in which woman becomes the empty placeholder of man's equally empty honour, is an ever-present threat to women's purity that comes from the outside – that is, from other men. Women are indeed portrayed as desiring, but desiring chastely – showing an immutable love for one man. In Lope de Vega's *El caballero de Olmedo* (*The Knight from Olmedo*), for instance, the love affair is between Alonso, brave knight from Olmedo, and Inés, beautiful and noble maid from Medina del Campo.[44] Inés, however, is betrothed to the treacherous Don Rodrigo, a friend of her father's. From the instant we are introduced to each of the main characters, Inés never expresses anything but disdain for Rodrigo, and is immediately attracted to the handsome stranger from Olmedo:

> DOÑA INÉS: Dime tú: si don Rodrigo
> ha que me sirve dos años
> y su talle y sus engaños
> son nieve helada conmigo,
> y en instante que vi
> este galán forastero

me dijo el alma: "Este quiero,"
y yo le dije: "Sea ansí,"
 ¿quién concierta y desconcierta
este amor y desamor?

([INÉS:])   Explain this, then. For two
Years now Rodrigo's been my suitor.
His looks and flattering words turn me
To ice. And yet, no sooner do I see
This handsome stranger than my soul
Informs me that I love him, and I
Reply that, yes, I must agree.
Who decides that we should love
One person, not another?)[45]

What provides excitement and dramatic tension for the spectators in this and other honour plays is the displacement that occurs from wonderment at the enormity of female desire to the more orchestrated competition between men for the prize of a woman's love and the honour it signifies. The political power of the king is reified directly in many of these plays as the source, the fountain, of the honour that now regulates the interactions of his subjects. These classic honour dramas depend upon a common structure of rupture, some offence against someone's honour, and closure, in the form of justice handed down by the king or some representative of his authority, as in *El caballero de Olmedo*. Upon hearing the story of Alonso's deceit and his subsequent murder at the hands of Rodrigo, the king ends the play by pronouncing sentence:

REY: Prendellos,
y en un teatro mañana
cortad sus infames cuellos.

([KING:])   Arrest them [the offenders]!
Tomorrow in a public place
Cut off their evil heads.)[46]

Fittingly, the king's righteous but deadly justice is to take place in a theatre, where it serves not only as punishment of the offenders but also as a representation to the people of the king's own role as the nexus between law and honour. Thus, the rearticulation of monstrous, uncontrollable female desire into a limited discourse of love over a foundation of honour serves the ends of a new form of political power, one that will spill over from the relation of subjects to monarchs to that of citizens to each other and to the state.

9

Her Weapon

So far, we have strived to identify, from the clues provided by early modern exemplary texts, a trend, beginning in the late fifteenth century in Spain, to eradicate the spectre of female desire and thereby legitimize a model of femininity based on chastity, marital love, and duty. As we saw in our reading of *La Celestina*, moralistic delimitations of the "proper" sexual mores arrive with equally rich explorations of "improper" or illicit attitudes and behaviour. As Guido Ruggiero argues in regard to Italy during the same period, "as that discourse of civic morality gained shape and power, it intersected with an increasingly articulated and important counterculture of the illicit, grown up partly in response to the inherent contradictions in the dominant cultural vision of the correct placement of sex in marriage."[1]

In the new cultural context, the "improper" element could be recognized as such and excluded outright, as in Fichte's later recommendation to simply expel all prostitutes from the state. Yet it could also be incorporated into satires and parodies, as well as new discursive forms such as the picaresque narrative, which build on the Celestinesque exploration of marginal spaces and countercultural mores. We discussed above Cervantes's theatrical response to the (deadly) serious treatment of the honour theme in his *Entremeses*. He explicitly thematizes the theatre in other works, including his full-length play *Pedro de Urdemalas*. Among his prose writings, *La tía fingida* (*The Pretended Aunt*) (attributed to him) would be a good example. This novella deals with many of the same themes that we have discussed apropos *La Celestina* but does so with a lighter touch and without the slightest hint of melodrama. *La tía fingida* is the story of a prostitute, or more accurately, of her elderly female handler, who masquerades as the venerable aunt of a young noblewoman. In the world of the *Comedia*, the conflation of aristocrats with prostitutes would be unthinkable. It is precisely the rigour of this distinction that sets the stage for Cervantes's parody, as when one of the young prostitute's ladies-in-waiting issues a proclamation as to her virtue, which is at the same time a sales pitch:

> – Huy, huy – dijo la dueña – , en eso por cierto está mi señora doña Esperanza de Torralba, Meneses y Pacheco. Sepa, señor mío, que no es de las que piensa, porque es mi señora muy principal, muy honesta, muy recogida, muy discreta, muy graciosa, muy música, y muy leída y escribida, y no hará lo que vuesa merced le suplica, aunque la cubriesen de perlas.

("Hey day! Very likely, indeed, my lady Doña Esperanza [de Torralba, Meneses y Pacheco] will do any such thing," said the dueña. "I would have you to know, good señor, she is not one of those you take her for. My lady is very genteel, very honourable, very correct, very discreet, very well read, and very well written; and she will not do what you ask: no, not though you were to cover her with pearls").[2]

Cervantes further accentuates the contrast between the dueña's feigned indignation and her asking price by thereafter referring to her as the "dueña del 'huy' y 'las perlas'" ("Hey Lady and Pearls").[3] It is important to note, however, that Doña Esperanza de Torralba is not a common prostitute but is, rather, sold by her aunt to wealthy men *as a noble virgin*; in other words, she is not only a sexual commodity but a *transgressive* commodity as well, in that, by "enjoying" her, her buyer can also enjoy what he (and others) perceive as the piercing of the sphere of honour. The aunt can repeatedly sell her as a virgin only if she can be certain to bleed each time she copulates – proof that honour has indeed been pierced – and this requires that she resort to Celestina's expertise, the reparation of maidenheads. The insight of Cervantes's discourse is this equivalence of honour and hymen; that both are liminal, undeniably subject to counterfeit, and each is a barrier that has meaning only insofar as it is always already transgressed or transgressable.

María de Zayas deals with some of the same themes in *El prevenido, engañado* (*The Forewarned Deceived*), although here, it is not so much the concept of honour that is satirized, as in Cervantes's work, but the absurdity of the expectation that women behave in accordance with the prevailing moralist discourse. *El prevenido, engañado* narrates the life story of a young and noble *granadino* as he travels the world trying to fulfil his sexual-marital expectations. The problem is that the nobleman, having been raised in the ideology of the sort espoused by Juan Luis Vives, truly believes that each woman with whom he falls in love will be a chaste vessel for his virile passion. Zayas seems to have a great deal of fun disabusing him of that notion, as each and every one of his amorous exploits results in the blatant revelation of his beloved's real, embodied, sexual desire, and, furthermore, her enactment of that desire with other men.

In a particularly amusing episode, Fadrique – the *granadino* – falls in love with a beautiful, free-spirited poet and, after exchanging a few well-wrought verses, lapses into daydreams of conjugal bliss:

Pasáronse muchos días en esta voluntad, sin extenderse a más los atrevimientos amorosos, que a sólo aquello que sin riesgo del honor se podía gozar, teniendo estos impedimentos tan enamorado a don Fadrique, que casi estaba determinado a casarse, aunque Violante jamás trató nada acerca desto, porque verdaderamente aborrecía el casarse, temerosa de perder la libertad que entonces gozaba.

(Many days passed with this understanding, without amorous boldness extending further than only to that which could be enjoyed without risking honor. These impediments [had] don Fadrique so enamored that he was almost determined to marry, although Violante never discussed anything regarding this, because she truly loathed marrying, fearful of losing the freedom she then enjoyed.)[4]

This passage offers several examples of inversions of the dominant order of representation. For one, a common trope would be to speak of a great love or passion hindered by social or material impediments, whereas Zayas makes the impediments entirely responsible for Fadrique's love. Second, it is the man who – naively expressing the official vinculum between marriage and sexual satisfaction – seeks matrimony, while the woman won't even give it serious consideration, so addicted is she to her freedom. By the end of the episode, Fadrique has found himself on the other side of the equation, helping his friend sleep with Violante's married cousin, while he himself is sleeping with Violante in the husband's house. Thinking he is at last on the inside track of desire, he will be dealt the most humiliating blow yet, when he finds out that Violante is cheating on him with yet another lover.

One cannot help but feel that Fadrique ultimately gets exactly what he deserves, the rewards of his nosiness: looking always beneath the rosy surface of decorum, he comes face to face with naked female desire. Zayas's strategy here is thus to highlight the hypocrisy of decorum, much as Cervantes's exposes the emptiness of honour. In their own distinctive ways, they are both examining their society's most fundamental assumptions concerning gender roles and gender relations and exposing them to scrutiny and even ridicule.

In their exposure of hypocrisy, Cervantes's and Zayas's novellas may remind us of the treatment of honour and morality in such picaresque narratives as *Lazarillo de Tormes* (1554) and *La pícara Justina* (*The Spanish Jilt*) (1605). While the voice of *Lazarillo* paints a dark picture of Spanish society of the mid-1500s and denounces the lack of charitable souls and the rampant corruption of "protective" masters and institutions such as the church and the state, the marginal gaze of the heroine of *Justina* focuses squarely on gender relations. Remarkably, her in-your-face first-person account comes through despite the misogyny of the presumed author, López de Ubeda – in his landmark 1987 study *The Antiheroine's Voice*, Friedman calls him "antifeminist."[5]

Justina's relentless undressing of (male) authority figures and her unapologetic claim to matrilineal picaresque royalty sets up an intriguing gender-inflected conflict between the burlesque voice of the *pícara*-narrator and the moralistic, admonishing, and accusatory authorial presence that struggles to contain her within the familiar frame of didactic literature. As Friedman writes, "the author superimposes himself on the structure of the narrative, poetically at the beginning of each section and morally at the end ... In the *aprovechamientos*, he appends instructive but commonplace adages to a blatantly antisocial text to remove *La pícara Justina* from the threat of inquisitorial stricture. The benefits are reciprocal in that the author enjoys moral superiority over his creation and the narrator enjoys a certain freedom of speech."[6]

Justina, like Lazarillo before her, is an unlikely narrator, a literary trope meant to represent the unspoken and unspeakable truth of a social body that's rotten to the core. But while Lazarillo's first-person narrative flows free, unconstrained, and unchallenged, even as it denounces the hypocrisy and corruption of abusive masters, the interventionist author of *La pícara Justina* brackets her voice within a moralistic watchtower perspective, similar to that of the "watchtower of human life" ("atalaya de la vida humana"), as in the subtitle of the second part of Mateo Alemán's *Guzmán de Alfarache*.[7] The watchtower author is meant to diagnose, isolate, and treat the cancer that's spreading through the social body; and the *pícara*'s life/gaze/voice is treated as both poison and antidote. This dual status of the *pícara* as venom and vaccine (*pharmakon*) explains why the author himself assumes the role of the (moral) doctor who must provide the proper medicine and dosage instructions for his patients or readers:

> Y advierto al lector que siempre que encontrare algún dicho en que parece que hay un mal ejemplo, repare que se pone para quemar en estatua aquello mismo, y en tal caso, se recorra al aprovechamiento que he puesto en el fin de cada número y a las advertencias que hice en el prólogo al lector, que si ansí se hace, sacarse ha utilidad de ver esta estatua de libertad que aquí he pintado, y en ella, los vicios que hoy día corren por el mundo.

> (Readers be warned that if they come across content that appears to contain a bad example, they must recall that this book is meant to burn such bad examples in effigy; and in case of doubt they should make use of the *aprovechamiento* that I have placed at the end of each section and also remember the prologue's warnings; for if they do this, they will surely profit from the effigy of freedom that I have here painted as a representation of the plague of vice that's spreading through the world.)[8]

Referring in another section to the *pícara*'s description of the religious festivities of León, the author makes the following comments: "personas mal intencionadas son como arañas, que de la flor sacan veneno, y así, Justina, de las fiestas santas no se aprovecha sino para decir malicias impertinentes" ("ill-intentioned people are like spiders who can produce venom from flower blossoms, and thus, Justina uses these sacred celebrations to spin her malicious web of impertinent storytelling").[9] The medical language is most explicit in those sections of the text that are reserved for authorial interventions. In fact, the presence of this kind of language has contributed to the book's attribution to Francisco López de Ubeda, a physician from Toledo of whom it is known that he accompanied Philip III to León in 1605. Here's an example from the introduction: "Si ello el libro está bueno, buen provecho les haga, y si malo, perdonen, que mal se puede purgar bien los enfermos si yo me pongo ahora muy de espacio a purgar a la pícara" ("If the book is good, may you profit from it, and if bad, may you excuse it, for it would not do the sick any good if I were to purge the *pícara* too rigorously").[10] As we can see here, the author pitches his picaresque book as medicine for the morally ill, which would lose its efficacy if he were to water down the active ingredient. In other words, the author must allow enough of the *pícara*'s voice and worldview to come through for the *pharmakon* to work – that is, for us to be properly inoculated against the plague of free women.

The first words of the *pícara*-narrator are understandably tentative. Justina feels vulnerable, out of her element, intimidated by the very writing instruments she must use to tell her story. She expects to be scorned and stigmatized by masculine authorities. Yet, by the end of her introduction, she is fully ready to go. If she entered the realm of writing as a fearful writer,[11] she soon feels empowered by the pen, as is indicated by the title of chapter 1, "De la escribana fisgada" ("Of the Snooped Scribe").[12] As noted by Nina Cox Davis and others,[13] the word "fisga" and its derivatives function as phallic markers of power in the burlesque context in which the standard male critic – mockingly named "fisgón medroso" – is disqualified as vane, intrusive, nosy, and overly scrupulous, even as he pompously claims professional expertise in every imaginable subject: "Yo, el licenciado Perlícaro, ortógrapho, músico, perspectivo, mathemático, arismético, geómetra, astrónomo, gramático, poeta, retórico, dialéctico, phísico, médico, flebótomo, notomista, metaphísico, y theólogo, que declaro ser este primer capítulo y todo el libro el segundo pecado nefando" ("I, Licentiate Perlícaro [the name is a clever word play meaning Pricy Pearl], orthographer, musician, perspectivist, mathematician, arithmetician, geometrician, astronomer, grammarian, poet, rhetorician, dialectician, physician, medic, phlebotomist, anatomist, metaphysician, and theologian declare that this chapter and indeed the entire book is but a sinful abomination").[14] In her response, Justina notes that, as a critic (and not a creator), her male accuser is a mere renter or borrower of words ("alquilador de verbos").[15] Her aggressive stance vis-à-vis masculine authority is best signified by the rallying cry that marks the start of her life story: "¡Agua va! Desvíense que lo tengo todo a punto, y va de historia" ("Look out! Take cover! Here it comes! Story time it is!").[16] The implications of this cryptic warning to watch out for dirty waters are fully fleshed out in chapter 5, when Justina instructs a college graduate (*bachiller*) to retrieve from under her bed a basket of honeycomb, which turns out to contain a pile of feces.

Justina's contempt for representatives of moral and cultural authority can be contextualized within her general view of men. In book 4, which deals with her search for a suitable groom, she identifies a series of masculine types including the presumptuous, the hypocritical, the self-centred, and the ostentatious. Justina seems to suggest that men are only good for money and sex, and possibly to provide cover under a good family name. Later, she playfully uses the list of Latin cases to mockingly paint a picture of her ideal man: he must be "dative" (obsequious) and "genitive" (sexually satisfying), as well as "nominative" (he must carry a reputable name).[17] As one of us argued in *(A)wry Views*, despite her initial hesitations in the presence of ink, pen, and paper, Justina comes to think of her writing as a weapon that she can skilfully wield to expose masculine hypocrisy, short-sightedness, egotism, and misogyny, even as her voice is ultimately contained within the profoundly anti-feminist frame provided by the author.[18]

Today, it is not difficult to find a similar understanding of a woman's voice as her weapon. Angie Thomas's best-selling novel *The Hate U Give* (2017), which inspired an equally popular motion picture, makes this point explicitly:

> "Who said talking isn't doing something?" she says. "It's more productive than silence. Remember what I told you about your voice?"
> "You said it's my biggest weapon."
> "And I mean that ... You want to fight the system tonight? ... Use your weapon."[19]

As for a feminine voice effectively competing for narrative space, we can think of no better example today than the Netflix series *Alias Grace*, which is based on Margaret Atwood's award-winning fictionalization of the life of Grace Marks, a poor Irish immigrant working as a domestic servant in colonial Canada who was convicted of the infamous 1843 double murder of her employer and his housekeeper. Grace's tragic life story is framed by a series of personal interviews conducted by Dr Simon Jordan. As was the case in *La pícara Justina*, the female protagonist is able to overcome her initial hesitation and take control of the narrative in an act of defiance that will force Dr Jordan to confront his own hidden fears, prejudices, and desires, pushing him to question his protective/authoritative role as expert inquirer, potential benefactor, and ultimate judge. The doctor's identity crisis is a direct consequence of the shattering of his own narrative frame, precipitated by a hypnotic session during which Grace channels a darkly aggressive persona, capable of the most scandalous insights – not unlike the spider-like gaze of the "poisonous" Justina. The tables are turned in this powerful scene, in which the subject of the scientific experiment undresses the good doctor, his companions, and, we would argue, the entire community. Dr Jordan asks the hypnotized Grace whether she ever had "relations" with her alleged co-conspirator and partner in crime. Her shocking response comes with a series of confessions uttered in a notoriously unchained voice that identifies itself as belonging to Mary Whitney, Grace's dead friend and confidante:

Relations? What do you mean? Really, Doctor, you're such a hypocrite! You want to know if I kissed him, if I slept with him, ... is that it? ... Whether I did what you'd like to do with that little slut who's got hold of your hand? You'd like to know that, so I'll tell you. Yes. I would meet him outside, in the yard. I'd press up against him and let him kiss me and touch me all over, Doctor, the same places you'd like to touch me, because I can always tell. I know what you are thinking when you sit in that stuffy sewing room with me. That was all, Doctor. That was all I let him do. I had him on a string ... After that, he'd say he'd do anything. But why? Oh, Doctor, you're always asking why. Poking your nose in, and not only your nose. You're such a curious man, Doctor. Curiosity killed the cat, you know? You should watch out for that little mouse beside you and her little furry mouse hole too! ... I am not Grace ... I told James to do it. I was there all along! ... Here. Where I am now, with Grace ... But Grace doesn't know, she's never known! They almost hanged her, that would have been wrong ... I wouldn't want to hurt her. You mustn't tell her ... Do you want to see her back in the asylum? ... You see? You're all the same. You won't listen, ... you won't hear.[20]

Whether a symptom of an acute case of multiple personality disorder (as the roguish hypnotist claims), a supernatural act of possession (as some members of the audience would want to believe), or a canny deception (as Dr Jordan suspects), Grace's hypnotic performance has the effect of reducing the doctor to silence and shame. The reputed physician was supposed to be able to penetrate the depths of Grace's psyche, access her lost memories, and ultimately author an objective judgment on her mental state and her involvement in the murders. But instead of the expected authoritative report that would have established Grace's innocence (or guilt), the eager addressees of Dr Jordan's letter (including the external audience) are left with nothing but the doctor's confession of utter impotence, wrapped in a myriad of conflicting feelings. If Dr Jordan's document speaks truth, this is not the truth of Grace's soul, but that of the physician's own shattered ego threatened by the mere existence of Grace, the whole of Grace:

> Was she really in a trance or was she play-acting and laughing up her sleeve? … The truth eludes me. Or Grace eludes me … I wonder if [hypnotism and mesmerism] provide an opportunity for women to say what they think and to express their true thoughts and feelings more boldly and in more vulgar terms that they could otherwise feel permission to. I wonder about Grace's violent childhood and her experience as a young woman, abused constantly, harassed on every side. I wonder how much repressed rage she must have carried with her as a result. The question is, was this rage directed toward Nancy Montgomery and Thomas Kinnear, resulting in their murder? Or at me, therefore making her confession during her hypnotism a fraud designed to hurt me? One thing is certain. I cannot write a report for your committee. I must forget Grace Marks.[21]

These powerful scenes from *Alias Grace* help illuminate certain passages of *La pícara Justina* in unexpected ways. Justina feels stripped in the presence of the pen and forced to stand naked in shame (*in puribus*) as the author piles on the blame. She is branded with the letter *P*, which signifies deviancy, poverty, shamelessness, stained genealogy, and venereal disease (*pícara, pobre, poca vergüenza, pelona y pelada*). Rather than retreating, however, the *pícara* manages to go on the offensive and return the blame. Thus, Justina suggests that the reason why the pen can brand her with this long list of stigmatizing marks and threaten her with yet one more *P*, the most definitive of all (prostitution, no doubt) is that the letter *P* lives inside its own name: "Qué he de esperar, sino que como la pluma tiene la P dentro de su casa y el alquiler pagado, me ponga algún otro nombre de P que me eche a puertas?" ("What could I expect if the Pen has the letter *P* inside its own house and the rent paid; will it not reach for that other *P* name to finish the job?").[22] Moreover, she comes to think of her stigmas as battle wounds or even hunting trophies to be exhibited rather than hidden: "Las manchas de la vida picaresca ... son como las del pellejo de pía, onza, tigre, pórfido, taracea y jaspe" ("The stains of the picaresque life ... are like those on a tiger, on porphyry, intarsia and jasper").[23] As with the scandalous confession that emerged from the depths of Grace's split voice, Justina's own "naked" confession works to expose the hypocrisy of her accusers and those moral and cultural authorities who hold power over her: "¿Seré yo la primera camuesa colorada por defuera y podrida por de dentro? ¿Seré yo el primer sepulchro vivo?" ("Am I really the first pippin apple that's nice and red on the outside and putrid in the inside? Will I be the first living grave?").[24]

Could it be that, by releasing Justina's voice, the moral doctor/author of *La pícara Justina* risks the same fate as Dr Simon Jordan in *Alias Grace*? We would argue that, as the voice of the *pícara* becomes stronger and more defiant, the commonplace accusations, warnings, and disclaimers of the male author can no longer be trusted to contain her. Thus, the readers of *La pícara Justina* (as those of *Lazarillo* before her), as well as the spectators of the film treatment of *Alias Grace* and the readers of Atwood's novel, might welcome the chance to see the world through the eyes of the accused, even if momentarily.

Some cultural commentators wonder if the scandals of the Trump presidency might not offer a real opportunity to address and fight against misogynistic practices and discourses, unequal treatment of women, sexual harassment, and other forms of abuse. As Spanish professors and early modern specialists, we would suggest that, in allowing the work of such authors as Cervantes and María de Zayas and such texts as *La pícara Justina* to speak to our medialogy, the Spanish Golden Age classroom can help contextualize and historicize our moment and encourage our students to ask not only "what then?" but "what next?" Understanding how we got here in the first place is half the battle; and the transhistorical and transcultural classroom can make us better prepared for the difficult conversations ahead. After all, as Margaret Atwood has recently reminded us in her urgent reflection "Am I a Bad Feminist?" – a title that resonates with uncanny accents when placed side by side with Sor Juana's confession, "Yo, la peor de todas" ("I, the worst of them all")[25] – the question of *what next* must be borne of honest self-examination, with the long view in sight; and fiction can help. If the ultimate aim of ideology is to eliminate all ambiguity, as Atwood notes, and thus confine everything and everyone in familiar models (of gender and otherwise), then "fiction writers are particularly suspect because they write about human beings, and people are morally ambiguous."[26]

The process, or trend, that we have outlined thus far while dealing with the rearticulation of femininity taking place in early modern Spain has another pole in the development of a properly modern subjectivity. As we saw earlier in our discussion of Fichte's philosophical writings, the Enlightenment, which could be defined as a programmatic project of formalization of modern subjectivity, was also engaged in the explanation of sexual difference, in which the definition of subjective reason was arrived at more often than not through an exclusion of female desire. As we have tried to show, this exclusion was bequeathed to the Enlightenment, and thus to contemporary Western mentality, via a process of change inherent to the period we call early modernity, a striking example of which occurs in Spain. The exclusion of the feminine that enables an "active" definition of subjectivity in the Enlightened work of Fichte is already a redundant one: the feminine being excluded is itself already the product of an earlier exclusion, one in which female sexual desire was removed – at the level of the licit, or proper – from the gender distinction of femininity.

The two processes are indirectly related, and mutually dependent: the normalization of a male subjective space, in which men are the monadic, semi-autonomous links in a larger social body called the state – an agglomerate of desire – implies a concomitant evacuation of female sexuality in order that women can serve a new function in a new social order. The symbolic power that enables the cohesion of the Spanish Empire and the ideology of honour that it propagates requires a space of illusory autonomy, a place where men could build the hearth of their identity and desire, from which they could participate in a state that they might never see embodied. This space was provided by the new femininity. The modern patriarchal subject is thus built, at least in part, on the apocryphal eradication of desire and agency from the feminine, which is why we would argue that, if we wish to understand this subject's role in contemporary society, it would be important to examine the cultural conditions of its emergence.

10

A Homeopathic Cure for Patriarchy

In the wider cultural context of the Spanish Golden Age, Justina's fictionalized account of a female writer fighting off male critics and moral watchtowers brings to mind the work of such women authors as Teresa de Jesús and Sor Juana Inés de la Cruz, both of whom were looked at with suspicion by their male superiors for their intrusion into the masculine realm of writing. In her *Respuesta a Sor Filotea* (*Reply to Sor Filotea*), Sor Juana defended the right of women to engage in intellectual pursuits and to teach other women. Indeed, she went on to suggest that male teachers should be kept away from young women in order to ensure women's safety and protect the moral health of the community. She countered the bishop's admonishment that she should devote herself to prayer and activities appropriate to her gender by paraphrasing Teresa de Jesús's assertion that one can very well philosophize in the kitchen while cooking dinner. Known as the "decima musa" ("tenth muse") and the "fenix de Mexico" ("phoenix of Mexico"), Sor Juana was a self-taught scholarly wonder who was equally comfortable discussing philosophy and science, composing music, and writing poetry.[1] Her denunciation of male hypocrisy and misogyny led to her official condemnation. Hence, in 1694 (a year before her death), Sor Juana ceased to write, under pressure from the bishop and other high-ranking officials whose censure forced her to repent her waywardness, undergo penance for her sins, and dispose of her books, scientific tools, and musical instruments.

As a poet, Sor Juana mastered the baroque style that had been popularized by Luis de Góngora and his followers while adding her own gender-inflected perspective. In her masterful sonnet known as "A su retrato," for example, she makes use of such baroque tropes as the passing of time and the illusory nature of youth and beauty to criticize the blind conventionality of her portrait (possibly Juan Carreño de Miranda's work) and make a point about art's airbrushing of women:

> Este que ves, engaño colorido,
> que del arte ostentando los primores,
> con falsos silogismos de colores
> es cauteloso engaño del sentido;
>   éste, en quien la lisonja ha pretendido
> excusar de los años los horrores,
> y venciendo del tiempo los rigores
> triunfar de la vejez y del olvido,
>   es un vano artificio del cuidado,
> es una flor al viento delicada,
> es un resguardo inútil para el hado:
>   es una necia diligencia errada,
> es un afán caduco y, bien mirado,
> es cadáver, es polvo, es sombra, es nada.

> (This that you see is a colourful deception,
> which, in displaying the charms of art,
> with the false syllogisms of its hues
> deceptively subverts the sense of sight;
>   this, in which false praise has vainly sought
> to veil the horrors of the passing years,
> safeguarding against the rigours of time
> to triumph over old age and oblivion,
>   it is a vein protective artifice,
> it is a fragile bloom caught in the wind,
> it is a useless safeguard against fate:
>   it is a thoughtless and erroneous project,
> it is a failing enterprise, and, rightly seen,
> it is corpse, dust, shadow, nothingness.)[2]

The final verse of Sor Juana's sonnet echoes Góngora's anamorphic unveiling of the tragic end of youth and beauty turned "en tierra, en humo, en polvo, en sombra, en nada" ("into earth, smoke, dust, shade, nothingness").[3] Yet, by focusing on her "colourful deception" ("engaño colorido"), Sor Juana redirects the anamorphic gaze to the representational medium, turning (her) poetry into a weapon against art(ifice). Thus, the truth that's revealed from the right angle ("bien mirado"/"rightly seen") in Sor Juana's poem is not (at least not only or primarily) the tragic end of aging flesh hidden behind youthful appearances, but the blind spot of (conventional) art. She seems to be implying that the lying conceits that erase the signs of aging from her face ("falsos silogismos de colores") hide her existential truth: her life as well as her impending death. This is the failure of man's art(ifice) wrapped in thoughtless flattery: *lisonja, vano artificio, necia diligencia errada.*

As with the previously discussed texts, Sor Juana's work can certainly inform and animate class discussions of gender roles, misogyny, and conventional representations of women in the age of Trump and in the context of the #MeToo and #TimesUp movements. With regards to representations of women, for example, the vast majority of the images produced today by the retail, fashion, and culture industries use photoshop tools to remove wrinkles, skin blemishes, and other signs of aging from women's faces and to alter the appearance of their bodies to fit unattainable ideals of shape, size, and proportion. This, despite the fact that the American Medical Association officially identified airbrushing as a health issue back in 2011 and discouraged "the altering of photographs in a manner that could promote unrealistic expectations of appropriate body image."[4]

At the same time, in examining the writings of Sor Juana in their own cultural context, we can see that she preserves and builds on certain aspects of the philosophical, artistic, and literary traditions of her predecessors while responding to or transgressing others. Her play *Los empeños de una casa* (*The House of Trials*) is a good example of her approach to (and dialogue with) the *Comedia Nueva.*

As previously discussed, within the larger sociological context of the *Comedia*, the so-called *dramas de honor* were powerful vehicles for the exemplary dramatization of moral issues. As Maravall suggests, these plays could indeed propagate or rearticulate what we might now refer to as "packages of values" or ideologemes around the subject of honour. Arguably, the most intense and sophisticated treatment of the honour theme in the Spanish baroque can be found in the work of Calderón de la Barca, which is often a direct point of reference for Sor Juana. Of particular interest to the reading of Sor Juana's *Los empeños de una casa* (and Zayas's *El verdugo de su esposa*) is Calderón's *El médico de su honra,* an especially dark play in which, as we explained in chapter 7, a high-ranking aristocrat orders the that his innocent wife be bled to death. At the risk of oversimplifying Calderón's intricate plot, we would characterize this play as building on two central themes, which are omnipresent in the baroque subgenre of the honour play: the absolute dominion of *reputación* over and above actual conduct, despite the well-reasoned protestations of such paradigmatic characters as Pedro Crespo (the well-known protagonist of *El alcalde de Zalamea*); and the justification (or at least the repeated thematization) of dire measures for the satisfaction of honour.

While Sor Juana's writing in New Spain is roughly a generation removed from Calderón's, her theatrical work emerges within a dramatic tradition clearly marked by his influence. At the same time, she manages to probe and ultimately question the "ethics" behind his treatment of the popular honour theme, particularly in *El médico de su honra*. In the second *sainete* of *Los empeños de una casa* (*The House of Trials*), Arias and Muñiz, two actors in the production of the same play, ridicule the supposed author as "un estudiante/que en las comedias es tan principiante,/y en la Poesía tan mozo,/que le apuntan los versos como el bozo" ("a student [who] wrote this comedy so trite,/… a novice playwright,/as ignorant of verses in his youth as his face is scant in whiskers") only to contrast the work to those of Calderón, Moreto, or Rojas.[5] In many respects, the play follows devotedly the conventions of *siglo de oro* drama by re-enacting conflicts of honour in pursuit of dramatic tension and successfully resolving these conflicts through the customary intervention of representatives of royal authority. Yet Sor Juana's play deviates from traditional standards in subtle but significant ways. One of the most striking elements that distinguishes *Los empeños de una casa* from the traditional honour play is that it explicitly problematizes the dominion of *reputación*, one of the centrepieces of baroque ideology as a whole.[6]

In classic honour plays, even when the validity of honourable "non-public" behaviour may be acknowledged, its importance is, for all practical purposes, overshadowed by the omnipresence of the public eye; in other words, it is not the actual conduct or behaviour but its appearance that rules the traditional baroque stage. Hence, a man's honour, which is repeatedly portrayed as more precious than any possession, more precious than life itself, is contingent on public opinion – that is to say, his identity is one with his reputation. The character in Sor Juana's play who perhaps most exemplifies the values of the classic honour drama is Don Rodrigo, the well-born but impoverished father of the beautiful and talented Leonor. As he says, in a conversation with Don Pedro:

> Bien habréis conjeturado
> que lo que puede, Don Pedro,
> a vuestra casa traerme
> es el honor, pues le tengo
> fiado a vuestra palabra;
> que, aunque sois tan caballero,
> mientras no os casáis está
> a peligro siempre expuesto;
> y bien veis que no es alhaja
> que puede en un noble pecho
> permitir la contingencia;
> porque es un cristal tan terso,
> que, si no le quiebra el golpe,
> le empaña sólo el aliento.

(Don Pedro, as you surely are aware, it is my honour that has brought me to your house, for it is now pawned to your word, and though you are indeed a gentleman, it remains exposed to danger until you two are married. I'm sure you can see that this is not a treasure that a noble heart can treat lightly, for it is such a fragile piece of crystal that, even if it's not broken by a blow, even the slightest breath can cloud it over.)[7]

The metaphoric equation of honou and fragile glass is anything but unusual in the tradition of the *Comedia*; what is truly innovative about this scene is the fact that Don Rodrigo's words are part of a negotiating ploy, not a statement of fact or fait accompli. Rather than opting to take revenge on Pedro, whom he believes has taken his daughter from him, Rodrigo, on the advice of his servant Hernando, decides to reason with Pedro in hopes of "making a deal" to protect his honour. This implies an awareness not only that honour and *reputación* are contingent on the sphere of public knowledge,[8] but that the borders of this sphere are themselves negotiable. In other words, public knowledge can be manipulated (the public eye can be fooled) to ensure a mutually agreeable non-violent resolution of the honour conflict.

Another way in which Sor Juana problematizes the ethics of the *Comedia* has to do with the way assumptions (of guilt) are treated within the play. In clear contrast to Mencía in *El médico de su honra*, for whom suspicion is tantamount to guilt and hence death, Leonor is here granted the benefit of the doubt by Carlos, who, in words that come very close to those in Sor Juana's own poetry, actually "theorizes" the injustice of the double standards that afflict women: he refuses to assume the worst of Leonor, and won't respond until he finds out how she came to be there, since "que si yo en la casa propia/estoy, sin estar culpado,/¿cómo quieres que suponga/culpa en Leonor? Antes juzgo/que la fortuna piadosa/la condujo adonde estoy" ("I'm in the very same house, and I've done nothing wrong, so why should I suspect Leonor of wrongdoing? Rather, I think merciful fortune must have brought her where I am").[9] From such a "reasoned" approach to the problem of perceived infidelity, one can see that Sor Juana is interested in representing a world in which the prescriptive force of honour, in particular its almost automatic condemnation of women, is far less straightforward than in the world of Calderón.

A second apparent point of contention for Sor Juana is the implicit justification in Calderón, among other authors of the *Comedia*, of extreme measures for the vindication of one's honour. In fact, if there is a "message" to the "wrap-up" of the final few pages of Sor Juana's play, it is that conflicts of honour may be solved by more reasoned, less drastic means. Don Rodrigo's words make a barely disguised reference to *El médico de su honra*, as he adopts a similar, anatomical metaphor:

> Tomad, hijo, mi consejo:
> que en las dolencias de honor
> no todas veces son buenos,
> si bastan sólo süaves,
> los medicamentos recios,
> que antes suelen hacer daño;
> pues cuando está malo un miembro,
> el experto cirujano
> no luego le aplica el hierro
> y corta lo dolorido,
> sino que aplica primero
> los remedios lenitivos.

> (Take my advice, my son: when one's honor is infirm, strong medicine isn't always the best recourse – indeed it can do great

harm – when a less toxic remedy would suffice. When one has an infected limb, an expert surgeon won't just amputate without first trying less drastic measures.)[10]

If the mere suspicion of dishonour demands the surgical removal of the "infected" member by the "doctor of his honour" in Calderón's drama, Sor Juana clearly favours a more "homeopathic" approach. Not only does she recommend searching out second opinions before deciding on a treatment, she is clearly quite circumspect about resorting to the knife.

Are the attitudes evident in *Los empeños de una casa* merely reflective of Sor Juana's feminine/feminist consciousness, or do they tell us something about *criollo* culture in baroque New Spain and its most prevalent social values? Or could they be due to a historical change in values that would be equally evident in Spanish literature and theatre of the same historical period? We would suggest that a complex combination of all three factors (and perhaps others) might be at play here. Nevertheless, we would argue that a sustain exploration of these questions will help explain the historical genealogy of guiding ideologemes and cultural attitudes and their transformation from baroque times to the present.

In his chapter on Sor Juana's *Respuesta a Sor Filotea de la Cruz*, a letter she wrote, ostensibly in response to certain public admonitions made against her by the bishop of Puebla, Octavio Paz suggests that Sor Juana shows herself to be in the grips of a pervasive contradiction, running through the very centre of her existence, as both a profoundly religious person and an intellectual. He quotes from the *Respuesta*: "He intentado sepultar con mi nombre mi entendimiento, y sacrificárselo sólo a quien me lo dio; y que no otro motivo me entró en religión, no obstante que al desembarazo y quietud que pedía mi estudiosa intención eran repugnantes los ejercicios y compañía de una comunidad" ("I have attempted to entomb my intellect together with my name and to sacrifice it to the One who gave it to me; and that no other motive brought me to the life of Religion, despite the fact that the exercises and companionship of a community were quite opposed to the tranquillity and freedom from disturbance required by my studious bent").[11] Paz "finds" a striking contradiction between, in the first instance, a desire to renounce her studious inclination, and, in the second instance, the claim that she joined the convent *despite* her knowledge that the conventual enclosure would not be conducive to a life of study. From this *explication de texte*, he teases out a deeper contradiction, namely, "la contradicción entre su vocación intelectual y la vida en el seno de una comunidad religiosa" ("the incompatibilities between her intellectual vocation and life in a religious community").[12]

Whether or not this contradiction indeed corresponds to the particulars of Sor Juana's "actual" life as potentially "exposed" in the *Respuesta*, signs of this existential struggle do not abound in her work. What is more striking is the way in which Paz must force through a reading of this passage in order to defend his thesis, an interpretation that, under closer examination, seems problematic. Paz reads the passage as meaning a renunciation of Sor Juana's inclination to study – "lo cual significa, justamente, la renuncia a su estudiosa inclinación."[13] By contrast, we would argue that what Sor Juana "confesses" here is that she has attempted to bury, with her name, her understanding, and to sacrifice it only to the one who gave it to her. To bury does not necessarily mean the same as to renounce, for it can also mean to hide from public knowledge, as she has done with her name. If she is to sacrifice her understanding, it must be to God alone, rather than to others.

We would agree that there is a contradiction apparent in this passage, and in all of the *Respuesta*, but it is a far more subtle one than that which Paz would claim against her. This contradiction lies in the medium of the letter itself, which undermines the official "renunciation" of her public role by making the very act of renunciation a public act. At the same instant in which she accepts the private, cloistered nature of women's knowledge, she is effectively carving for herself a discursive space in a public realm and participating in a knowledge and a power of which she has been ostensibly deprived.

Two models of ideological discourse that are similar in fundamental ways bear mentioning here: Althusser's interpellation and the genealogy of the confession proposed in Foucault's *Histoire de la sexualité*, both of which emphasize the act of responding on the part of the subject of ideology: responding to a call or a naming in Althusser's model, and to a questioning in Foucault's.[14] In both models, the self is subjected to an *identity*, a prestructured place in an ideological order or a "grid" of power relations, by means of a response to a query by some representative of power. We would argue that such an understanding of the interpellative function of the symbolic law or of power is incomplete. Hence, we essentially agree with Slavoj Žižek's critique of Althusser, in which he claims that what is truly constitutive of subjectivity is the fact that the interpellation, the call of the symbolic order of representation, always misses its mark; it is always stained by some irreducible excess.[15] From this perspective, the central or primary "contradiction" present in the *Respuesta* could be seen as an insightful illustration of just this dialogic and constitutive relation between the call of power and the response that situates a subject in relation to that call – and, in some fundamental way, in excess of it.

One of the great lines of argumentation in the *Respuesta* is Sor Juana's defence of her desire for knowledge, ranging from the autobiographical detail of childhood anecdotes to her erudite statements on the nature of a woman's right to knowledge. Each of these arguments is organized around a specific caveat or escape-clause: that Sor Juana's pursuit of knowledge is a private affair, and that all incursions of her work into a public realm have not been her doing. Even her defence of women's pursuit of knowledge acknowledges that it should be private: "Y al fin [Doctor Arce (digno profesor de Escritura)] resuelve, con su prudencia, que el leer públicamente en las cátedras y predicar en los púlpitos, no es lícito a las mujeres; pero que el estudiar, escribir y enseñar privadamente, no sólo les es lícito, pero muy provechoso y útil" ("Arce [worthy professor of Scripture] at last resolves, in his prudent way, that women are not allowed to lecture publicly in the universities or to preach from the pulpits, but that studying, writing, and teaching privately is not only permitted but most beneficial and useful to them").[16]

Yet, while couching her defence of a woman's right to study in these terms – the terms "demanded" by propriety, values, patriarchy, in short, the symbolic order of power – Sor Juana reinscribes the contradiction previously discussed: the very act of proclaiming the necessary privacy of a woman's knowledge is, at the same time, an act of public reason, by virtue of being a persuasive polemic launched against a representative of power. Thus, in her narrative account of herself, in which she describes that self in relation to certain parameters of acceptability, she creates a discursive space that enters into problematic tension with the normative space dictated by the interpellative discourse, producing an excess of self that remains unaccounted for.

In the work of both Žižek and Lacan, this excess of ideology is produced by the splitting of the subject into the "I" of the utterance and the ever-receding *sujet d'énonciation*. It is precisely this latter subject that inhabits the excess and escapes the standardization that discursive power seeks to impose. Toward the end of the *Respuesta*, in an often-cited passage, Sor Juana claims never to have written of her own volition, "de tal manera, que no me acuerdo haber escrito por mi gusto sino es un papelillo que llaman *El Sueño*" ("so much so that I recall having written nothing at my own pleasure save a trifling thing they call the *Dream*").[17] It is, of course, commonplace to refer to the *Repuesta* as a prose version of that epic quest for knowledge; but it is not so common to remark that, in this very statement, the contradiction has returned: that the same words that announce this lack of volition in her writing are written entirely of her own volition. We would argue that these are the words of that *other* subject, that place of enunciation that, while straining to account for "a Sor Juana" who would fit the precepts of her ideological environs, nonetheless exceeds those very limits in the narration of a self who is never entirely accountable.

PART THREE

A Cervantine Toolkit for the Post-Truth Age

11

Revelations of a Glass Man

As others before him, most notoriously Erasmus, Cervantes looks to the subject of madness as an analytical instrument. Whether we think of Don Quixote, Cardenio, or the protagonist of *El licenciado vidriera* (*The Glass Graduate*), Cervantes's madmen are tools in his literary toolkit or table of tricks (*mesa de trucos*). They open oblique views (literally ex-centric viewpoints) that reveal the nonsense of comforting narratives and commonplace notions. Hence, in walking with Cervantes's madmen, we may risk a bit of our own reason and our grounding in reality (in the reality we think we know and share). As Maurice Molho pointed out, these fictional madmen work as "clarividentes tangenciales" ("tangential clairvoyants");[1] yet, we should note that Cervantes's madmen are decidedly distinct from one another, even if they all "embody" outside-the-box visions.

A few years ago, one of us developed a pedagogical project pairing *Don Quixote* with some the most popular (and controversial) road movies of the last four decades, including *Easy Rider*, *Thelma and Louise*, *The Motorcycle Diaries*, *Into the Wild*, and *Borat*. The goal of this inter-discursive, trans-historical and cross-cultural experiment was not only to foreground the road as a central presence in Cervantes's fictional world, but also to show that, in reading *Don Quixote* alongside *Easy Rider*, *The Motorcycle Diaries*, and *Into the Wild*, we are likely to experience the madness of the protagonist very differently than when we read it with *Thelma and Louise* or *Borat*. While *Easy Rider* might illuminate culture-war hot-button issues with an emphasis on freedom, communal values, and law and order, *Thelma and Louise* provides an opportunity to examine misogynistic attitudes and commonplace assumptions about gender roles in literature, art, and society. The idealistic framings of *The Motorcycle Diaries* and *Into the Wild* are likely to focus our attention on those passages of the novel that elicit the reader's identification with Don Quixote's higher purpose and his "heroic" refusal to accept the mundane reality enforced by the agents of normalcy; here, we would be inching closer to the "Romantic reading" of the novel. Viewed through the lens of *Borat*, on the other hand, the eccentric protagonist would emerge as a misguided fool, rather than a principled hero. But even when we laugh at his foolish eccentricity, the Cervantine madman retains much of his "tangential clairvoyance" as a reality agitator whose mere presence can often lift the veil of the alibis and enforcers of social normality and normativity:

> The radical eccentricity of the "road character" played by comedian, writer, and producer Sacha Cohen reveals aspects of our social "normality" that would otherwise remain under the (political) radar. I would venture that a close examination of the episodes of *Don Quixote* II that take place in the country-house of the duke and duchess in light of the scene in which Borat dines with the social elites of a Southern U.S. town, for example, could help us focus the discussion on the critical engagement of social issues in Cervantes's novel … A comparative analysis of the tonal structuring of both texts around the eccentricity of their protagonists would provide interesting ways to reflect on issues of reader positioning in connection with the mechanics of humor.[2]

The key question is this: What do we laugh at when we read *Don Quixote* and watch *Borat*, and what kind of (political) statements do we make by laughing? Here, we follow this comparative thread to shed light on the raison d'être of the Glass Graduate, arguably the most problematic of Cervantes's madmen. The protagonist of *El licenciado vidriera* certainly qualifies as an eccentric character, at least for the duration of his madness, but is he really a tangential clairvoyant in the sense in which Molho uses the term in *Cervantes: raíces folkóricas*?

As George Shipley has noted, *El licenciado vidriera* is not just the story of an eccentric, but an eccentric story told by a flawed narrator who provides virtually no guidance to its readers.[3] Critics continue to disagree about the real target of Cervantes's satire. We propose a reading of this exemplary novel as an anamorphic text that speaks to two different audiences: the spectators who celebrate the madman's act, his playful mocking and vilification of others in line with common biases and traditional forms of scapegoating; and the critical readers who might gaze at this "freak show" sponsored by a wealthy gentleman from an oblique perspective – "si bien lo miras" ("if you consider this carefully"), as Cervantes encouraged his reader to do in his introduction.[4] These issues seem just as relevant in our time of demagoguery and divisiveness.

Regarding *Don Quixote*, we argued in *Medialogies* (and earlier in "Don Quixote and Political Satire") that the all-out defence of the 1609–14 mass exile of the Moriscos enunciated by the notorious character known as Ricote (himself a Morisco convert) should not be taken at face value, but rather as an expression of the satirical strategy of "excesiva ortodoxia" ("excessive orthodoxy"), which Stephen Colbert would master in our own day on *The Colbert Report*.[5] The fact that Ricote is basically cheering the monarchical cause of racial cleansing that resulted in his own exile should certainly clue us in; and then there's the piling on of mythical images of the racial other as tainted, poisonous, rotten, duplicitous, and corrupt, which is reminiscent of Cohen's satirical craft. Recall the segment that takes place at the bed-and-breakfast where Borat and his producer Azamat had arranged to spend the night. Their realization that their kindly hosts were Jewish led them to believe that they were been poisoned. The scene culminates in the most preposterous way as Borat and Azamat throw dollar bills at a pair of cockroaches and run for their lives.

An exposé published by Willa Paskin and David Marchese in *Salon* offers an interesting perspective that could prove helpful as we attempt to wrap our minds around Ricote's "defence" of the politics of racial cleansing in *Don Quixote* and, even more so, the Glass Man's brand of shooting-from-the-hip hate speech in *El licenciado vidriera*. According to Paskin and Marchese, the Jewish owners of the bed-and-breakfast featured in *Borat* were never in on the joke. As far as Mariam and Joseph Behar knew, they had rented out three rooms to a documentarian and his film crew; yet, once they saw the film, the couple showed a great deal of appreciation for the mock-documentary and especially for Cohen's satirical craft, which they did not consider to be anti-Semitic: "Speaking on the telephone, Joseph, with Mariam chatting in the background, says they saw the film and thought it 'was not anti-Semitic at all. It was outstanding. [Cohen] is a genius.'"[6]

The key point to make here – which was not lost on Joseph and Mariam Behar – is that the target of Cohen's satire is, quite obviously, not Jews but the anti-Semites who traffic in hate speech and stock images of the Jewish other. Similarly, when Ricote piles on stock images of the Morisco other (his own "poisonous race") in the fictional world of *Don Quixote*, it seems safe to assume that Cervantes is challenging his readers to reflect on the nonsense of the fundamentalist Christian rhetoric and scapegoating politics that had led to the mass deportation of tens of thousands of Spanish citizens in the early 1600s.

We would apply a similar approach to the controversial exclamations of the madman who is the focus of *El licenciado vidriera*. The storyline of this exemplary tale has been described as little more than a shallow shell that serves as narrative frame for the madman's purported witticisms. An abandoned boy who goes by the name of Tomás Rodaja impresses two well-to-do college students, and they are persuaded by his quick wit to sponsor his studies at the prestigious university in Salamanca. Having earned a law degree, Tomás embarks on a long European trip of cultural enrichment in the company of an army officer. Back in Salamanca, Tomás is exposed to the obsessive attention of a woman of dubious reputation, who resorts to a love potion to secure his affections. The potion backfires, rendering him ill and causing him to believe he is made of fine glass. Vidriera (this is the name given to the protagonist during this section of the narrative) is convinced that his glass intellect is sharper and more refined than the mind of the common man, even if his body is naturally fragile and easily breakable.

The central part of the story is devoted to the madman's improvised judgments and opinions. People crowd around him to hear his witticisms, which for the most part turn out to be recycled satirical observations, mean-spirited put-downs, and racist and misogynistic pronouncements. As Shipley writes, Vidriera's witticisms are little more than "mean-minded, if oft-repeated, bad-mouthing, scarcely elevated above coarse and shallow prejudice by sporadic infusions of verbal and conceptual wit."[7]

Beyond his "mad" phase, Tomás's life story amounts to a few lines of text describing his cure at the hands of a charitable friar, his failed attempts to secure gainful employment as a man of sound reason and deep scholarly preparation in the same courtly circles that had embraced his manic alter ego, and his eventual death as the soldier he had never aspired to be. Shipley faults the "incurious and inattentive narrator" for the story's imbalances.[8] He argues that neither Vidriera, who suffers from acute madness or lack of judgment (in the text, "sin juicio"), nor the narrator, who takes sides with the uncritical crowd, can be said to speak for the author. But where does that leave the readers of this strange tale? Will they align themselves with Vidriera's mob of admirers or with the author "who sought repeatedly in his art to teach us to be wary of the coercive authority of narrators"?[9]

We agree that the narrator's failure to distance himself from the mob who celebrates Vidriera's satirical comments can be read as a version of the conceit of the "unreliable narrator," which is one of the key instruments in the Cervantine table of tricks. After all, the most consistent targets of Vidriera's verbal attacks are low-level trade labourers, racial and religious minorities, street urchins, and women, the last of whom he classifies according to a familiar misogynistic taxonomy: prostitute, procuress, shrew, unfaithful.

In spite of this (or perhaps because of it), the allure of Vidriera's aggressive rhetoric has endured well beyond his time to inspire the unwavering admiration of certain critics who see the Glass Graduate as a clever mask that allows Cervantes to offer his own opinions and moralizing correctives – "noble afán moralizante" ("noble moralizing purpose").[10] According to this view, which can be traced back to the work of nineteenth-century critics, Cervantes would have mobilized the literary conceit of the wise fool to escape the strictures of social and cultural etiquette (we might now call it political correctness) and to unscrupulously target individuals and social groups deserving of scorn. As recently as the 1990s, Lúdovic Osterc maintained that Vidriera's satirical comments were meant to express the author's own sentiments and beliefs and his laudable condemnation of not just corrupt individuals, especially "mujeres libertinas" ("libertine women"), but also "las costumbres perversas y vicios sodomitas" ("perverse manners and sodomite vices").[11] Contrary to this view, we argue that Vidriera is not Cervantes's mouthpiece, but rather a clever showcase of communal prejudice whose transparency focuses our gaze on the biases of the enabling crowd.

We would insist that there's nothing morally edifying about the type of hate speech that's celebrated by Vidriera's audiences (including in courtly circles), promoted by princely sponsors, and dutifully recorded by the (failed or unreliable) narrator. As a notorious member of the Cervantine gallery of madmen, Vidriera retains a degree of "tangential clairvoyance," but not because he violates the rules of polite society to tell it like it is or speak the truth of the "silent majority,"[12] but because his presence reveals the prejudice and blind spots of that majority's worldview. This is the type of critical discernment that's needed today to expose the familiar forms of hate speech and demagoguery that have taken hold of so much political culture in the age of social media.

As an example, the following quote illustrates how racist attitudes and discriminatory practices can be masked as "drain-the-swamp" calls for "fairness."[13] The passage is particularly effective in exposing the hypocrisy of the demagogue who projects onto others his own moral failings:

– ¿Qué es esto, señor Licenciado, que os he oído decir mal de muchos oficios, y jamás lo habéis dicho de los escribanos, habiendo tanto que decir? ...
– Aunque de vidrio, no soy tan frágil que me deje ir con la corriente del vulgo, las más veces engañado ... Los maldicientes, por donde comienzan a mostrar la malignidad de sus lenguas es por decir mal de los escribanos y alguaciles y de los otros ministros de la justicia, siendo un oficio el del escribano sin el cual andaría la verdad por el mundo a sombra de tejados, corrida y maltratada ... Es el escribano persona pública, y el oficio del juez no se puede ejercitar cómodamente sin el suyo. Los escribanos han de ser libres, y no esclavos, ni hijos de esclavos; legítimos, no bastardos, ni de ninguna mala raza nacidos. Juran de secreto fidelidad y que no harán escritura usuaria; que ni amistad, ni enemistad, provecho o daño les moverá a no hacer su oficio con buena y cristiana conciencia.

(– Is it possible, Mr Graduate, that I've heard you speak ill of so many professions and yet you have made no mention of scribes, about whom there's so much to say? ...
– Although made of Glass, I am not so fragile as to let myself be swayed by the current of the mob, which is most easily deceived ... Those prone to slander first show the evil intent of their tongues by bad-mouthing scribes, law enforcement and justice officials, even as their offices are of such importance that without them the truth would remain hidden in the shadows of the world, victimized and mistreated ... Scribes are public officials without whom judges could not easily carry out the

duties of their office. They must be free, not slaves or descendants of slaves; legitimate, not bastards or born of an inferior race. They have sworn loyalty against corruption, and do not allow friendship or enmity, profit or loss, to interfere with their handling of their office in good Christian conscience.)[14]

In a characteristically Cervantine turn, we can see that despite Vidriera's public commitment to resist the current of the mob, it doesn't take long (merely a paragraph) for the Glass Graduate to change his tune and lead the crowd in its trashing of public officials, prosecutors, and attorneys (*solicitadores*). He refers to them all as ignorant, negligent, self-interested, and corrupt, to great acclaim.[15] As Shipley notes, "Vidriera seldom resists going with the flow of common ridicule and vilification, which his enthusiastic following (among whom our narrator is prominently positioned) take to be common sense."[16]

Most crucially, Vidriera's speech turns the victims of racist and discriminatory policies into the "real" perpetrators. As the Glass Graduate explains, those who are contaminated by social and racial maladies (*bastardos* or *de mala raza nacidos*) could not, by virtue of their inferiority, be trusted in the administration of justice, since they lack the necessary inclination to fairness that's inherent in a good Christian conscience.

We hear in these passages the clear echoes of the anti-immigrant and minority-bashing nativism that has taken hold in American political culture. Recall Trump's assertion that a judge of Mexican heritage could not possibly be trusted to remain neutral in the legal case involving Trump University in the face of the president's own attacks on Mexicans as rapist animals. Similarly, he routinely slandered the law enforcement officials and prosecutors in charge of the government probe into Russian meddling in the 2016 presidential election as well as a wide swath of politicians and officials when promulgating the myth of his landslide victory in 2020. Indeed, the lessons of *El licenciado vidriera* seem as relevant and timely as ever in our own day, as the former president repeatedly cried "witch hunt" and "Russia hoax" with respect to investigations into the 2016 election and then continually claimed "an attempt to steal a landslide win" and "the lie of the year" about the "rigged" 2020 election, despite incontestable evidence to the contrary.

Faced with the demagogue's blame game, might we bring the game back to its transparent origin, as Cervantes taught us to do? After all, weren't the "Russia hoax," "witch hunt," "attempt to steal," and "lie of the year" actually the White House's ludicrous denials and the relentless attacks carried out by the president, his allies in Congress, and the far-right media machine against the "very conflicted" and "biased" public officials in charge of the Russia investigation and the 2020 election certification process?[17]

It is tragically ironic that the man crying "witch hunt" is the same politician who stoked the infamous anti–Hillary Clinton chant "lock her up!" in countless campaign rallies. And what about his slandering of media outlets and his characterization of any reporting of facts he doesn't like as "fake news"? This coming from a man who has traded in conspiracy theories and fabrications for decades (he called them "truthful exaggerations" in *The Art of the Deal*) and rode the wave of "alternative facts" all the way to the presidency of the United States of America.

If *Don Quixote* taught us a fundamental lesson about alternative facts, media framing, and the shifting nature of truth and reality, the *Exemplary Novel of the Glass Graduate* would be our Cervantine "tangential clairvoyant" of choice to illuminate the arts of the demagogue, especially his weaponizing of prejudice and hate speech.

12

A Posthumous Lesson

Cervantes's treatment of otherness and what Counter-Reformation society widely conceived of as threats of moral, racial, or religious contamination is remarkably consistent across his work. Whether we examine his dramas of captivity or his comedic interludes, his beloved *Galatea*, his exemplary tales, or his long novels, we can see that the Cervantine world is populated by *familiar others* – that is, stock images of religious, moral, and racial contamination and social and political antagonism. Yet these familiar images are consistently bracketed in Cervantes's tales as artificial constructs that say more about the cultural anxieties of his day and the limitations of common literary and theatrical conventions than about the social agents they ostensibly represent.

For example, when rogues and scullions are revealed to have been people of noble birth, such revelations trouble the very idea of an insidious and alien underlayer of urban life that was the favoured subject of the literature we call the picaresque, at least since Mateo Alemán's *Guzmán de Alfarache* (1599–1604). If, as suggested by *Guzmán* and its brethren, *pícaros* were conceived of as a sickness to be eradicated from society, Cervantes's outcasts and his take on deviancy of any kind indicate a different attitude, according to which even criminal behaviour is not simply projected onto an external other, but rather understood as part of the very fabric of society, encompassing even the highest levels of political and ecclesiastic power.

Cervantes hammers this point home again and again in his great posthumous novel, *Los trabajos de Persiles y Sigismunda* (*The Trials of Persiles and Sigismunda*) (1617). The plot of the *Persiles* revolves around a group of pilgrims from an unidentified northern country who are on their way to Rome, centre of the Catholic faith that they, minorities in their own barbaric land, have practised in secret until now. However, when the pious Periandro finally arrives in the Holy City, he finds himself on the wrong side of the Vatican's justice:

> Acertaron a estar en la calle dos de la guarda del Pontífice, que dicen pueden prender en fragrante, y como la voz era de ladrón, facilitaron su dudosa potestad y prendieron a Periandro; echáronle mano al pecho y, quitándole la cruz, le santiguaron con poca decencia: paga que da la justicia a los nuevos delincuentes, aunque no se les averigüe el delito.

> (Two of the pope's guards just happened to be in the street – the ones they say can arrest people caught in the act – and since the shouting was about a thief they made use of their questionable authority and arrested Periandro. They reached into his jacket and took out the cross, slapping him around in the bargain; such is the payment the law makes to those just arrested, not even bothering to find out if they've committed a crime.)[1]

This passage gives us cause to reflect on Cervantes's brushes with his own nation's legal system and his resulting stints in prison on false, or at least unjustified, charges. Still, at the denouement of an ostensibly religious pilgrimage, showing the pope's guards as thugs dedicated to harassing people having sex in the street or, more specifically, prostitutes at work, certainly undermines the assumed authority of the church and its officers.

The fact that this parody is perhaps a shade subtler than *Don Quixote*'s may account in part for the rather irregular critical reception of Cervantes's last novel, published some months after his death, about which he wrote that it might end up being either the worst or, most likely, the best book of entertainment ever composed in the Spanish language: "El cual ha de ser o el más malo o el mejor que en nuestra lengua se haya compuesto, quiero decir de los de entretenimiento; y digo que me arrepiento de haber dicho *el más malo*, porque según la opinión de mis amigos ha de llegar al estremo de bondad posible" ("It will be either the worst or best ever composed in our language, I mean, of those written for diversion; I must say I regret having said *the worst*, because in the opinion of my friends it is bound to reach the extremes of possible goodness").[2] In fact, for quite some time after its author's death, the *Persiles* was even more successful than the *Quixote*. But over the past centuries, Cervantes's posthumous work has slipped into relative obscurity, as its baroque style and fantastical plot and characters jarred the sensibilities of a more modern readership. Recent critics, in contrast, have started to see the *Persiles* as a daring literary adventure that may surpass even *Don Quixote* in some respects, especially in its mockery of the most intolerant religious and social practices and beliefs of Cervantes's time.[3]

The movement of the soul toward the rewards of heaven, the Christian motif that would seem to inspire and parallel the journey of the protagonists toward Rome, turns out to be driven by far baser desires. Thus, the protagonists' quest is anamorphically recalibrated near the end of the novel (book 4, chapter 12) when the narrator drops the proverbial Cervantine bomb, letting the reader in on the family's little secret – namely, that the pilgrimage on which Persiles and Sigismunda (or Periandro and Auristela, as they are referred to throughout much of the text) had embarked was nothing but an excuse, a clever justification concocted by the mother of Persiles, Queen Eustoquia, to give her younger son a chance to win over the heart of his brother's fiancé: "Concertaron que se ausentasen de la isla antes que su hermano viniese, a quien darían por disculpa, cuando no la hallase, que había hecho voto de venir a Roma a enterarse en ella de la fe católica, que en aquellas partes setentrionales andaba algo de quiebra" ("[The mother and son] planned for the couple to leave the island before his brother should come back. When he didn't find her there, they'd give him the excuse that she'd made a vow to go to Rome to learn more about the Catholic faith, which in those northern regions is somewhat in need of repair").[4]

What should we make of the frequent discussion of religious commonplaces then? As we look back with new eyes and hear with new ears, the meaning of this ever-expansive tale of tales becomes increasingly elusive. We would argue that the narrator's belated revelation forces us to adjust our perspective and make different sense of a host of other passages, even entire episodes, which become unhinged from the Christian backbone of the story.

We come across the familiar notion of the Christian life as a journey in search of spiritual solace at the beginning of book 3, when the narrator reminds us that "están nuestras almas siempre en continuo movimiento y no pueden parar ni sosegar sino en su centro, que es Dios" ("our souls are in continual movement and can't stop or rest except at their center – which is God").[5] But, as we are attuned now to the possibility of perspective shifts, we are more likely to remember a previous variation of the conventional Christian motif. Indeed, in book 2, Auristela uses the same language to describe a woman's sexual desire for a man:

> Bien sé que nuestras almas están siempre en continuo movimiento, sin que puedan dejar de estar atentas a querer bien a algún sujeto a quien las estrellas las inclinan ... Dime, señora, a quién quieres, a quién amas y a quién adoras: que, como no des en el disparate de amar a un toro, ... como sea hombre el que, según tú dices, adoras, no me causará espanto ni maravilla. Mujer soy como tú; mis deseos tengo y, hasta ahora, por honra del alma, no me han salido a la boca, que bien pudiera, como señales de la calentura.

> (Just as I ... know the soul of each of us is always in continual movement, unable to avoid wanting that someone toward whom the stars incline us ... Tell me, my lady, whom you want, whom you love and whom you adore, for as long as you haven't succumbed to the madness of falling in love with a bull ..., and as long as it's a man you adore – as you put it – it won't shock or amaze me. I'm a woman like you and have my own desires; until now, in order to protect my soul's honor, they haven't left my mouth, though it's true I easily could have let them slip out during my fever.)[6]

Shockingly, for the time and in the context of what Alban Forcione famously termed Cervantes's "Christian romance,"[7] Auristela implies that, as long as the desire in question isn't for an animal – and here she doesn't shy away from citing examples from antiquity – well, it's fine by her. And this is before she confesses to her own sexual heat ("calentura").

While these semantic coincidences or confluences and their ironic implications may have gone unnoticed in a straightforward reading of *Persiles* as a Christian romance, they are harder to ignore in light of the revelations of the final book. Thus, the knowledge that *Los trabajos de Persiles y Sigismunda* is not much of a spiritual pilgrimage after all invites interpretations more attentive to the ironic bracketing of conventions that we associate with other (more explicitly or recognizably humorous) works authored by Cervantes, among them, *Don Quixote*, his exemplary novel *El coloquio de los perros* (*The Dialogue of the*

Dogs), and several of his *entremeses*, including *El retablo de las maravillas, La elección de los alcaldes de Daganzo, El viejo celoso* (*The Jealous Old Man*), and *El juez de los divorcios* (*The Divorce Court Judge*). We would argue that *Persiles* contains as much hard-hitting irony as any of these works, even if it is not designed to make us laugh in the same way – which itself may be a function of the genre that *Persiles* is meant to parody.

Literary genres such as the picaresque and pastoral are dialectically entwined with the beliefs and prejudices they both represent and supplement. To take the example of pastoral literature in Cervantes's time, the image of the Golden Age worked as a distraction from the endemic corruption in a growing urban society. City life may be dirty and dangerous, the tradition went, but that's because the people have abandoned the towns and the countryside; because administrators are corrupted by greed; because foreigners have taken over. Return to the land, obey the law of both monarch and God, and you will realize that now is the true Golden Age. Just like the ideals of honour and chivalry, the ideal of Arcadia was an illusion meant to distract people from the injustice of their own existence, to show them an image of country life as purer and better than the city and court, even while the same court was feeding on their livelihood like a parasite.

That is not to say that there weren't plenty of critical voices explicitly decrying the real corruption in Spanish society.[8] But what Cervantes did so differently was to show the Golden Age as factually false and nevertheless a worthy ideal and goal, and thus a reminder of how much could be improved. In other words, Cervantes was both touting the value of the ideal and calling attention to our failure to realize it in the present. In this sense, we agree with Anthony Cascardi's characterization of "Cervantes' literary investigation of the foundations of political thought," in which context Don Quixote's famous speech to the goatherds serves both "to debunk the power of myth as 'mere' fantasy that cannot possibly say anything meaningful about the world [and] to offer an alternative to political theory in the form of a vision that derives its force from the essence of fantasy, i.e., from its ability to negate one world and hypothesize another."[9]

While Cervantes's first exploration of the theme of corruption and utopia was in the *Galatea*, he returns to it repeatedly in his later works, including both the *Quixote* and *Los trabajos de Persiles y Sigismunda*. Toward the beginning of the first part of *Don Quixote*, the knight errant and his squire happen to approach a group of goatherds seated on the ground enjoying a simple meal. When the goatherds invite the travellers to eat with them, Don Quixote promptly sits down while Sancho stands at his side, as a good squire ought to do, at which point his master tells him to join them as an equal: "Quiero que aquí a mi lado y en compañía desta buena gente te sientes, y que seas una mesma cosa conmigo, que soy tu amo y natural señor; que comas en mi plato y bebas por donde yo bebiere, porque de la caballería andante se puede decir lo mesmo que del amor se dice: que todas las cosas iguala" ("I want you to sit here at my side and in the company of these good people, and be the same as I, who am your natural lord and master; eat from my plate and drink where I drink, for one may say of knight errantry what is said of love: it makes all things equal").[10]

But while the goatherds and their simple fare inspire Don Quixote to dream of a golden age prior to distinctions in social status, his reverie is immediately troubled by Sancho's casual acceptance of his own simplicity. As he puts it, "sé decir a vuestra merced que como yo tuviese bien de comer, tan bien y mejor me lo comería en pie y a mis solas como sentado a par de un emperador" ("I can tell your grace that as long as I have something good to eat, I'll eat it just as well or better standing and all alone as sitting at the height of an emperor").[11] In fact, Sancho's retort goes considerably further, as he confesses his preference for solitude and freedom so as not to be limited by the sorts of manners that would be required in more refined company: "Mucho mejor me sabe lo que como en mi rincón sin melindres ni respetos, aunque sea pan y cebolla, que los gallipavos de otras mesas donde me sea forzoso mascar despacio, beber poco, limpiarme a menudo, no estornudar ni toser si me viene gana, ni hacer otras cosas que la soledad y la libertad traen consigo" ("What I eat, even if it's bread and onion, tastes much better to me in my corner without fancy or respectful manners, than a turkey would at other tables where I have to chew slowly, not drink too much, wipe my mouth a lot, not sneeze or cough if I feel like it, or do other things that come with solitude and freedom").[12] While Don Quixote thus revels in court society's popular fantasy of the simple country life in which all are equal and, naturally, equally noble, Sancho's response reveals that the Quixotic dream of pre-social equality is nothing other than just that, a dream.

After forcing Sancho to sit down next to him, Don Quixote then launches into a diatribe touting every known cliché about a past golden age in a crescendo of hyperbole:

Eran en aquella santa edad todas las cosas comunes: a nadie le era necesario para alcanzar su ordinario sustento tomar otro trabajo que alzar la mano y alcanzarle de las robustas encinas, que liberalmente les estaban convidando con su dulce y sazonado fruto ... [,] las solícitas y discretas abejas, ofreciendo a cualquiera mano, sin interés alguno, la fértil cosecha de su dulcísimo trabajo ... Las doncellas y la honestidad andaban, como tengo dicho, por dondequiera, sola y señera, sin temor que la ajena desenvoltura y lascivo intento le menoscabasen, y su perdición nacía de su gusto y propia voluntad.

(In that blessed age all things were owned in common; no one, for his daily sustenance, needed to do more than lift his hand and pluck it from the sturdy oaks that so liberally invited him to share their sweet and flavorsome fruit ... Diligent and clever bees established their colonies, freely offering to any hand the fertile harvest of their sweet labor ... Maidens in their modesty wandered, as I have said, wherever they wished, alone and mistresses of themselves, without fear that another's boldness or lascivious intent would dishonor them, and if they fell it was through their own desire and will.)[13]

The narrator dismisses the speech in short order as absurd, and blames it on the acorns that the goatherds were eating, which brought to Don Quixote's mind the past golden age and, with it, the desire to make a useless speech that could very well have been omitted: "Toda esta larga arenga (que se pudiera muy bien escusar) dijo nuestro caballero, porque las bellotas que le dieron le trujeron a la memoria la edad dorada, y antojósele hacer aquel inútil razonamiento a los cabreros, que, sin respondelle palabra, embobados y suspensos, le estuvieron escuchando" ("This long harangue – which could very easily have been omitted – was declaimed by our knight because the acorns served to him brought to mind the Golden Age, and with it the desire to make that foolish speech to the goatherds, who, stupefied and perplexed, listened without saying a word").[14] There is no doubt, then, about the absurdity of the speech and thus the absurdity of believing in the ideal of the golden age as portrayed in pastoral literature; the real question concerns the relation of the ideal to social reality. For, if Don Quixote is making a speech that we readers laugh at, and that perplexes the "real" goatherds who are sitting beside him, that is because we readers and those goatherds share a common reality from which we can mock Don Quixote's beliefs.

The next morning, Don Quixote and Sancho are invited by a companion of the goatherds to the "real" funeral of Grisóstomo, a nobleman who pretended to be a shepherd in order to woo the beautiful and disdainful Marcela, a noblewoman who has renounced society to live like a shepherdess on the land. The question is then, how can we laugh at the absurdity of Don Quixote's fantasies, supposedly from the vantage of reality, if that same reality features people who are behaving exactly as if they were characters in the knight's pastoral fantasies? As if to underscore the point, Cervantes describes the effect Marcela had on the noblemen in shepherd garb in precisely the same kind of language that Don Quixote had just been using, and that the narrator had ridiculed:

> Aquí sospira un pastor, allí se queja otro; acullá se oyen amorosas canciones, acá desesperadas endechas. Cuál hay que pasa todas las horas de la noche sentado al pie de alguna encina o peñasco, y allí, sin plegar los llorosos ojos, embebecido y transportado en sus pensamientos, le halló el sol a la mañana; y cuál hay que sin dar vado ni tregua a sus suspiros, en mitad del ardor de la más enfadosa siesta del verano, tendido sobre la ardiente arena, envía sus quejas al piadoso cielo.
>
> (Here a shepherd sighs, there another moans, over yonder amorous songs are heard, and farther on desperate lamentations. One spends all the hours of the night sitting at the foot of an oak tree or a rocky crag, not closing his weeping eyes, and the sun finds him in the morning absorbed and lost in his thoughts; another gives no respite or rest to his sighs, and in the middle of the burning heat of the fiercest summer afternoon, lying on the burning sand, he sends his complaints up to merciful heaven.)[15]

As they make their way to the funeral, Don Quixote and Sancho meet up with other travellers, who immediately grasp that he is insane when he refers to himself as a knight errant. Yet the very same travellers accept without question that they are surrounded by noblemen dressed as shepherds suffering the unrequited love of an impossibly beautiful and unattainable shepherdess. What the novel thus questions is not merely the truth of the scenarios within its interior frames, but also, and more importantly, the very social reality that its readers believe they inhabit. Cervantes is thus showing how that same reality rests on beliefs that are in many ways as absurd as Don Quixote's.

What might those beliefs be in the case of Grisóstomo's suicide over the unrequited love of the non-shepherdess Marcela? As the real and fake shepherds, along with the travellers, gather to listen to Ambrosio as he reads the last poem Grisóstomo wrote to Marcela before he took his life, Marcela appears at the top of a nearby hill and descends upon the funeral. She then embarks on a spirited defence of her liberty from the desires and expectations of men, declaring in conclusion, "yo, como sabéis, tengo riquezas propias, y no codicio las ajenas; tengo libre condición, y no gusto de sujetarme" ("as you know, I have wealth of my own and do not desire anyone else's; I am free and do not care to submit to another").[16] Struck by her courage and dignity, Don Quixote publicly vows to defend her against all those present, proclaiming that she deserves to be respected for her extraordinary virtue: "es justo que, en lugar de ser seguida y perseguida, sea honrada y estimada de todos los buenos del mundo, pues muestra que en él ella es sola la que con tan honesta intención vive" ("It is just that rather than being followed and persecuted, she should be honored and esteemed by all good people in the world, for she has shown herself to be the only woman in it who lives with so virtuous a desire").[17] Once again, Cervantes has managed to ridicule social illusions and, at the same time, recall and exalt ideals worthy of emulation.

This pattern of portraying ideals as honourable while dismissing as absurd fantasy the thought that they might actually exist in reality is a constant in Cervantes's writing. To take another example from *Don Quixote*, in his famous speech on arms and letters, the theme of *justicia distributiva* (distributive justice) gets exactly the same kind of treatment;[18] and it should be clear why it does: while the Golden Age fantasy of equality among all social strata is a beautiful ideal well worth pursuing, the notion that it may already exist in reality – a notion propagated by the ideology of the honour code at the time – justifies quiescence in the face of social inequalities that make a real difference to people's lives.

Just as Don Quixote incurs ridicule for his fanatical devotion to truly worthy ideals, characters and situations in other of Cervantes's books affirm radical and even democratic notions of equality while ridiculing these notions in the same breath. In *Persiles*, we are thus regaled about an island kingdom whose inhabitants choose their own ruler: "[El reino] no se hereda ni viene por sucesión de padre a hijo; sus moradores le eligen a su beneplácito, procurando siempre que sea el más virtuoso y mejor hombre que en él se hallara, y sin intervenir de por medio ruegos o negociaciones, y sin que los soliciten promesas ni dádivas, de común consentimiento de todos" ("[The kingdom is] not inherited or passed down by succession from father to son. Its inhabitants choose as their ruler whomever they think best, always striving to insure he's the best and most virtuous man to be found in the kingdom. Without the intervention of pleasings and negotiations, and without being wooed by promises or bribes, the king emerges from the common consensus").[19] The lack of corruption in this society leads those who aren't monarchs to try to be virtuous, while kings are encouraged to achieve even higher degrees of virtue: "Y con esto, los que no son reyes procuran ser virtuosos para serlo y, los que lo son, pugnan serlo más, para no dejar de ser reyes" ("Because of this, those who aren't kings try to be virtuous in order to become one, while those already kings strive to be even more virtuous so they won't be obliged to stop ruling").[20] Such a land is free of ambition and greed, or so we are told: "Con esto se cortan las alas a la ambición, se atierra la codicia" ("Thanks to this, soaring ambition's wings are clipped, greed is grounded").[21] This kingdom is also a model of justice, mercy, charity, and fairness. In the words of the narrator, "con esto los pueblos viven quietos, campea la justicia y resplandece la misericordia, despáchanse con brevedad los memoriales de los pobres y, los que dan los ricos, no por serlo son mejor despachados" ("as a result the people live in peace, justice triumphs and mercy gleams, and the petitions of the poor are handled with dispatch while those of the rich are not dispatched one bit better because of their wealth").[22]

While such sentiments reflect a serious study on Cervantes's part of treatises dealing with the legitimacy of kingship,[23] the scenario he then inserts ends up disrupting the very possibility of a society like that ever existing. For when an exceptional and beautiful young man comes to join the island nation's Olympic games and bests the native youth in every endeavour, "comenzó luego la invidia a apoderarse de los pechos de los que se habían de probar en los juegos, viendo con cuánta facilidad se había llevado el estrangero el precio de la carrera" ("on seeing how easily the stranger had carried off the prize for running, envy began to take possession of his competitors' hearts").[24] Thus, while this society is described as one where peace, justice, and mercy rule, the excellent youth who competes to be the strongest and most virtuous crowns his achievement by shooting a dove in flight at a great distance, at once demonstrating his superior skills and piercing the heart of the symbol of peace. Our ideals, Cervantes is telling us, be they of excellence, virtue, or equality and honour, should be esteemed and recognized – but as ideals. The belief that they already exist, as opposed to being goals to which we can aspire, can only deprive us of the very bounty they promise.[25]

The traditional reading of *Persiles* as a Christian romance, even as a straightforward defence of Counter-Reformation utopianism, clearly would have Cervantes upholding a vision of Catholic, monarchical Spain as the embodiment of the ideal kingdom. In the past few decades, however, a series of revisionist readings have emerged. These new interpretations, with which we very much concur, have called attention to the presence of a powerful irony in those passages which, at first glance, would have appeared to reinforce the Catholic ideals that sustained Spain's imperial enterprise. As the pilgrims are about to set foot on the western edge of the Iberian peninsula, Antonio reminds his daughter Costanza that Iberia showers the heavens with saintly tributes: "Ésta es la tierra que da al cielo santo y copiosísimo tributo" ("This is a land that pays abundant holy tribute to Heaven").[26] Moreover, on arrival on the peninsula, the work's narrator writes, "les pareció que ya habían llegado a la tierra de promisión que tanto deseaban" ("it seemed to them they'd already arrived at the Promised Land they so longed for").[27] These notions are seemingly reinforced by Auristela, as she paints a lovely picture of Spain as the most peaceful and saintly region of the world: "Ya los cielos, a quien doy mil gracias por ello, nos ha[n] traído a España ...; ya podemos tender los pasos, seguros ... porque, según la fama que, sobre todas las regiones del mundo, de pacífica y santa, tiene ganada España, bien nos podemos prometer seguro viaje" ("Heaven, which I heartily thank, has already brought us to Spain ...; we can now stride forward safe ... Judging by the fame it has as the most peaceful and holy region on earth, [Spain] can certainly promise us a safe journey").[28] What happens next, however, is the kind of narrative turn that one might expect inside the parodic frame of *Don Quixote*. Remarkably, the pilgrims are first treated to the violent death of a young man, a sword deeply buried in his back, and then subjected to the customary roughing up at the hands of Inquisition officials and the extortionist practices of Spanish "sátrapas de la pluma" ("foxy pen-pushers") – legal professionals – "como es uso y costumbre" ("as is their usual crafty style").[29] As one of us argued in *(A)wry Views*, these narrative developments serve to provide a perspective adjustment that cuts through the self-serving mythology of Spanish imperialism while opening an abyss right where Christian readers might have expected reality to match up with the ideals quoted by Antonio, Auristela, and even the work's narrator.[30]

Indeed, the travellers' experiences while in Spain and later on in Rome are nothing like the *seguro viaje* (safe journey) that Auristela had anticipated. Instead, the pilgrims will be first-hand witnesses of (as well as actors in) the kind of misadventures that we would expect to take place in *other* spaces, among barbarians. Thus, for all practical purposes, the Catholic lands of Spain and Rome turn out to be more of the same when compared to the reality of the Northern region that was home to the protagonists, or even the morally corrupt space of Policarpo's palace, in which everyone was contaminated by selfishness, depravity, and lust. As a matter of fact, the narrator's reflections on the lifestyle of the inhabitants of Policarpo's island could just as well apply to the once-mythologized Catholic lands: "Estas revoluciones, trazas y máquinas amorosas andaban en el palacio de Policarpo y en los pechos de los confusos amantes ... Todos deseaban, pero a ninguno se le cumplían sus deseos: condición de la naturaleza humana" ("These amorous disturbances, schemes, and machinations were on the move in Policarpo's palace and in the hearts of the confused lovers ... All of them had desires, but no one's desires were fulfilled, for it is a condition of human nature").[31]

We would argue that the narrator's philosophical digression here is key to understanding the Cervantine corrective to the perfect ideal of the Christian journey and the conventions of the Christian romance. Whether we are talking about Christian Spaniards or about *others*, what defines and shapes common humanity is ultimately human desire; and what people do with this persistent and pervasive desire is what gives meaning to individual and collective existence. Whether male or female, Christian or *other*, wealthy or poor, strong or weak, powerful or powerless, all major and minor characters of the *Persiles* are indeed in constant movement; yet what accounts for that movement is the great equalizing force of desire. This is our common human condition at work: the *movement of being* pushing conventional ideals to their breaking point. But again, it is not the ideal of the Christian life itself that's the target of the Cervantine irony, but the notion that

Catholic Spain or Rome is the true historical embodiment of the ideal of the Christian life.

There are times when – as Diana de Armas Wilson, among others, has noted – Christian Spain seems uncannily reminiscent of the Barbaric Isle of book 1 of *Persiles*.[32] Remarkably, the human sacrifices described in *Persiles* 1.2 are inspired by the belief that a mighty king is destined to conquer the world, a notion that would be familiar to anyone subjected to the propagandistic providentialism of the Spanish monarchy:

> [Esta insula] es habitada de unos bárbaros, gente indómita y cruel, los cuales tienen entre sí por cosa inviolable y cierta ... que de entre ellos ha de salir un rey que conquiste y gane gran parte del mundo. Este rey que esperan no saben quién ha de ser y, para saberlo, aquel hechicero les dio esta orden: que sacrificasen todos los hombres que a su ínsula llegasen, de cuyos corazones (digo, de cada uno de por sí) hiciesen polvos y los diesen a beber a los bárbaros más principales de la ínsula, con expresa orden que el que los pasase, sin torcer el rostro ni dar muestras de que le sabía mal, le alzasen por su rey. Pero no ha de ser este el que conquiste el mundo, sino un hijo suyo.

> (The island is inhabited by barbarians, a savage and cruel people, who hold as a certain and inviolable truth ... that from among them a king will come forth who will conquer and win a great part of the world. They don't know who this king is that they await, but, in order to find out, the sorcerer gave them the following order: they must sacrifice all the men who come to their island, grind the hearts of each of them into powder, and give these powders in a drink to the most important barbarians of the island with express orders that he who should drink the powders without making a face or showing any sign that it tasted bad would be proclaimed their king. However, it wouldn't be this kind who'd conquer the world, but his son.)[33]

While this quote incorporates familiar images of an *absolute other* – that is, barbarians defined by their ritualized human sacrifices and cannibalistic practices – the ironic overtones of the passage would be hard to miss for readers attentive to the Cervantine table of tricks. For starters, there is the issue of predestined imperial greatness, which could indeed bring to mind familiar claims of historical and providentialist exceptionalism in Counter-Reformation and imperial Spain. But if this weren't enough, this picture of perfect barbarism is effectively undone in the same way that the ideal of the Golden Age was ridiculed in the previously quoted passages of *Don Quixote*. Life (the life of the flesh and the senses) refuses to be contained by either conventional ideals or caricaturesque images of otherness.

As we suggested earlier, Sancho's incontinent body had made a mess (literally at times) of the regressive ideal of the Golden Age. Recall the scatological passages of the fulling hammers episode (book 1, chapter 20), which foregrounded most graphically the materiality of Sancho's body just ahead of his parodic reproduction of his master's proclamation that he is destined to resurrect the golden age of times past:

> Sancho … tuvo necesidad de apretarse las ijadas con los puños, por no reventar riendo …; de lo cual ya se daba al diablo don Quijote, y más cuando le oyó decir, como por modo de fisga:
> – "Has de saber, ¡oh Sancho amigo!, que yo nací por querer del cielo en esta nuestra edad de hierro para resucitar en ella la dorada, o de oro. Yo soy aquel para quien están guardados los peligros, las hazañas grandes, los valerosos fechos…"
> Y por aquí fue repitiendo todas o las más razones que don Quijote dijo.
>
> (Sancho … had to press his sides with his fists to keep from bursting with laughter …; by now Don Quixote was sending him to the devil, especially when he heard him say, in a derisive tone:
> "Sancho my friend, know that I was born, by the will of heaven, in this our iron age, to revive the one of gold, or the Golden Age. I am he for whom are reserved dangers, great deeds, valiant feats …"
> And in this fashion he repeated all or most of the words that Don Quixote had said.)[34]

The materiality of the body and the life of the senses are similarly foregrounded in *Persiles*, even in those passages and situations that seem to mimetically reproduce conventional images of self and other, good and evil. The notion that what makes a barbaric family line eligible for world domination is the ability of one of its members to swallow human-heart paste while showing no sign of displeasure or distaste is patently ridiculous and can only be interpreted as a Cervantine wink, an indication that we need to take the whole barbarian scene with a grain of salt. This is basically what we mean when we say that, while images of familiar *others* abound in Cervantes's work, they are consistently bracketed as artificial constructs, revealed as ideologically charged reductions of the world.

This brings us to the Cervantine treatment of moral and racial contamination. We can find countless examples of "moral corruption" in *Persiles*, involving such male characters as King Policarpo and Rutilio, and females like Rosamunda. King Policarpo sets his own kingdom on fire as part of a Machiavellian plan to hook up with Auristela; Rutilio manipulates a young student into running away with him; and Rosamunda is one of several female characters who are driven by scandalous sexual desires that cannot be contained by the moral codes of honour and virtue. Yet readers (at least those readers who have made it all the way through to the end of the novel) can plainly see that these and other "fringe" characters who fall victim to the madness of lust are no different than Auristela and Periandro, the hero/heroine couple, which ultimately raises the question, how do we separate heroes from villains and spiritual health from contamination and corruption in this peculiar Christian romance? Our answer is that we don't, or rather, we can't, at least not in any absolute way, since everyone is shown to be contaminated by desire, the defining trait of the human experience ("condición de la naturaleza humana").

To be sure, we can certainly find characters who want to think of themselves as watchdogs of the moral order; but they generally do not fare well in the textual world of *Persiles*. Clodio, for example, plays the role of "watchtower" that we might associate with the narrative presence of the repentant Guzmán in Alemán's *Guzmán de Alfarache: Atalaya de la vida humana* (*Guzmán de Alfarache: Watchtower of Human Life*) or with the authorial presence that frames the life story of the first female *pícara* in *La pícara Justina*. As a member of the moral police, Clodio "el maldiciente" ("the slanderer") – this is how the narrator refers to him – offers a scathing characterization of the lustful Rosamunda as the very effigy of corruption and decay: "Rosa inmunda" ("filthy rose").[35] No doubt Clodio would have had a better time of it inside a picaresque novel of the *Guzmán* variety, but he gets no sympathy from the narrator of *Persiles*. His reward for his watchtower zeal comes in the form of a stray arrow that pierces his murmuring and admonishing tongue. The narrator's perfectly unsympathetic description of the instant of his death tells us all we need to know: "Pero no fue el golpe de la flecha en vano, que a este instante entraba por la puerta de la estancia el maldiciente Clodio, que le sirvió de blanco, y le pasó la boca y la lengua, y le dejó la vida en perpetuo silencio: castigo merecido a sus muchas culpas" ("The arrow's force wasn't wasted, however, for at that very instant the slanderer Clodio was entering the door to the room and became its target. It drove through his mouth and tongue, silencing his life forever – just punishment for his many faults").[36] Again, when the narrator speaks of Clodio's many sins or *culpas*, he is referring to the character's determination to offer unsolicited moral advice, as when he admonishes Arnaldo that, "entre la gente común tiene lugar de mostrarse poderoso el gusto, pero no le ha de tener entre la noble" ("among the common people personal taste is very powerful, but it shouldn't be among the nobility").[37] Arnaldo's reaction to Clodio's "sound" advice (sound from a moral-watchtower position) matches the narrator's impatient dismissiveness: "No me aconsejes más, porque tus palabras se llevarán los vientos" ("Don't advise me anymore, for your words will just be swept away with the wind").[38]

With regards to the familiar theme of racial contamination, those passages of *Persiles* dealing with Morisco characters are among the best illustrations we could find of Cervantes's oblique treatment of conventional images of otherness. Thus, the eloquent Zenotia paints a mythical portrait of herself as a Morisco witch, effectively recalling the stock images that circulated in Christian circles for decades, leading up to the infamous expulsion of hundreds of thousands of such converts from 1609 to 1614: "Mi estirpe es agarena; mis ejercicios, los de Zoroastes, y en ellos soy única … Pídemelo, que haré que a esta claridad suceda en un punto escura noche; o ya, si quisieres ver temblar la tierra, pelear los vientos, alterarse el mar" ("I come from Mohammedan stock; my spiritual exercises are those of Zoroaster and I'm matchless in them … Just ask, and in a twinkling I'll make this brightness turn to darkest night; or if by chance you'd like to see the earth tremble, the winds quarrel with each other, the sea turn rough").[39] But Zenotia deploys these stock images of the Morisco other in the midst of a life story that otherwise foregrounds her unenviable role as a victim of inquisitorial persecution and unimaginable hardship: "La persecución de los que llaman inquisidores en España me arrancó de mi patria: que, cuando se sale por fuerza della, antes se puede llamar arrancada que salida" ("That persecution in Spain by those known as Inquisitors tore me from my homeland, for when one is forced to leave it, one doesn't simply leave but feels torn away").[40] Zenotia's description of her forced departure from her beloved fatherland as a heartbreaking "tearing" adds a tragic dimension to her speech.

While the stock images of racial contamination are, of course, impersonal, Zenotia's deeply personal life story puts pressure on the conventional images of Morisco otherness by inviting readers to relive the tragedy of the expulsion from the individualized perspective of one of the victims. After all, mythical effigies do not suffer, people do! Remarkably, the narrator refers to the Morisco character Zenotia as "Spanish Zenotia" ("la española Zenotia"), in a gesture that could be read as an attempt at symbolic restoration.[41] But it falls to another Morisco, known as "el jadraque," to mobilize Cervantes's trademark strategy in dealing with the cultural production of otherness, his excessive orthodoxy.[42] Indeed, this Morisco character appears to appeal for and justify most passionately the mass expulsion decreed by King Philip in what the narrator ironically describes as a heavenly trance:

¡Ea, mancebo generoso; ea, rey invencible! Atropella, rompe, desbarata todo género de inconvenientes y déjanos a España tersa, limpia y desembarazada desta mi mala casta, que tanto la asombra y menoscaba! … ¡Llénense estos mares de tus galeras, cargadas del inútil peso de la generación agarena; vayan arrojadas a las contrarias riberas las zarzas, las malezas y las otras yerbas que estorban el crecimiento de la fertilidad y abundancia cristiana! … No los esquilman las religiones, no los entresacan las Indias, no los quintan las guerras; todos se casan, todos, o los más, engendran, de do se sigue y se infiere que su multiplicación y aumento ha de ser innumerable. ¡Ea, pues, vuelvo a decir, vayan, vayan, señor, y deja la taza de tu reino resplandeciente como el sol y hermosa como el cielo!

(Oh, noble youth! Oh, invincible king! Trample down, break through, and push aside every obstacle and leave us a pure Spain, cleaned and cleared of this evil caste of mine that so darkens and defames it! … Let the seas be filled with your galleys loaded with the useless weight of the descendants of Hagar; may these briars, brambles, and other weeds hindering the growth of Christian fertility and abundance be flung to the opposite shore! … The religious orders don't harvest them, the Indies don't thin them out, wars don't draft them. They all get married and all or most of them have children. From this it follows and can be inferred that the multiplications of and additions to them will unquestionably be incalculable. So I repeat, make them go; make them go, sir, leaving the tranquil surface of the fountain of your kingdom shining like the sun and as beautiful as the sky!)[43]

If this passage from *Persiles* sounds familiar to readers of *Don Quixote*, it's simply because there's little difference between *el jadraque*'s heavenly trance and Ricote's well-known tongue-in-cheek defence of King Philip and the official in charge of the expulsion, Don Bernardino de Velasco, for their dedication to protecting the Christian purity and racial health of the Spanish nation. In fact, both speeches (Ricote's in *Don Quixote* and *el jadraque*'s in *Persiles*) work exactly in the same way, by piling on the mythical imagery of Morisco otherness in the midst of passionate defences of an auto-genocide that are incongruously attributed to the victims themselves. If the caricaturesque piling on of stock images were not enough to undress the emperor, so to speak, the choice of carriers for this overwrought imagery would surely clue in the reader that these passages are not meant to be taken at face value.

It is not just our literary genres that are populated by stock characters: knights errant, giants, and damsels in distress in the case of chivalry novels; shepherd-lovers and unreachable maidens in pastoral literature; morally corrupt social types and their victims in picaresque narratives. On the contrary, in *Persiles*, as in his *Novelas ejemplares* and, most famously and effectively, in *El retablo de las maravillas*, Cervantes establishes explicit connections between literary, theatrical, and artistic conventions and social conventions. In the process, he makes us aware of the fact that our reality is itself anchored in stock images and that those stock images are likely to structure our desires as well as our field of vision. This is a point that Richard Sherwin has made recently in his discussion of visual media literacy, when he writes that social conventions "frame the visible and invisible alike – establishing the one by virtue of the other."[44] Hence, we would argue that Cervantes's treatment of conventional ideals and stock images of otherness as artificial constructs in many of his works, most notoriously in *Persiles*, put the spotlight on the cultural processes that inform and condition our understanding of the world and ourselves in it. Indeed, what we ultimately propose here is a reading of *Los trabajos de Persiles y Sigismunda*, among other Cervantine texts, as a series of highly effective lessons in metafiction, media framing, and reality literacy.

13

Surviving the Post-Truth Age

"Truth isn't truth," is how Donald Trump's TV lawyer, Rudy Giuliani, responded to Chuck Todd's probing on *Meet the Press* during a conversation about whether the then president would agree to be interviewed by Special Counsel Robert Mueller.[1] According to Giuliani, the president's "version of the truth" would make him vulnerable to a perjury trap.[2] Giuliani's statement is simply one more link in a chain of White House pronouncements that goes back to Kellyanne Conway's "alternative facts" and contains many presidential nuggets about the "fake news media," including such tweets as "any negative polls are fake news" and this warning to the attendees of a Veterans for Foreign Wars convention in Kansas City in 2018: "Just remember: What you're seeing and what you're reading is not what's happening."[3] If this sounds like an Orwellian line, that's because it's just that: "The Party told you to reject the evidence of your eyes and ears. It was their final, most essential command" and "Whatever the Party holds to be truth *is* truth."[4]

The Orwellian echoes of this kind of presidential and White House rhetoric were not lost on political and cultural commentators, many of whom, including Representative Adam Schiff, took to Twitter to sound the alarm on what they see as authoritarian language: "Today, Giuliani added to Orwell's liturgy: War is Peace. Slavery is Freedom. Ignorance is Strength. Truth isn't Truth."[5] But one of the most interesting comments came from horror fiction writer Stephen King, who dug up a bit of Giuliani's employment history to make sense of his cavalier disregard for truth: "Let's not forget that Rudy Giuliani – old Mr. Truth Isn't Truth – worked for Purdue Pharma in 2002. Thanks in part to his efforts, sales of OxyContin continued, and the opioid epidemic was born. Just another rat thriving in the swamp Trump promised to drain."[6]

The connection to Big Pharma here allows us to circle back to Erich Fromm's insightful afterword to *1984*, particularly his discussion of Alan Harrington's notion of the "mobile truth" in *Life in the Crystal Palace*, originally published in 1959. In Harrington's conceptualization, the "mobile truth" of the crystal palace has nothing to do with epistemological relativism in any traditional sense, or with the probing of reality that we associate with post-structuralist (or neo-baroque) critical and philosophical inquiry. Instead, Harrington's "mobile truth" names a form of service (or servitude) to the corporation that forecloses the very possibility of *truth* outside of its "moral obligation" to protect the interests of shareholders.[7] As Nostrum Pharmaceutical founder and president Nirmal Mulye explained as part of his justification for his company's 400 per cent price hike of an antibiotic mixture, he has a "moral requirement to sell the product at the highest price," adding – in what may sound as a simple truism – that his business, like any other, is ultimately about making money.[8]

Mulye further made his point by defending "Pharma Bro" Martin Shkreli, who was once known as the "most hated man in America" after his pharmaceutical firm raised the price of an AIDS drug over 5,000 per cent in 2015: "I agree with Martin Shkreli that when he raised the price of his drug he was within his rights because he had to reward his shareholders."[9] The fact that Shkreli is serving a seven-year prison sentence for fraud due to his mismanaging of hedge funds notwithstanding, Mulye's defence of the profit-at-all-cost business model as a *moral obligation* predicated on the need to reward shareholders should not surprise anyone. This is the logical endgame of the market society.[10]

From this perspective, we can indeed say that Trump made good on his promise to run the US government like a business (i.e., to make America great again for his political shareholders) when he dismantled environmental regulations and consumer protections and cut taxes on the wealthy; when he mobilized racist and misogynist sentiments against his political opponents; and when he railed against news outlets and scientific findings that stand in the way of his "version of the truth." Denouncing him as "amoral" and "unprincipled" misses the point. When he puts out "alternative facts," he is simply pursuing his self-interest and the interests of his political/economic shareholders in the same way that the propaganda machine funded by the Koch brothers spreads disinformation on climate change to protect their industrial ventures from inconvenient truths. This is precisely the danger of the "mobile truth" in the crystal palace that Alan Harrington warned us against over half a century ago.

An important point to make, though, is that, for this kind of disinformation to be effective, the "mobile truth" of Trump and the Koch brothers must be able to reach large audiences. This is why the agents of the corporate "truth" are always, first and foremost, "attention merchants."[11] As historian Tim Wu explains, industry "took note of what captive attention could accomplish" in the aftermath of the two world wars.[12] Industrialists learned from the devastating effectiveness of government propaganda that attention is a "precious resource ..., a commodity, like wheat, pork bellies, or crude oil," "a form of currency they could mint."[13] Wu's compelling history of "attention" as a resource to be bought and sold in the marketplace shows that the rise of attention merchants over the past hundred years has been intricately tied to the mass media that spreads their mobile truth, from newspapers and radio in the first half of the twentieth century, to television in the second half, and to the digital devices that are omnipresent in our own time.

Wu suggests that the unprecedented success of present-day attention merchants has resulted in a public health crisis that afflicts us all: "It is no coincidence that ours is a time afflicted by a widespread sense of attentional crisis, at least in the West – one captured by the phrase 'homo distractus,' a species of ever shorter attention span known for compulsively checking his devices."[14] In following Wu's argument to its ultimate consequences, one comes away with the impression that this crisis could threaten basic human survival. Hence, he urges us to press the pause button and reflect on the kinds of lives we are living and how much of our time and our choices have effectively been turned over to an industry whose sole purpose is to capture and redirect our attention: "We are certainly at an appropriate time to think seriously about what it might mean to reclaim our collective consciousness ... As William James observed, ... when we reach the end of our days, our life experience will equal what we have paid attention to, whether by choice or default. We are at risk, without quite fully realizing it, of living lives that are less our own than we imagine."[15] While much of Wu's book is explicitly aimed at understanding "how the deal went down," starting with the advertisers and venture capitalists of the nineteenth century, he hints at earlier attention-harvesting spectacles, agents, and institutions, from the early modern theatre to the church. It is interesting that some of his examples of the merchandising of attention in the first half of the nineteenth century involve one-man acts of deception, often by former preachers who had learned the art of attention harvesting and redirecting in their previous line of work.

Beyond this specific connection with religious messaging and his nods in the direction of theatrical spectacles, there is little discussion of earlier forms of political and cultural propaganda in Wu's book. Instead, he focuses on the rise of modern attention merchants in the ecosystem of the capitalist (media) market. What we have proposed here, by contrast, is an opening of the historical lens in an effort to learn from the cultural wars of another age of media saturation, an age that preceded our own by about four hundred years but whose symbolic constructs and institutional structures changed the world forever, in part due to the rise of an unprecedented attention-harvesting culture, which has been defined as the guided, mass-oriented, and spectacular culture of the baroque.[16] We are especially interested in the work of those literary "discontents" of the 1600s who warned their "discreet readers" against the numbing effects of the nascent culture of the spectacle and urge them to wise up and stand guard in the presence of the new con artists of attention.

This warning is, as we have argued, the central lesson of Cervantes's meta-theatrical *Stage of Wonders*, the most salient example of this type of cultural red-flagging in the early seventeenth century. Indeed, the creators of this travelling spectacle of wonders are explicitly portrayed as attention merchants and con artists who traffic in racist, religious, and misogynist biases. But we have identified a host of additional works of the Spanish Golden Age that deal with these issues either directly or indirectly, from Cervantes's full-length novels, including his masterpiece *Don Quixote* (1605; 1615) and his posthumous *Persiles* (1617), to his *Novelas ejemplares* (1613); from the masterful collections of novellas authored by María de Zayas, especially her *Desengaños amorosos* (1647), to the multifaceted work of Sor Juana Inés de la Cruz and the "unauthorized voice" of the female narrator of *La pícara Justina* (1605), among others.

As we look to survive the post-truth age and escape the annihilating loss of consciousness of the "homo distractus" at the hands of modern-day attention merchants in our media ecosystem, we would do well to search for allies in Orwell's, Huxley's and Atwood's dystopian parables, but we can also arm ourselves with Zayas's awakening terrors and Cervantes's undressing parodies. Let's put "the classics" to work (and not just in the classroom)!

If it is true – as Albert Einstein famously stated – that "imagination is more important than knowledge," in that it allows us to transcend the limits of what we know or think we know,[17] then art and literature can surely help as much as history, philosophy, and the other humanistic disciplines. Indeed, we need them all to illuminate the frames that bind us. Einstein thought of himself as "enough of the artist to draw freely upon [his] imagination."[18] We would argue that today's scientists, artists, and humanists must draw on their collective imagination as much as their expertise to break through the frame of a market society that has embraced the corporate version of the mobile truth. As chemists Jingxiang Yang, Michael Ward, and Bart Kahr have recently argued, today good science is not enough to advance knowledge and influence public policy; scientists must learn to push back against the falsification of knowledge and the cynical denialism that's being pedalled by special interests, snake oil salesmen, and, yes, former presidents. Speaking of the Cato Institute, which is funded by the petrochemical industries of the Koch brothers, they write:

> Opponents of science now have the loudest voices, and they are not constrained by facts or the preponderance of evidence ... We must push back against the falsification of science ... We must not allow those with vested interests to deconstruct hard-won facts, while we are busy trying to establish new ones ... Science is messy, particularly environmental science. The difference between scientific experts and polemicists is that the former group is typically cautious, obligated to embrace all the evidence, which is sometimes in conflict, while the latter can choose with surety only work that supports a predetermined rhetorical argument. This puts scientists at a spectacular disadvantage in affecting policy.[19]

This is not to say that, with the right kind of public pressure and educated consumer demand, market forces could not potentially veer in a different (environmentally sensitive) direction. As environmental historian Adam Rome has recently noted, "in the last thirty years, many U.S. corporations have committed to becoming more environmentally sustainable. They have worked to conserve energy, reduce waste and toxic emissions, and develop eco-friendly products," but "the rules of the market worked against the success of green initiatives."[20] Rome's research aims at illuminating the limits of market-driven efforts to make businesses more sustainable. His case study, which focuses on DuPont Industries, shows that, while there's no reason to think that green couldn't be gold in ideal market conditions, the fact is that "businesses respond to incentives, and too many aspects of the market still penalize environmental leadership."[21]

In terms of our media market, which is currently dominated by attention merchants, strident speech and demagoguery are routinely rewarded over expertise and genuine leadership, including in the so-called climate change debates, a misleading misnomer meant to suggest that there are broad scientific disagreements in an area that is acutally characterized by overwhelming consensus. As atmospheric science expert and director of the Earth Systems Science Center at Penn State University Michael Mann recently stated,

> the term *skeptic* has been hijacked, especially in the climate change debate ... It is used as a way to dodge evidence that one simply doesn't like. That, however, is not skepticism but rather contrarianism or denialism, the wholesale rejection of validated, widely accepted scientific principles on the basis of opinion, ideology, financial interest, self-interest, or all these things together ... When it comes to the fractious debate over policy-relevant areas of science, the Bozos are too often the ones with the megaphones.[22]

The "Bozos" that Mann has in mind here are no doubt a version of the attention merchants featured in Wu's book. Mann appears to be aware of the need to enlist humanists and artists in the fight against the powerful anti-science megaphones of our day and the financial interests behind them. This would explain why, in *The Madhouse Effect*, he makes prominent use of the satirical commentary of graphic artist Tom Toles. For their part, the creators of the environmental film *Merchants of Doubt* (based on the eponymous 2010 non-fiction book authored by historians of science Naomi Orestes and Erik Conway) went even further in enlisting non-scientists to their public-educating cause when they entrusted to a magician (a professional of the arts of illusion and deception) the actual framing of the story (i.e., the decades-long history) of anti-science denialism.

The connection with the con artists behind the magical spectacle of *The Stage of Wonders* is nothing short of astonishing. As explained by the professional illusionist in *Merchants of Doubt* (and artfully demonstrated by the producers of *The Stage of Wonders*), mass deception works by redirecting our attention *elsewhere* – that is, by fixing our gaze on the distractions that blind us. In discussing his craft in the author's prologue to his *Exemplary Tales* (*Novelas ejemplares*), Cervantes referred to his writer's toolkit as a "mesa de trucos" – a table of tricks.[23] Who better than the actual professionals of illusion to unmask the deception games of the attention merchants? We argue that this is precisely the stated goal of much of Cervantes's work, including his theatrical compilation published with the title *Eight Plays and Eight Interludes, Never Performed* (*Ocho comedias y ocho entremeses nunca representados*). As his character Miguel (a clear stand-in for Cervantes himself) explains in the "Adjunta al Parnaso," the goal of his collection of plays and interludes, which he says he plans to deliver to the printing press (not the stage), is to refocus our attention on the (dis)simulations of the *Comedia Nueva*, so that we may carefully examine what the fast actions of the new theatrical spectacles veil or cover over:

> PANCRACIO: Y agora, ¿tiene vuesa merced algunas [comedias]?
> MIGUEL: Seis tengo, con otros seis entremeses.
> PANCRACIO: Pues ¿por qué no se representan?
> MIGUEL: Porque ni los autores me buscan, ni yo les voy a buscar a ellos.
> PANCRACIO: No deben de saber que vuesa merced las tiene.
> MIGUEL: Sí saben; pero, como tienen sus poetas paniaguados y les va bien con ellos, no buscan pan de trastrigo. Pero yo pienso darlas a la estampa, para que se vea despacio lo que pasa apriesa, y se disimula, o no se entiende, cuando las representan. Y las comedias tienen sus sazones y tiempos, como los cantares.

> (PANCRACIO: Now, does Your Grace have any [plays]?
> MIGUEL: I have six, with another six interludes.
> PANCRACIO: So why are they not being performed?
> MIGUEL: Because the impresarios are not seeking me out, nor am I looking for them.
> PANCRACIO: They must not know that Your Grace has them.

MIGUEL: They do; but they have their servile poets and are doing well with them; they are not looking for anything that goes against the grain. But I am determined to take them to the press so that readers can examine at their leisure what happens too fast and is dissimulated or not understood when they perform them. Theatre plays, like songs, are subject to fashion and change with the times.)[24]

In a memorable passage from his landmark novel *Don Quixote*, we find a similar discussion of the new public theatre, which focuses on its commercial aspects. Here, the cultural scene of the *Comedia* is explicitly described as an industry that deals in cultural commodities: "mercadería vendible" ("salable merchandise").[25] Cervantes sees the emerging market of the culture of the spectacle as a threat to conceptual or ideas-based theatre.[26] In its reliance on fast-paced action and its appeal to raw emotions, the *Comedia Nueva* would thus foreclose (or dramatically shrink) the necessary deliberative space, the critical distance that makes thinking possible. By contrast, the theatrical instruments in Cervantes's toolkit work to slow things down and to open spaces for reflection, understanding, and deliberation "para que se vea despacio lo que pasa apriesa, y se disimula, o no se entiende, cuando las representan" ("so that we may attentively examine [*despacio*: literally, *with space*] that which is represented in haste, 'dissimulated,' or cannot be comprehended").[27]

As we have argued throughout our book, Cervantes's work may serve as an example of countercultural critique in our own day, as could the work of María de Zayas, Sor Juana Inés de la Cruz, and other authors of the Spanish Golden Age. Their insightful lessons in media manipulation and the truth-blurring effect of the culture of the spectacle prove particularly useful in our media markets. Take the social media phenomenon. As media studies professor Siva Vaidhyanathan has recently noted, Facebook and other social media platforms are effective in riling people up and confirming their worldviews, but they do little to encourage reflection or deliberation.[28] In effect, social media platforms and the frenzied news markets that they have either created or dramatically reshaped have contributed to the spread of informational silos and the erosion of evidence-based knowledge, reflection, and deliberation, all of which has had a devastating effect on public discourse.

When we consider the zombie-like status of *truth* in our age of inflationary media, the problem is much bigger than fake news. Vaidhyanathan addresses this issue directly, while commenting on a study dealing with the impact of fake news on the 2016 election, published by Harvard's Berkman Klein Center for Internet and Society: "Defining the problem as fake news is inadequate and distracting. The problem is garbage of all sorts – fake news, half-fake news, exaggerated claims, conspiracy theories, hate speech, extremist propaganda, harassment, all of which creates cacophony – constant screaming. The problem is not that some people might believe something that's not true. The problem is that most people might stop caring if anything is true."[29]

The disinformation plague spreading in social media silos is one thing, but what about other digital media tools, like search engines? While Vaidhyanathan warned against the "Googlization" of knowledge and information in his 2012 book *The Googlization of Everything (And Why We Should Worry)*, communications scholar Safiya Umoja Noble has further underscored the role that search engines (and the algorithms that run them) play in reinforcing biases in *Algorithms of Oppression: How Search Engines Reinforce Racism*. But the most comprehensive and outright terrifying overview of the destructive power of algorithms has arguably come, not from a humanist, but from mathematics professor and data scientist Cathy O'Neil. Her sobering exposé of the invisible "prejudice, misunderstanding, and bias" that are embedded in "the software systems that increasingly managed our lives" is, once again, eerily reminiscent of the behind-the-scenes look of *The Stage of Wonders*:

> By 2010 or so, mathematics was asserting itself as never before in human affairs, and the public largely welcomed it. Yet I saw trouble ... Many of these [mathematical] models encoded human prejudice, misunderstanding, and bias into the software systems that increasingly managed our lives. Like gods, these mathematical models were opaque, their workings invisible to all but the highest priests in their domain: mathematicians and computer scientists. Their verdicts, even when wrong or harmful, were beyond dispute or appeal. And they tended to punish the poor and the oppressed.[30]

The pseudo-magical preconditions that determine who is worthy of "going to college, borrowing money, ... finding and holding a job," and even who is sentenced to prison and for how long – just like the rules of the magic tableau – "define their own reality and use it to justify their results."[31] In what could be interpreted as a powerful indictment of "life in the crystal palace" (to use Harrington's evocative expression one last time), O'Neil makes use of a preponderance of evidence to effectively show that, in the Big Data economy, "profits end up serving as a stand-in, or proxy, for truth."[32] With all this evidence in mind, mathematicians, scientists, social scientists, artists, and humanists need to stand together as knowledge-seeking professionals against the conversion of universities into veritable markets of cultural commodities – "mercadería vendible," as Cervantes would have it. Moreover, they/we must go on the offensive to expose and denounce the dark forces behind the market fundamentalism that is threatening democratic institutions, reinforcing and justifying inequalities, and turning us into zombie-like agents of planetary destruction.

As we worked on the final revisions of this concluding chapter in the aftermath of the Capitol assault of 6 January 2021, Trump had been deprived of his favorite social media megaphones, amidst public calls to combat the spread of violence-inducing claims of election fraud. He has been impeached twice, a historical first for a president. In the post-election environment, a growing segment of the mainstream news media is recognizing in Trump's conspiracy-mongering rants the manipulative lies of a demagogue. Quotable Voltaire is presently making the rounds in liberal circles: "Any one who has the power to make you believe absurdities has the power to make you commit injustices."[33] Yet, as we take stock of the incalculable damage of the Trump presidency and his right-wing partners and allies in this (long overdue) moment of reckoning, it is important to keep in mind that, as CNN's Boris Sanchez put it in his "off-script" reaction to a surreal Fox News interview with Trump, "This is not about the marketplace of ideas. This is about the marketplace of realities."[34] Indeed, this is about what we have called the most dangerous promise/product of the market society: *reality entitlement.*

As one of us has recently argued, the particular version of reality entitlement that fuelled the Trump presidency and would light the fuse of the January 6th insurrection is anchored in racist mythologies of national resurgence and "feel-good" white grievance narratives weaponized by the algorithms that run the most effective confirmation-bias machine in history.[35] This is what our current, deeply siloed version of the Internet has become in the age of social media: the perfect marketplace of alt-realities. Understanding that Trump and Trumpism are but symptoms of this much wider age-defining phenomenon is a fundamental first step in the direction of reality literacy today.

EPILOGUE

Looking for Relevance in All the Right Places

An esteemed colleague once paid us the head-scratching compliment that our work engaged with pressing contemporary issues while "avoiding the trap of relevance." In what way, we asked each other, is it a trap for one's work to be relevant – and, for that matter, relevant to what? From our colleague's perspective, relevance could be a trap insofar as the study of literature, especially literature of the past, should be focused on that literature itself, and not on the possible relevance it may have for contemporary concerns. This is a reasonable worry, one that becomes all the more palpable in a time of apparently endless crisis that advances humanistic studies as the first sacrifice to the gods of fiscal prudence. By articulating the relevance of what we do in an attempt to stave off that sacrifice, do we humanists – and, more to the point, scholars of literature and language – unwittingly sacrifice something more precious, the very essence of what we study?

In the literary humanities, Hispanic studies has been for some time one of the few growth industries, spurred by the demand in the United States for instruction in the nation's unofficial second language.[1] As Roy Ketchum points out, Spanish-language learning, "in particular, is promoted for its instrumental value and its marketability."[2] While this demand is undoubtedly economic and instrumental in nature, the curious unintended consequences are, to a certain extent, obvious: increasing demand for language courses leads universities either to expand the graduate student corps in Spanish departments and programs or, what is more likely, to hire more lecturers. The former directly affects the number of scholars doing advanced work in Hispanic language and literatures; but the latter's impact is also inevitable, as a greater demand for lecturers, at least some with PhDs, reverberates through a field with shrinking demand in other language areas.

The result is that, rather than staying at the margin of debates concerning the relevance of our scholarly practices, Hispanists' considerations of methodological and pedagogical challenges have a particular urgency. Thus, as we are forced to confront the dilemmas of relevance, it is worthwhile that we do so head on, as it were.

What exactly is the problem with relevance? Stanley Fish's typically acerbic and provocative version takes this form: "to the question 'of what use are the humanities?', the only honest answer is none whatsoever.'"[3] By contrast, Martha Nussbaum's book *Not for Profit* is an anthem of opposition to this perspective.[4] Along similar lines, we could also recall Joshua Landy's pithy response to Fish: "Is this supposed to help? Let's put it this way: if the most prominent humanists are publicly proclaiming their belief in the utter uselessness of what they do, what reason could a cash-strapped administrator possibly have for not shutting down their departments?"[5] Landy and Nussbaum offer many solid arguments for why the humanities are not only useful but indispensable, and some of these include questions of marketability, to use a crass term. As Landy points out, "employers, it turns out, actually like philosophy BAs."[6]

Fish's characteristic hyperbole and contrarianism notwithstanding, it seems unlikely that he could really be so far apart from his colleagues on such a vital issue. Jonathan Mayhew brings clarity to the debate by, in a sense, rephrasing the Fishian position. As he suggests (and we are paraphrasing here), the study of the most accomplished products of human intelligence is an inherently valuable activity that does not require justification through such appeals. Listening to Mozart might make your baby smarter, but staking the value of Mozart on the capacity of his music to stimulate infantile intelligence raises the question of what intelligence is *for* in the first place. Why do we want our babies to be smarter, if not to be able to exercise their intelligence in meaningful ways, such as being able to listen intelligently to Mozart? Training in the humanities may or may not always foster a sort of intelligence that is directly useful for other areas of life, but it trivializes such training to justify it by appealing to an aspirational shopping list of tangential benefits.[7] Indeed, Landy prefaces the economic argument when he states, "Don't get me wrong, I would hate to imply that the humanities *need* an economic reason," indicating an implicit agreement that direct usefulness "for other areas of life" does, in fact, imply a trivialization of humanistic training.[8]

The point, we think (and this is clearly what Landy is arguing), is that neither position is exclusive of the other. To embrace the inherent value of literary study, as Mayhew does, it is not necessary to claim, à la Fish, that the humanities are useless. They can be both inherently valuable *and* useful for other purposes. Most skills usually are.

The worry about making one's work relevant also may stem from a protective attitude toward the very texts we study. As critics scramble to find some kind of new ethical and/or political grounding, from multiculturalism to eco-feminism to human rights, the "innocent" classics (so the argument goes) are used and abused in favour of, and against, political ends specific to our own time and place. Under such a critical gaze, we may be subjected to criticism that our "ahistorical" or "transhistorical" readings risk erasing the text and substituting it with the type of content that fits our political agendas and professional aspirations. Moreover, there seems to be a new cloud of suspicion hanging over this type of "literary politicking,"[9] which is perceived in some quarters as an empty performance with no stakes or impact in the "real world" – that is, an academic practice that may have more to do with professional positioning (*medro*) than with genuine political or ethical concerns. In this – so the charge goes – we abuse not just the text but also the endless list of "others" for whom we claim to speak.

With respect to these criticisms, if the issue is whether we can have direct, unabridged access to the original truth of the text, the answer is of course a resounding *NO*, insofar as the observer is unavoidably present in the product of observation – as Maravall pointed out as early as 1956 in his *Teoría del saber histórico* (*Theory of Historical Knowledge*). But we should not forget that this is a two-way street – that Borges's famous story about how an apocryphal French author, Pierre Menard, reproduced verbatim some chapters of *Don Quixote* is as much a Cervantine reading of postmodernity as it is a postmodern reading of *Don Quixote*. It is well known that, from the very Prologue of Cervantes's novel, the text calls attention to the fact that any act of speech is, for all practical purposes, a negotiation with authority. On these grounds, one could conceivably reflect on why someone like Pat Robertson could call for the assassination of Hugo Chavez on national TV and have the statement go uncensored, while Kanye West's remarks about George W. Bush during an NBC show for the relief of the victims of Hurricane Katrina – "George Bush doesn't care about Black people"[10] – were erased from the West Coast airing. To be sure, it wouldn't be a case of "what would Cervantes say if he were Pierre Menard?" but of how reading the *Quixote*, for example, trains us to better understand this particular *why,* since, as we have been arguing, the Cervantine text asks similar *whys* about the nature of authority and the media.

We believe that Walter Benjamin got it right with his thesis against "positivistic" historicism, when he suggested that a historical reading must convey a sense of urgency and immediacy, precisely because the past is alive in our dreams and aspirations, as well as in our nightmares. Is not an essay that deals with the Cervantine take on the Morisco question all the *more* complete, all the *more* Cervantine, and all the *more* historical when it incorporates a reflection on what it means for the Spanish prime minister, José María Aznar, to state at Georgetown University, in the aftermath of Madrid 3/11, that Spain has been fighting Islamic terrorists since the beginning of the Reconquest? Is our reading not *more* historical, *truer* to the Cervantine point about the media framing of reality and the silencing of *off-script voices* when we allow Marcela's words in *Don Quixote* (book 1, chapter 14) to meet not only with Sor Juana's *Respuesta* but also with Kanye West's censored rant against Bush's handling of Katrina? Their voices were not heard, precisely because they were pre-emptively framed as "off-script rants." And finally, isn't the Cervantine ironization of prejudice in his time best applied to and against the prejudices of our time?

One way to make this point in terms of the urgency of the present would be to refer to the historical memory debates that have been raging in Spain in the past few decades and to the symptomatic search for Lorca's remains. At the height of these debates and of the search efforts for the elusive body of the poet, someone pasted an unpublished poem on the trunk of an olive tree just inside a park erected in Lorca's memory, where some believe his body was buried in an unmarked grave outside his hometown. The poem, signed "Anselmo," urged visitors to let the dead rest in undisturbed peace and blissful *silence*. These verses resonate with uncanny accents as we reconsider the place of history and literature today:

El OLIVO
Federico

¡Dejad el olivo!,
dejad el olivo,
que guarde sus secretos
en el hondo de la madre tierra.

Dejar los secretos que guarden
sus silencios en el alma del olivo,
que alma y alma universal
se abracen en el abrazo de la vida
...
¡Que nos regalen la vida!,
de todos los cantes,
de la ciudad de Grana,
de la sierra de Grana,
del aire de Grana.
...
Dejad que los hombres mansos
reposen en la cama de la Tierra,
dejad que sus almas naveguen
por la blanca luz de los cielos.
Dejad que los muertos reposen en paz.
Dejad a los malditos abrazando
la muerte que un mal día sembraron

(THE OLIVE TREE
Federico

Leave the olive tree alone!
leave the olive tree
to guard its secrets
in the depths of mother earth.
Leave the secrets to keep
their silence inside the soul of the olive tree,
so that soul and universal soul
may come together in the embrace of life
...
May they present to us the gift of life
of all the songs
of the city of Granada
of the mountains of Granada
of the air of Granada.
...
Leave the tame men
to their rest in the bed of the earth,
leave their souls to sail through

the white light of the heavens.
Leave the dead to rest in peace.
Leave the accursed
in their embrace of the death
they sowed that terrible day.)[11]

The last two verses of the poem come remarkably close to the climactic scenes of Guillermo del Toro's 2001 film *El espinazo del diablo* (*The Devil's Backbone*). In the film, which has been widely acclaimed as an insightful commentary on the Spanish Civil War and its place in history, the ghost of Santi drags his killer down to the bottom of the pool, where their bodies come to rest together, interlocked in an inert embrace. Yet, as one of us has argued elsewhere, the ghosts of the orphanage do not rest in peace, will not rest in peace, until the narrative is transformed and the place is redeemed by a generation of children who find the courage to face the past and join its victims in their quest for justice.[12] The open door of the orphanage leading to a new horizon at the conclusion of the film is the polar opposite of the resting place that the poet Anselmo wishes for the dead Federico. The silent communion of the dead with the motherland in the depths of the earth might indeed allow us to "hear" the dreamed "songs of Granada," but the echoes of these "songs of the city of Granada, of the mountains of Granada, of the air of Granada" might require the same kind of commemorative "silencing" of dissenting (off-script) voices as the ceremonial burial of Grisóstomo in *Don Quixote*.[13]

Not too far from the commemorative park where "Anselmo" made his poetic plea, a minimalist plaque stands on the side of the road, marking the spot where Lorca is believed to have been executed by a firing squad in August 1936, alongside a schoolteacher, Dióscoro Galindo, and two *banderilleros*, Francisco Galadí Melgar and Joaquín Arcollas Cabezas. A short farewell authored by Lorca himself offers passersby a Marcela-like (off-script) response to Anselmo:

DESPEDIDA
Si muero,
dejad el balcón abierto.
El niño come naranjas.
(Desde mi balcón lo veo).
El segador siega el trigo.
(Desde mi balcón lo siento).

¡Si muero,
dejad el balcón abierto!

(FAREWELL
If I die
leave the balcony open.
The child eats oranges.
(I watch him from my balcony.)
The reaper harvests the wheat.
(I hear him from my balcony.)
If I die,
leave the balcony open!)[14]

In contrast with Anselmo's plea to let the poet rest in peace, this voice from beyond the grave asks to remain present in the world of the living, refusing to be laid to rest. This ghostly presence rejects "the depths of the motherland" and "the white light of the heavens" and expresses a desire to stay put at his open balcony, watching over the living fields of the present and the future.

Del Toro's *The Devil's Backbone* comes to mind again. The ghost of yet another poet (Casares) refuses to abandon the civil war orphans. The dead poet stands guard at the open window of the orphanage in ruins, ready to fight for the future alongside the victimized children. "¡Nunca me iré de este lugar!" ("I will never leave this place") is Casares's promise.[15] As an allegory of the cosmopolitan intellectual of the 1930s caught at the turbulent crossroads of the Spanish Civil War, the ghostly figure of Casares, who is determined to remain a historical agent, even in death (or perhaps more so in death), throws into high relief Lorca's demand that we leave his balcony open. This dramatic demand for historical relevance comes with a sense of urgency today, in the context of the work of the Asociación para la Recuperación de la Memoria Histórica, which seeks to reopen all unmarked graves of civil war victims. Are open graves not the ultimate remainders (and reminders) of the off-script voices that monumental sites and national spectacles are often designed to erase or literally bury?

Yet, open graves can also become public spectacles of national mourning, subject to the same ideological trappings as devotional sites. A satirical piece by novelist and poet Manuel Vilas, flippantly titled "Lorca Reloaded," touches on this seemingly unavoidable paradox:

Federico García Lorca es por fin un espectáculo del siglo XXI, es nuestro Mich[a]el Jackson, o algo así. Necesitábamos encontrar la materia de que estaba hecho el poeta. Necesitábamos sus huesos, los huesos más amados de nuestra historia. Sin huesos, el cuerpo es ficción. El mito Lorca se agranda. Lorca nos alegra. Es nuestro hit internacional. Me fascina que no aparezcan sus huesos porque eso convierte a Lorca en una ilusión muy posmoderna, muy thriller, muy CSI. Pero amo los huesos de Lorca y quiero verlos antes de morirme.

(Federico García Lorca is at last a spectacle for the twenty-first century, our Michael Jackson or something of that sort. We needed to find the matter of which the poet was made. We needed his remains, the most beloved remains of our history. Without his remains, his body is a fiction. The myth of Lorca grows. Lorca makes us happy. He is our international hit. I am fascinated by the fact that his remains have not appeared because that makes Lorca a postmodern illusion, a CSI-type thriller. But I love Lorca's remains and want to see them before I die.)[16]

What will we see if/when the remains of the poet are finally found? Will Lorca's remains become relics on which to build another commemorative (yet silencing) site? Will the findings inspire mystifying songs or denunciations of ongoing injustice? Will the discoveries function as monumental landmarks or will they reveal open wounds in the present historical landscape?

This brings us to our key question about (and exploration of) the place of history and literary studies today. To set up a kind of dual-straw-man opposition, some would argue that the primary purpose of a literary reading or study is to enlighten us about the original meaning of the text; for others, the real objective is to enlighten us about something outside the text – say, its political context, or even our own. But this opposition itself seems to rest on the fallacy that there is a strict distinction to be made between the meaning of a text and what is outside it. To steal a line from Derrida and twist it around a bit: *il n'y a QUE hors texte*, there is nothing BUT the outside of the text. The text, in other words, was never an innocent classic; rather, it was always engaged with its multiple contexts – political, theological, philosophical. Moreover, we cannot have access to it except through the lens of our own reading context – that is, our own state of emergency, to use Benjamin's insightful image. And this is why if we, as readers of literature, look for meaning in the original, pristine text, then we are like the proverbial lover looking for love in all the wrong places, or, worse yet, looking for meaning in the one place we'll never find it.

Notes

PROLOGUE

1. "Donald Trump Campaign Rally," 14:40.
2. Dawsey, "Trump Profanely Derides."
3. Ibid.
4. Ibid.
5. Ann Coulter, *Twitter*, 12 January 2018, twitter.com/anncoulter/status/951570094580170753.
6. Donald Trump, *Twitter*, 12 January 2018, *Trump Twitter Archive*, version 2, thetrumparchive.com/?searchbox=%22the+language+used+by%22.
7. Edelman, "Trump Denies Haiti Slur."
8. Collinson and Gaouette, "World Wonders."
9. E. Cohen, "The Truth."
10. Ibid.
11. Ibid.
12. Ibid.
13. Ibid.
14. Ibid.
15. Sun and Eilperin, "CDC Gets List."
16. Collinson, "Trump Divines His Own Truth."
17. Orwell, *1984*, 212–13.
18. Ibid., 265.
19. De Freytas-Tamura, "George Orwell's '1984.'"
20. Orwell, *1984*, 34–5.
21. Donald Trump, "The FAKE NEWS media (failing @nytimes, @NBCNews, @ABC, @CBS, @CNN) is not my enemy, it is the enemy of the American People!" *Twitter*, 17 February 2017, *Trump Twitter Archive*, version 2,

thetrumparchive.com/?searchbox=%22the+fake+news+media+failing+nytimes+nbcnews+abc%22&results=1.
22 White, "Metro Detroit Man."
23 Donald Trump, *Twitter*, 25 November 2017, *Trump Twitter Archive*, version 2, thetrumparchive.com/?searchbox=%22foxnews+is+much+more+important%22.
24 Donald Trump, *Twitter*, 27 November 2017, *Trump Twitter Archive*, version 2, thetrumparchive.com/?searchbox=%22we+should+have+a+contest%22.
25 Donald Trump, *Twitter*, 9 December 2017. *Trump Twitter Archive*, version 2, thetrumparchive.com/?searchbox=%22cnn+slogan%22.
26 "Read Sen. Jeff Flake's Speech."
27 Fromm, "Afterword," 321.
28 Orwell, *1984*, 299–300.
29 "2006 White House Correspondents' Dinner," 0:56:25.
30 Castillo and Egginton, *Medialogies*, 9.
31 Ibid.; Suskind, "Without a Doubt."
32 Suskind, "Without a Doubt."
33 "Conway," 1:59.
34 Fromm, "Afterword," 326.
35 Harrington, *Life in the Crystal Palace*, 227.
36 Fromm, "Afterword," 321–2.
37 "The Moral Limits of Markets."
38 Fromm, "Afterword," 325.
39 N. Postman, *Amusing Ourselves*, xix.
40 Teare, "Amusing Ourselves."
41 A. Postman, "My Dad Predicted Trump in 1985."
42 Orwell, *1984*, 35 and 4.
43 A. Postman, "My Dad Predicted Trump in 1985."
44 Beck, "During Speech at UB."

CHAPTER ONE

1 Zabala, "Trump's Call."
2 Sarlin, "Comey Disclosures."
3 Dan Rather, "It is understandable that Donald Trump's twitter attack on President Obama early this morning would immediately be consumed …" *Facebook*, 4 March 2017, facebook.com/thedanrather/posts/10158295903900716."

4 Anderson, "Combatting Misinformation."
5 Balibar, *Citizen Subject*, 24.
6 Rorty, *Achieving Our Country*, 90.
7 "Trump: "My Primary Consultant," 0:25.
8 Castillo and Egginton, *Medialogies*, 215.
9 "Donald Trump Is a Pro Wrestler"; Duff, "Why Wall Street Loves Trump."
10 Castillo and Egginton, *Medialogies*, 216; Leibniz, *New Essays*, 355.
11 Castillo and Egginton, "The Screen," 141.
12 C. Kelly et al., "The Bubble," 0:31.
13 Ibid., 1:33.
14 Almodóvar, *All about My Mother*, 1:18:32; our translation.
15 Castillo and Egginton, *Medialogies*, 207–17.
16 Herling, "The Incredible World," 2:15 and 2:03–13, italics original.
17 Morozov, "The Perils of Perfection."
18 Breitenbach, "Syrian Refugee."

CHAPTER TWO

1 Nietzsche, *Writings*, 7.60.
2 Lepore, "After the Fact."
3 Ibid.
4 Ibid.
5 Colbert, Drysdale, et al., "The Word," 0:13.
6 Correspondence between the intellect and the things.
7 Aquinas, *Questions*, 1.1.
8 Baudrillard, *Simulacra*, 6.
9 Morris, "Simulacra in the Age of Social Media," 1.
10 Snyder, "The American Abyss."
11 Lepore, "After the Fact."
12 Ibid.
13 Nietzsche, *Writings*, 7.60; Vattimo, *Of Reality*, 16.
14 Lacan, *Television*, 3.
15 Lepore, "After the Fact."
16 Ibid.
17 Vattimo, *Of Reality*, 114.
18 Wheeler, "The Computer," 564.
19 Vattimo, *Of Reality*, 108; Zabala, "Trump's Call to Order."
20 Vattimo, *Of Reality*, 108.
21 Ibid., 110.

CHAPTER THREE

1 *Apocalypse and the End Times*, 04:52.
2 Home page, Prophecy Depot Ministries, 15 March 2017, web.archive.org/web/20170315141252/http://www.prophecydepotministries.net.
3 "Donald Trump: The Candidate of the Apocalypse."
4 Feffer, "Trump's Apocalyptic Message."
5 Trump, "Inaugural Address."
6 Lozano, *Historias y leyendas*, 2:64–65. Translations from this text are our own.
7 Ibid., 2:52.
8 Tate, "Mythology in Spanish Historiography," 14–15.
9 Trump, *Trump*, 40.
10 *OED Online*, s.v. "demagogue, *n.*"
11 Trump with Schwartz, *Trump*, 39–40.
12 Gracián y Morales, *El criticón*, 3.6.
13 Gracián y Morales, *Oráculo*, maxim 64.
14 Trump, *Trump*, 43–44.
15 Gracián y Morales, *Oráculo manual*, maxim 122, our translation.
16 Gracián y Morales, *El héroe*, chapter 12, our translation.
17 Gracián y Morales, *El criticón*, 1.6.
18 Ibid., 2.5, our translation.
19 Quevedo y Santibáñez Villegas, *Poesía completa*, 1:30, our translation.
20 Gracián y Morales, *El criticón*, 2.4 and 2.7.
21 The title of Las Casas's volume is *An Account, Much Abbreviated, of the Destruction of the Indies*.
22 Rodríguez de la Flor, "Sacrificial Politics," 247 and 250.
23 Ibid., 252.
24 Mendieta, *Historia eclesiastica indiana*, 2:122, our translation.

CHAPTER FOUR

1 Kelley, "The Nephilim."
2 Prata, "Genetic Modification."
3 Starr, "Explosive Hypothesis."
4 "Trump Apocalypse Watch."
5 Nagesh, "People Think Donald Trump Is the Antichrist"; Burr, "Nostradamus Predicted Trump Victory."
6 Lamar Duckworth and Williams, "Humble," 1:43–53.

7 Scott-Heron, *Now and Then*, 77.
8 Ibid.
9 Ibid., 78.
10 Poniewozik, "The Rise of Surreality TV."
11 Ibid.

CHAPTER FIVE

1 Farley, "Kaleidoscope," 24:47, 24:54, 24:56, 22:42.
2 Ibid., 48:20.
3 Deggans, "Television's New Antiheroes."
4 Greenberg and Schlattmann, "Truth Be Told," 04:07.
5 Deggans, "Television's New Antiheroes."
6 Walley-Beckett, "Más," 26:08.
7 Kant, *Groundwork for the Metaphysics of Morals*, 42.
8 Calderón, *El alcalde*, 1.875.
9 For an introduction to this concept and its application to ideology, see Žižek, *The Sublime Object*, 87–131.
10 Calderón, *El alcalde*, 1.874–6, our translation.
11 Maravall, *Teatro y literatura*, 40.
12 See Vega y Carpio, *El villano*, lines 517–18 ("... rey del campo que gobierno/me soléis todos llamar") ("... king of the fields I govern/you all call me"); and Claramonte, *La Estrella*, line 1100 ("sólo mi honor reina en mí"; "only my honour rules over me").
13 Walter Poesse, in his article "Utilización de las palabras 'honor' y 'honra' en la comedia española" (298), cites the following passage from Lope de Vega y Carpio (*Los comendadores de Córdoba*, 3:1251): "honra es aquella que consiste en otro;/ningún hombre es honrado por sí mismo,/que del otro recibe la honra un hombre;/ser virtuoso hombre y tener méritos,/no es ser honrado; pero dar las causas/para que los que tratan les den honra" ("Honour is such that it depends on another; no man's honour is self-dependent, for honour is bestowed on him by another; to be a man of virtue and merit is not enough to be honoured, but to give others good reasons to honour him"). For Poesse ("Utilización de las palabras," 303), as well as for us, there is no distinction between *honor* and *honra* as used by the poets of the Baroque theatre ("los poetas no distinguen en ningún grado perceptible entre 'honor' y 'honra'").
14 "We Are the 99 Percent,"; Cullors, "Black Lives Matter."
15 Rucker, "Sen. DeMint."

CHAPTER SIX

1 Cervantes, *Entremeses*, 151; Smith, *Eight Interludes*, 45 (translation slightly altered to convey the pun in "su Jamestad").
2 Cervantes, *Entremeses*, 156; Smith, *Eight Interludes*, 48.
3 Cervantes, *Entremeses*, 157; Smith, *Eight Interludes*, 48.
4 Cervantes, *Entremeses*, 149; Smith, *Eight Interludes*, 45.
5 Cervantes, *Entremeses*, 149n28.
6 Ibid., 156–7; Smith, *Eight Interludes*, 48.
7 Cervantes, *Entremeses*, 221; Honig, *Interludes*, 114.
8 Gerli, "*El retablo de las maravillas*," 485.
9 Cervantes, *Entremeses*, 218; Honig, *Interludes*, 112.
10 Cervantes, *Entremeses*, 219; Honig, *Interludes*, 112.
11 Cervantes, *Entremeses*, 219; Honig, *Interludes*, 112.
12 Cervantes, *Entremeses*, 220; Honig, *Interludes*, 113.
13 Cervantes, *Entremeses*, 225; Honig, *Interludes*, 114–15.
14 Cervantes, *Entremeses*, 225; Honig, *Interludes*, 116.
15 Zimic, "*El retablo.*"
16 Cervantes, *Entremeses*, 230; Honig, *Interludes*, 119.
17 Cervantes, *Entremeses*, 234; Honig, *Interludes*, 122.
18 Castro, *De la edad conflictiva*, 77–8, our translation.
19 Cervantes, *Entremeses*, 229; Honig, *Interludes*, 118.
20 Maravall, *Poder, honor y élites*, 118–19, our translation.
21 Ibid., 127.
22 See ibid., 130: "Lo cierto es que los pecheros de condición mecánica no lograron imponerse sobre los conversos, cuando éstos poseían riquezas suficientes. Tampoco, aunque se atrevieran a lanzar expresiones insolentes contra los nobles, lograron aquéllos por su parte dar un paso hacia arriba" (Troy Tower's translation: "The truth is that the mechanical-class commoners failed to establish themselves over the *conversos*, when they themselves had sufficient wealth. So too did they fail to step up to the nobles, even if they did hurl insolence their way").
23 Maravall, *Teatro y literatura*.

CHAPTER SEVEN

1 Juan Manuel, *Libro de los ejemplos*, 162. Translations from this text are our own.
2 Ibid.
3 Ibid.

4 Miguel, "Amarte es un placer," 1:03, our translation.
5 Maravall, *Teatro y literatura*, 48, translation by Troy Tower.
6 Busto puts it in very clear terms in Claramonte's *La Estrella de Sevilla* (line 743): "... el honor es cristal puro/que con un soplo se quiebra" ("Honour is pure crystal that breaks with a breath").
7 Calderón, *El medico de su honra*, 3:890–1 and 3:897–9, our translation.
8 Gilbert and Gubar, *The Madwoman in the Attic*, 85.
9 Zayas, *Novelas completas*, 287. Translations from this text are our own unless otherwise noted.
10 Williamsen, "Engendering Interpretation," 646.
11 Zayas, *Novelas completas*, 330.
12 Castillo, *Baroque Horrors*, 118.
13 Russell, "Preface," xiv, italics in original; Caputi and Russell, "Femicide," 15.
14 Nelson, "The Aesthetics of Rape," 66, italics original.
15 Larsson, *The Girl with the Dragon Tattoo*, 182.
16 Nelson, "The Aesthetics of Rape," 67.

CHAPTER EIGHT

1 Foucault, *The Order of Things*, 385, italics in original.
2 Fichte, *The Science of Rights*, 394.
3 Ibid., 398, italics in original.
4 See ibid., 429: "Now, if a woman should assign prostitution as her means of support, she would properly be considered insane ... It is, therefore, the same as if she had assigned no business; *and this is the reason* why she can be expelled from the state unless she chooses to reform" (emphasis in original).
5 Maravall, *El mundo social*, 24. Translations from this text are our own.
6 Maravall, *Estudios de historia del pensamiento español*, 83.
7 Castillo and Egginton, "The Perspectival Imaginary."
8 The royal seal best illustrates the omnipresence of the monarch's authority, acting as a reproducible signifier of his imaginary power throughout the empire. As Percy Schramm documents, by the time of Philip II, the crown was rarely used as a public representation of royal power, as the royal seal had taken its place as the true signifier of royalty; see Schramm, *Las insignias de la realeza*, 76–7.
9 Zimmermann, "The *Querelle des Femmes*."
10 Jordan, *Renaissance Feminism*, 87.
11 Ibid.
12 Ibid., 104; italics in original.
13 Parker, "Fantasies of 'Race' and 'Gender,'" 84, italics in original.

14 Ibid.
15 Kritzman, *The Rhetoric of Sexuality*, 58.
16 Ibid., 33; Rabelais, *Le tiers livre*, 1:539; J. Cohen, *Histories of Gargantua and Pantagruel*, 378.
17 Kritzman, *The Rhetoric of Sexuality*, 33.
18 Rabelais, *Le tiers livre*, 1:516; J. Cohen, *Histories of Gargantua and Pantagruel*, 362–3.
19 Kritzman, *The Rhetoric of Sexuality*, 35.
20 Maravall, *El mundo social*, 18.
21 Ibid.
22 Rojas Zorrilla, *La Celestina*, 64; Singleton, *La Celestina*, 9–10.
23 It is important to remember that we are not speaking of "realities" here; we would not wish to claim that the medieval world was any less violent than that of the Renaissance. Rather we are referring to different ways of thinking about the world, which would emphasize individual existence over that of the community, for example.
24 Gossy, *The Untold Story*, 26.
25 Gerli, *Celestina*, 6.
26 Rojas Zorrilla, *La Celestina*, 124; Singleton, *La Celestina*, 64.
27 Gerli, *Celestina*, 92.
28 Singleton, *La Celestina*, 261–2n18.
29 Vives, *The Education of a Christian Woman*, 71.
30 Rojas Zorrilla, *La Celestina*, 158; Singleton, *La Celestina*, 98.
31 Rojas Zorrilla, *La Celestina*, 183; Singleton, *La Celestina*, 124, italics in original.
32 Rojas Zorrilla, *La Celestina*, 183; Singleton, *La Celestina*, 125.
33 Perry, "Magdalens and Jezebels," 124.
34 Ibid., 128.
35 Nor does Perry argue for such a direct role in so many words. We are suggesting a clarification that she might indeed agree with.
36 Ibid., 124.
37 Bergmann, "The Exclusion of the Feminine," 125.
38 Ibid.
39 Ibid., 127.
40 Vives, *The Education of a Christian Woman*, 85.
41 Bergmann, "The Exclusion of the Feminine," 128.
42 Vives, *The Education of a Christian Woman*, 180, italics added.
43 "Quilting point" is the English translation of *point de capiton*, a term from Lacanian discourse theory. For a detailed discussion of the quilting point as the stabilizing knot for an ideological field of meaning, see Žižek, *The*

Sublime Object, 87–131. We are interpreting Jameson's term *ideologeme* in approximately the same way, although in his definition it pertains to the narrower context of class antagonism. For his explanation, see Jameson, *The Political Unconscious*, 76.
44 See also Lope's plays *Fuenteovejuna* and *Peribáñez y el comendador de Ocaña*.
45 Vega y Carpio, *El caballero*, 37; Edwards, *The Knight*, 89.
46 Vega y Carpio, *El caballero*, 118; Edwards, *The Knight*, 167.

CHAPTER NINE

1 Ruggiero, "Marriage," 11.
2 Cervantes, *La tía fingida*, 106; W. Kelly, *The Pretended Aunt*, 473.
3 Cervantes, *La tía fingida*, 107, translated by Troy Tower.
4 Zayas, *El prevenido, engañado*, in *Novelas completas*, 158; Greer and Rhodes, *Exemplary Tales*, 128.
5 Friedman, *The Antiheroine's Voice*, 92.
6 Ibid.
7 Alemán, *Guzmán de Alfarache*, 2:104.
8 López de Úbeda, *La pícara Justina*, 466. Translations from this text are our own.
9 Ibid., 247.
10 Ibid., 79.
11 See ibid., 51, where she is referred to as a "melindrosa escribana" ("hesitant scribe").
12 Ibid., 83.
13 Davis, "Breaking the Barriers," 146–8.
14 López de Úbeda, *La pícara Justina*, 83 and 87.
15 Ibid., 90.
16 Ibid., 69.
17 Ibid., 448.
18 Castillo, *(A)wry Views*, 54–70.
19 Thomas, *The Hate U Give*, 410–11.
20 Polley, *Alias Grace*, Part 6, 14:52–23:42.
21 Ibid., 26:21–29:24.
22 López de Úbeda, *La pícara Justina*, 62.
23 Ibid., 55.
24 Ibid., 57.
25 Juana, *Obras completas*, 876; Lavrin, "Unlike Sor Juana," 71.
26 Atwood, "Am I a Bad Feminist."

CHAPTER TEN

1. Castorena y Ursúa, *Fama*, translation by Troy Tower.
2. Juana, *Obras completas*, 134, our translation.
3. Góngora, *Obras completas*, 1:27; Chaffee-Sorace, *Góngora's Shorter Poetic Masterpieces*, 107.
4. American Medical Association, "Body Image."
5. Juana, *Los empeños de una casa*, in *Obras completas*, 675; McGaha, *Los empeños de una casa*, 171.
6. Aside from the *Comedia* tradition, see the works of Baltasar Gracián, especially *Oráculo manual*.
7. Juana, *Los empeños de una casa*, in *Obras completas*, 693; McGaha, *Los empeños de una casa*, 229.
8. Consider Hernando's line earlier in the play (Juana, *Los empeños de una casa*, in *Obras completas*, 647): "el remedio es bien se aplique/antes que el mal que pasa se publique" (McGaha, *Los empeños de una casa*, 71: "you'd best be quick, before what's happened can become public").
9. Juana, *Los empeños de una casa*, in *Obras completas*, 663; McGaha, *Los empeños de una casa*, 127. See Juana's satire beginning "Hombres necios que acusáis" (*Obras completas*, 109), as well as the monologue by Carlos in *Los empeños de una casa* 2:1 (*Obras completas*, 658).
10. Juana, *Los empeños de una casa*, in *Obras completas*, 694; McGaha, *Los empeños de una casa*, 233–5.
11. Juana, *La Respuesta*, in *Obras completas*, 830; Paz, *Sor Juana Inés de la Cruz*, 5:492; Arenal and Powell, *The Answer*, 47–9.
12. Paz, *Sor Juana Inés de la Cruz*, 5:152; Sayers Peden, *Sor Juana*, 110.
13. Paz, *Sor Juana Inés de la Cruz*, 5:492.
14. Althusser, *Lenin and Philosophy*, 121–73; Foucault, *Histoire de la sexualité*, vol. 1.
15. Žižek, *The Sublime Object*, 87–131.
16. Juana, *La Respuesta*, in *Obras completas*, 840; Arenal and Powell, *The Answer*, 81.
17. Juana, *La Respuesta*, in *Obras completas*, 845; Arenal and Powell, *The Answer*, 97.

CHAPTER ELEVEN

1. Molho, *Cervantes*, 168, our translation.
2. Castillo, "The Literary Classics," 40–1.
3. Shipley, "Garbage In, Garbage Out," 7.

4 Cervantes, *Novelas ejemplares*, 1:52; Grossman, *Exemplary Novels*, 4.
5 Castillo and Egginton, *Medialogies*, 67–8; Castillo, "*Don Quixote* and Political Satire"; Giménez Caballero, *Genio de España*, 40, translated by Troy Tower.
6 Paskin and Marchese, "What's Real in 'Borat.'"
7 Shipley, "Garbage In, Garbage Out," 19.
8 Ibid., 38.
9 Ibid.
10 Zimic, *Las novelas ejemplares*, 183, our translation.
11 Osterc, *La verdad*, 228 and 231, our translation.
12 Fandos, "Donald Trump Defiantly Rallies a New 'Silent Majority'."
13 Garcia, "A History of 'Draining the Swamp'."
14 Cervantes, *Novelas ejemplares*, 2:69–70, our translation.
15 Ibid., 2:70.
16 Shipley, "Garbage In, Garbage Out," 19.
17 Trump, "Remarks … before Marine One Departure"; Trump, "Sleazy Adam Schiff, the totally biased Congressman looking into 'Russia,' spends all of his time on television pushing the Dem loss excuse!" *Twitter*, 24 July 2017, *Trump Twitter Archive*, version 2, thetrumparchive.com/?searchbox=%22sleazy+adam%22.

CHAPTER TWELVE

1 Cervantes, *Los trabajos*, 686; Weller and Colahan, *The Trials*, 327.
2 Cervantes, *Don Quijote*, 678; Grossman, *Don Quixote*, 454.
3 We are referring to criticism such as Armstrong-Roche, *Cervantes' Epic Novel*; Wilson, *Allegories of Love*; Fuchs, *Passing for Spain*; Baena, *El círculo y la flecha*; and Childers, "Quixo-Journalism"; among others.
4 Cervantes, *Los trabajos*, 717; Weller and Colahan, *The Trials*, 344.
5 Cervantes, *Los trabajos*, 427; Weller and Colahan, *The Trials*, 193.
6 Cervantes, *Los trabajos*, 289–90.
7 Forcione, *Cervantes' Christian Romance*.
8 Márquez Villanueva, *Menosprecio*, 273.
9 Cascardi, *Cervantes*, 77.
10 Cervantes, *Don Quijote*, 131; Grossman, *Don Quixote*, 75.
11 Cervantes, *Don Quijote*, 131; Grossman, *Don Quixote*, 75–6.
12 Cervantes, *Don Quijote*, 131–2; Grossman, *Don Quixote*, 76.
13 Cervantes, *Don Quijote*, 133–5; Grossman, *Don Quixote*, 76–7.
14 Cervantes, *Don Quijote*, 135; Grossman, *Don Quixote*, 77–8.
15 Cervantes, *Don Quijote*, 146; Grossman, *Don Quixote*, 85.

16 Cervantes, *Don Quijote*, 169; Grossman, *Don Quixote*, 100.
17 Cervantes, *Don Quijote*, 170; Grossman, *Don Quixote*, 101.
18 Cervantes, *Don Quijote*, 1228; Grossman, *Don Quixote*, 570.
19 Cervantes, *Los trabajos*, 260–1; Weller and Colahan, *The Trials*, 92.
20 Cervantes, *Los trabajos*, 261; Weller and Colahan, *The Trials*, 92.
21 Cervantes, *Los trabajos*, 261; Weller and Colahan, *The Trials*, 92.
22 Cervantes, *Los trabajos*, 261; Weller and Colahan, *The Trials*, 92.
23 Cascardi, *Cervantes*, 148–50.
24 Cervantes, *Los trabajos*, 265; Weller and Colahan, *The Trials*, 95.
25 Wilson, "Uncanonical Narratives."
26 Cervantes, *Los trabajos*, 431; Weller and Colahan, *The Trials*, 195.
27 Cervantes, *Los trabajos*, 430; Weller and Colahan, *The Trials*, 194.
28 Cervantes, *Los trabajos*, 460; Weller and Colahan, *The Trials*, 210.
29 Cervantes, *Los trabajos*, 470; Weller and Colahan, *The Trials*, 214.
30 Castillo, *(A)wry Views*, 107–8.
31 Cervantes, *Los trabajos*, 296; Weller and Colahan, *The Trials*, 114.
32 Wilson, *Allegories of Love*, 130–50.
33 Cervantes, *Los trabajos*, 126–7; Weller and Colahan, *The Trials*, 21.
34 Cervantes, *Don Quijote*, 239; Grossman, *Don Quixote*, 150.
35 Cervantes, *Los trabajos*, 331 and 215; Weller and Colahan, *The Trials*, 136 and 67.
36 Cervantes, *Los trabajos*, 331–2; Weller and Colahan, *The Trials*, 136.
37 Cervantes, *Los trabajos*, 295; Weller and Colahan, *The Trials*, 113.
38 Cervantes, *Los trabajos*, 295; Weller and Colahan, *The Trials*, 114.
39 Cervantes, *Los trabajos*, 327; Weller and Colahan, *The Trials*, 134.
40 Cervantes, *Los trabajos*, 329; Weller and Colahan, *The Trials*, 135.
41 Cervantes, *Los trabajos*, 329.
42 Castillo, "*Don Quixote* and Political Satire."
43 Cervantes, *Los trabajos*, 558–60; Weller and Colahan, *The Trials*, 258.
44 Sherwin, *Visualizing Law*, 23.

CHAPTER THIRTEEN

1 "Giuliani," 0:34.
2 Ibid., 0:27.
3 Donald Trump, "Any negative polls are fake news, just like the CNN, ABC, NBC polls in the election. Sorry, people want border security and extreme vetting," *Twitter*, 6 February 2017, *Trump Twitter Archive*, version 2, thetrumparchive.com/?searchbox=%22any+negative+polls%22; Trump,

"Remarks ... at the Veterans of Foreign Wars of the United States National Convention."
4 Orwell, *1984*, 81 and 249, italics in original.
5 Adam Schiff, "Today, Giuliani added to Orwell's liturgy: War is Peace. Slavery is Freedom. Ignorance is Strength. Truth isn't Truth," *Twitter*, 19 August 2018, twitter.com/repadamschiff/status/1031233428459536386.
6 Stephen King, *Twitter*, 19 August 2018, twitter.com/stephenking/status/1031286369941905410.
7 Harrington, *Life in the Crystal Palace*, 227; "The Moral Limits of Markets."
8 Crow, "Pharma Chief Defends 400% Drug Price Rise."
9 Ibid.
10 "The Moral Limits of Markets."
11 Wu, *The Attention Merchants*.
12 Ibid., 5–6.
13 Ibid., 6.
14 Ibid.
15 Ibid.
16 Maravall, *La cultura del barroco*.
17 "What Life Means to Einstein," 117.
18 Ibid.
19 Yang, Ward, and Kahr et al., "Abuse of Rachel Carson," 10030.
20 Rome, "DuPont and the Limits of Corporate Environmentalism," 76–8.
21 Ibid., 99.
22 Mann and Toles, *The Madhouse Effect*, 1–2, italics in original.
23 Cervantes, *Novelas ejemplares*, 52.
24 Cervantes, *Viaje del Parnaso*, 314. Translations from this text are our own.
25 Cervantes, *Don Quijote*, 608; Grossman, *Don Quixote*, 417.
26 Friedman, *The Unifying Concept*, 16.
27 Cervantes, *Viaje del Parnaso*, 314.
28 Vaidhyanathan, *Anti-Social Media*.
29 "Facebook and the Newsroom."
30 O'Neil, *Weapons of Math Destruction*, 3.
31 Ibid., 13 and 7.
32 Ibid., 12.
33 Voltaire, "On Absurdities," 277.
34 "I'm Going Off Script," 2:07–12.
35 Castillo, *Un-Deceptions*.

EPILOGUE

1 According to an MLA report, Spanish enrolments in US postsecondary institutions increased by over 10 per cent between 2002 and 2006. While overall enrolment in foreign languages increased during the period, the authors note that "numbers of students attending institutions of higher education and enrollments in language courses are not equivalent groupings" (Furman, Goldber, and Lusin, "Enrollments in Languages Other Than English," 2), and hence it is difficult to ascertain whether the overall increase represents relative increases or merely part of greater enrolments in postsecondary education.
2 Ketchum, "Reading from the Periphery," 170.
3 Fish, "Will the Humanities Save Us?"
4 Nussbaum, *Not for Profit*.
5 Landy, "SUNY Albany."
6 See ibid., which references Shepherd, "I Think, Therefore I Earn."
7 Mayhew, "José-Miguel Ullán."
8 Landy, "SUNY Albany," italics in original.
9 Kostelanetz, *The End of Intelligent Writing*, 21.
10 "Flashback: Kanye West Attacks George W. Bush," 0:24.
11 Anselmo, "El Olivo," in Castillo, "Monumental Landscapes," 10–11.
12 Castillo, "Monumental Landscapes."
13 Cervantes, *Don Quijote*, book 1, chapter 14.
14 Lorca, *Canciones*, 188, our translation.
15 Del Toro, Trashorras, and Muñoz, *El espinazo del diablo*, 1:27:40, our translation.
16 Vilas, "Lorca Reloaded," our translation.

Bibliography

Alemán, Mateo. *Guzmán de Alfarache*. Edited by Benito Brancaforte. Madrid: Cátedra, 1979.

Almodóvar, Pedro, dir. and screenwriter. *All about My Mother*. Columbia TriStar, 2000.

Althusser, Louis. *Lenin and Philosophy*. Translated by Ben Brewster. London: NLB, 1971.

American Medical Association. "Body Image and Advertising to Youth H-60.928." 2011. policysearch.ama-assn.org/policyfinder/detail/body%20image?uri=%2FAMADoc%2FHOD.xml-0-5022.xml.

Anderson, Chris. "Combatting Misinformation in a World of Alternative Facts." *Iowa State Daily*, 31 January 2017. iowastatedaily.com/news/politics_and_administration/article_f0a6932e-e80d-11e6-8788-6346e819f601.html.

Apocalypse and the End Times, season 5. Interview of Bill Salus by Paul McGuire. GOD TV, 12 November 2017. god.tv/video/apocalypse-and-the-end-times-bill-salus/zype.

Aquinas, Thomas. *Questions disputées De veritate*. Edited by Roberto Busa and Enrique Alarcón. Translated by André Aniorté. Le Barroux, FR: Sainte-Madeleine, 2011.

Arenal, Electra, and Amanda Powell, trans. and ed. *The Answer/La respuesta: Including Sor Filotea's Letter and New Selected Poems*. 2nd ed. By Juana Inés de la Cruz et al. New York: Feminist Press, 2009.

Armstrong-Roche, Michael. *Cervantes' Epic Novel: Empire, Religion, and the Dream Life of Heroes in "Persiles."* Toronto: University of Toronto Press, 2009.

Atwood, Margaret. "Am I a Bad Feminist? Canadian Author Margaret Atwood Examines How She Landed in Such Hot Water among Her

Peers for Signing an Open Letter Regarding UBC's Handling of a Sexual Abuse Case." *Globe and Mail*, 13 January 2018. theglobeandmail.com/opinion/am-i-a-bad-feminist/article37591823.

Baena, Julio. *El círculo y la flecha: principio y fin, triunfo y fracaso del Persiles*. Chapel Hill: University of North Carolina Press, 1996.

Balibar, Étienne. *Citizen Subject: Foundations for Philosophical Anthropology*. Translated by Steven Miller. Oxford: Fordham University Press, 2016.

Baudrillard, Jean. *Simulacra and Simulation*. Translated by Sheila Faria Glaser. Ann Arbor: University of Michigan Press, 1994.

Beck, Julia. "During Speech at UB, Atwood Stresses the Importance of the Humanities." *Buffalo News*, 19 March 2018. buffalonews.com/2018/03/19/during-speech-at-ub-atwood-stresses-the-importance-of-the-humanities.

Bergmann, Emilie. "The Exclusion of the Feminine in the Cultural Discourse of the Golden Age: Juan Luis Vives and Fray Luis de León." In *Permanence and Evolution of Behavior in Golden-Age Spain: Essays in Gender, Body, and Religion*, edited by Alain Saint-Saëns, 124–36. Lewiston, NY: Edwin Mellen Press, 1991.

Breitenbach, Dagmar. "Syrian Refugee Takes Facebook to Court in Germany." *DW News*, 6 February 2017. dw.com/en/syrian-refugee-takes-facebook-to-court-in-germany/a-37090822.

Burr, Edmondo (pseud.). "Nostradamus Predicted Trump Victory and the Apocalypse." *YourNewsWire*, 10 November 2016. yournewswire.com/nostradamus-predicted-trump-victory-and-the-apocalypse.

Calderón de la Barca, Pedro. *El alcalde de Zalamea*. Edited by José Montero Reguera. Madrid: Castalia, 1996.

– *El médico de su honra*. In *Dramas de honor*, edited by Ángel Valbuena Briones, 2:11–118. Madrid: Espasa-Calpe, 1956.

Caputi, Jane, and Diana Russell. "Femicide: Sexist Terrorism against Women." In *Femicide: The Politics of Woman-Killing*, edited by Jill Radford and Diana Russell, 13–21. Toronto: Maxwell Macmillan Canada, 1992.

Cascardi, Anthony. *Cervantes, Literature, and the Discourse of Politics*. Toronto: University of Toronto Press, 2012.

Castillo, David. *(A)wry Views: Anamorphosis, Cervantes, and the Early Picaresque*. West Lafayette, IN: Purdue University Press, 2001.

– *Baroque Horrors: Roots of the Fantastic in the Age of Curiosities*. Ann Arbor: University of Michigan Press, 2010.

– "*Don Quixote* and Political Satire: Cervantine Lessons from Sacha Baron Cohen and Stephen Colbert." In *Approaches to Teaching*

Cervantes's "Don Quixote," edited by James Parr and Lisa Vollendorf, 171–7. New York: Modern Languages Association of America, 2015.
- "The Literary Classics in Today's Classroom: *Don Quixote* and Road Movies." In *Cervantes in Perspective*, edited by Julia Domínguez, 29–44. Madrid: Iberomamericana/Vervuert, 2013.
- "Monumental Landscapes in the Society of the Spectacle: From Fuenteovejuna to New York." In *Spectacle and Topophilia: Reading Early Modern and Postmodern Hispanic Cultures*, edited by David Castillo and Bradley Nelson, 3–18. Nashville, TN: Vanderbilt University Press, 2012.
- *Un-Deceptions: Cervantine Strategies for the Disinformation Age.* Forthcoming.

Castillo, David, and William Egginton. *Medialogies: Reading Reality in the Age of Inflationary Media.* London: Bloomsbury, 2017.
- "The Perspectival Imaginary and the Symbolization of Power in Early Modernity." *Indiana Journal of Hispanic Literatures* 8 (1996): 75–93.
- "The Screen Behind the Screen: A Penultimate Response to a Polemical Companion." *Hispanic Issues On Line Debates* 8 (2017): 132–46. cla.umn.edu/sites/cla.umn.edu/files/hiold_08_10_castillo_and_egginton.pdf.

Castorena y Ursúa, Juan Ignacio de, ed. *Fama, y obras posthumas del fenix de Mexico, decima musa, poetisa Americana.* By Juana Inés de la Cruz. Madrid: Manuel Ruiz de Murga, 1700.

Castro, Américo. *De la edad conflictiva: crisis de la cultura española en el siglo XVII*, 3rd ed. Madrid: Taurus, 1972.

Cervantes, Miguel de. *Don Quijote de la Mancha.* Edited by Francisco Rico with Joaquín Forradellas, Gonzalo Pontón et al. Madrid: Cátedra, 2015.
- *Entremeses.* Edited by Nicholas Spadaccini. Madrid: Cátedra, 1982.
- *Novelas ejemplares*, 8th ed. Edited by Harry Sieber. Madrid: Cátedra, 1985.
- *La tía fingida.* In *Novelas ejemplares*, edited by Jorge Luis Borges, 635–57. Buenos Aires: Emecé, 1946.
- *Los trabajos de Persiles y Sigismunda.* Edited by Carlos Romero Muñoz. Madrid: Cátedra, 1997.
- *Viaje del Parnaso.* Edited by Miguel Herrero García. Madrid: Consejo Superior de Investigaciones Científicas, 1983.

Chaffee-Sorace, Diane, trans. *Góngora's Shorter Poetic Masterpieces in Translation.* By Luis de Góngora. Tempe, AZ: ACMRS, 2010.

Childers, William. "Quixo-Journalism." *Hispanic Issues On Line Debates* 8 (2017): 91–110. cla.stg.umn.edu/sites/cla.umn.edu/files/hiold_08_07_childers_0.pdf.

Claramonte, Andrés de. *La Estrella de Sevilla*. In *La Estrella de Sevilla; El gran rey de los desiertos*, edited by Alfredo Rodríguez López-Vázquez, 141–315. Madrid: Cátedra, 2010.
Cohen, Elizabeth. "The Truth about Those 7 Words 'Banned' at the CDC." *CNN*, 31 January 2018. cnn.com/2018/01/11/health/cdc-word-ban-hhs-document.
Cohen, John Michael, trans. *The Histories of Gargantua and Pantagruel*. By François Rabelais. Harmondsworth: Penguin, 1955.
Colbert, Stephen, Eric Drysdale, et al. "The Word – Truthiness." *The Colbert Report*, season 1, episode 1, 17 October 2005. comedycentral.com.au/throwbacks/videos/the-colbert-report-the-very-first-episode-clips#the-word-truthiness.
Collinson, Stephen. "Trump Divines His Own Truth without Consequences." *CNN*, 6 May 2018. cnn.com/2018/05/07/politics/donald-trump-presidency.
Collinson, Stephen, and Nicole Gaouette. "World Wonders If Trump Is Eroding US 'Moral Authority.'" *CNN*, 12 January 2018. cnn.com/2018/01/12/politics/trump-shithole-world-fallout.
"Conway: Press Secretary Gave 'Alternative Facts.'" *Meet the Press*, NBC, 22 January 2017. nbcnews.com/meet-the-press/meet-press-01-22-17-n710491.
Crow, David. "Pharma Chief Defends 400% Drug Price Rise as a 'Moral Requirement.'" *Financial Times*, 11 September 2018. ft.com/content/48b0ce2c-b544-11e8-bbc3-ccd7de085ffe.
Cullors, Patrisse. "Black Lives Matter." Patrisse Cullors: Artist, Organizer, Freedom Fighter, 2019. patrissecullors.com/black-lives-matter.
Davis, Nina Cox. "Breaking the Barriers: The Birth of López de Úbeda's *Pícara Justina*." In *The Picaresque: Tradition and Displacement*, edited by Giancarlo Maiorino, 137–58. Minneapolis: University of Minnesota Press, 1996.
Dawsey, Josh. "Trump Profanely Derides Immigrants' Nations of Origin." *Washington Post*, 12 January 2018. wapo.st/2AQVXfR.
De Freytas-Tamura, Kimiko. "George Orwell's '1984' Has a Sales Surge." *New York Times*, 26 January 2017. nyti.ms/2ktMk2O.
Deggans, Eric. "Television's New Antiheroes: Creating Sympathy for the Devilish." *WBUR*, 15 December 2011. wbur.org/npr/143753533/televisions-new-antiheroes-creating-sympathy-for-the-devilish.
Del Toro, Guillermo, Antonio Trashorras, and David Muñoz, screenwriters. *El espinazo del diablo*. Directed by Guillermo del Toro. Criterion, 2013.
"Donald Trump: The Candidate of the Apocalypse." *Washington Post*, 22 July 2016. wapo.st/2azypk4.

"Donald Trump Campaign Rally in Hilton Head, South Carolina." C-SPAN, 30 December 2015. c-span.org/video/?402610-1/donald-trump-campaign-rally-hilton-head-south-carolina.

"Donald Trump Is a Pro Wrestler Masquerading as Commander-in-Chief." *Economist*, 13 April 2019. economist.com/united-states/2019/04/13/donald-trump-is-a-pro-wrestler-masquerading-as-commander-in-chief.

Duff, Turney. "Why Wall Street Loves Trump." CNBC, 14 August 2015. cnbc.com/2015/08/14/why-wall-street-loves-trump-commentary.html.

Edelman, Adam. "Trump Denies Haiti Slur amid Fallout from 'Shithole' Comment." NBC *News*, 12 January 2018. nbcnews.com/politics/donald-trump/trump-appears-deny-shithole-slur-defends-tough-immigration-stance-n837056.

Edwards, Gwynne, trans. and ed. *The Knight from Olmedo*. In *Fuente Ovejuna; The Knight from Olmedo; Punishment without Revenge*, by Lope de Vega y Carpio, 81–167. Oxford: Oxford University Press, 1999.

Fandos, Nicholas. "Donald Trump Defiantly Rallies a New 'Silent Majority' in a Visit to Arizona." *New York Times*, 11 July 2015. nyti.ms/1ISmDhu.

Farley, Ryan, screenwriter. "Kaleidoscope." Directed by Ellen Kuras. *Ozark*, season 1, episode 8. Netflix, 21 July 2017.

Feffer, John. "Trump's Apocalyptic Message: Biblical Prophecy, Survivalist Ideologue and Racist Conspiracies in One Package." *AlterNet*, 13 October 2016. alternet.org/2016/10/trumps-apocalyptic-message-biblical-prophecy-survivalist-ideolog-and-racist.

Fichte, Johann Gottlieb. *The Science of Rights: Grundlage des Naturrechts nach Principien der Wissenschaftslehre*. Translated by Adolph Ernst Kroeger. New York: Harper & Row, 1970.

Fish, Stanley. "Will the Humanities Save Us?" *New York Times*, 6 January 2008. opinionator.blogs.nytimes.com/2008/01/06/will-the-humanities-save-us.

"Flashback: Kanye West Attacks George W. Bush Over Katrina Response." *Today Show*, 27 August 2015. nbcnews.com/feature/flashback/video/flashback-kanye-west-attacks-george-w-bush-over-katrina-response-514568771962.

Forcione, Alban. *Cervantes' Christian Romance: A Study of "Persiles y Sigismunda."* Princeton, NJ: Princeton University Press, 1972.

Foucault, Michel. *Histoire de la sexualité*. 3 vols. Paris: Gallimard, 1976–84.

— *The Order of Things*. Translated by Alan Sheridan[?]. New York: Vintage, 1994.

Friedman, Edward. *The Antiheroine's Voice: Narrative Discourse and Transformations of the Picaresque*. Columbia: University of Missouri Press, 1987.
– *The Unifying Concept: Approaches to the Structure of Cervantes' Comedias*. York, SC: Spanish Literature Publications, 1981.
Fromm, Erich. "Afterword." *1984*, by George Orwell, 313–26. New York: Signet Classics, 1961.
Fuchs, Barbara. *Passing for Spain: Cervantes and the Fictions of Identity*. Urbana: University of Illinois Press, 2003.
Furman, Nelly, David Goldberg, and Natalia Lusin. "Enrollments in Languages Other Than English in United States Institutions of Higher Education, Fall 2006." MLA, 13 November 2007. mla.org/pdf/06enrollmentsurvey_final.pdf.
Garcia, Eric. "A History of 'Draining the Swamp.'" *Roll Call*, 18 October 2016. rollcall.com/2016/10/18/a-history-of-draining-the-swamp.
Gerli, E. Michael. *Celestina and the Ends of Desire*. Toronto: University of Toronto Press, 2011.
– "*El retablo de las maravillas:* Cervantes' 'Arte nuevo de deshacer comedias.'" *Hispanic Review* 57, no. 4 (1989): 477–92.
Gilbert, Sandra, and Susan Gubar. *The Madwoman in the Attic: The Woman Writer and the Nineteenth-Century Literary Imagination*, 2nd ed. New Haven, CT: Yale University Press, 2000.
Giménez Caballero, Ernesto. *Genio de España: exaltaciones a una resurrección nacional y del mundo*. Madrid: La Gaceta Literaria, 1932.
"Giuliani: 'Truth Isn't Truth.'" Rudolph Giuliani interview with Chuck Todd. *Meet the Press*, 19 August 2018. nbcnews.com/meet-the-press/video/giuliani-truth-isn-t-truth-1302113347986.
Góngora, Luis de. *Obras completas*, 2nd ed. Edited by Antonio Carreira. Madrid: Fundación José Antonio de Castro, 2000.
Gossy, Mary. *The Untold Story: Women and Theory in Golden Age Texts*. Ann Arbor: University of Michigan Press, 1989.
Gracián y Morales, Baltasar. *El criticón*. In *Obras completas*, edited by Evaristo Correa Calderón, 421–840. Madrid: Aguilar, 1944.
– *El héroe*. In *Obras completas*, edited by Evaristo Correa Calderón, 1–24. Madrid: Aguilar, 1944.
– *Oráculo manual y arte de prudencia*. In *Obras completas*, edited by Evaristo Correa Calderón, 353–420. Madrid: Aguilar, 1944.
Greenberg, Drew, and Tim Schlattmann, screenwriters. "Truth Be Told." Directed by Keith Gordon. *Dexter*, season 1, episode 11. Colleton/Clyde Phillips Productions/John Goldwyn, 10 December 2006.

Greer, Margaret R., and Elizabeth Rhodes, trans. and eds. *Exemplary Tales of Love and Tales of Disillusion*. By María de Zayas. Chicago: University of Chicago Press, 2009.

Grossman, Edith, trans. *Don Quixote*. By Miguel de Cervantes. New York: HarperCollins, 2003.

– *Exemplary Novels*. By Miguel de Cervantes. Edited by Roberto Gonzáles Echevarría. New Haven, CT: Yale University Press, 2016.

Harrington, Alan. *Life in the Crystal Palace*. New York: Knopf, 1959.

Herling, Jan. "The Incredible World of Diminished Reality." *YouTube*, 9 September 2010. youtu.be/FgTq-AgYlTE.

Honig, Edwin, trans. and ed. *Interludes*. By Miguel de Cervantes. New York: Signet Classics, 1964.

"'I'm Going Off-script': Boris Sanchez Reacts to Donald Trump's Fox News Interview." *CNN*, 29 November 2020. cnn.com/videos/politics/2020/11/29/trump-fox-news-interview-boris-sanchez-reacts-nr-vpx.cnn.

Jameson, Frederic. *The Political Unconscious: Narrative as a Socially Symbolic Act*. Ithaca, NY: Cornell University Press, 1980.

Jordan, Constance, trans. and ed. *Renaissance Feminism*. Ithaca, NY: Cornell University Press, 1990.

Juan Manuel. *Libro de los ejemplos del conde Lucanor y de Patronio*. Edited by Pedro Henríquez Ureña. Buenos Aires: Losada, 1939.

Juana Inés de la Cruz. *Obras completas*, 3rd ed. Edited by Francisco Monterde. Mexico City: Porrúa, 1975.

Kant, Immanuel. *Groundwork for the Metaphysics of Morals*, 2nd ed. Translated and edited by Allen Wood. New Haven, CT: Yale University Press, 2018.

Kelley, Jack. "The Nephilim." *Grace thru Faith*, 6 August 2018. gracethrufaith.com/end-times-prophecy/the-nephilim.

Kelly, Chris, Sarah Schneider, Bryan Tucker, et al. "The Bubble." *Saturday Night Live*, season 42, episode 6, 12 November 2016. nbc.com/saturday-night-live/video/the-bubble/3428577.

Kelly, Walter, trans. *The Pretended Aunt*. In *The Exemplary Novels ...: to Which Are Added El buscapié, or, The Serpent; and La tía fingida, or, The Pretended Aunt*, by Miguel de Cervantes, 469–84. London: Henry Bohn, 1855.

Ketchum, Roy. "Reading from the Periphery: Ricardo Piglia and the Liberal Arts." *Hispanic Issues On Line* 8 (2011): 170–85. cla.stg.umn.edu/sites/cla.umn.edu/files/hiol_08_11_ketchum_rading_from_periphery_0.pdf.

Kostelanetz, Richard. *The End of Intelligent Writing: Literary Politics in America*. New York: Sheed and Ward, 1973.
Kritzman, Lawrence. *The Rhetoric of Sexuality and the Literature of the French Renaissance*. New York: Columbia University Press, 1991.
Lacan, Jacques. *Television*. Translated by Denis Hollier, Rosalind Krauss, and Annette Michelson. In *Television: A Challenge to the Psychoanalytic Establishment*, edited by Joan Copjec, 1–46. New York: Norton, 1990.
Lamar Duckworth, Kendrick, and Michael Len Williams II, composers. "Humble." Directed by Dave Meyers, Dave Free, and Kendrick Duckworth Lamar. TDE Films/FREENJOY, 2017. youtu.be/tvTRZJ-4EyI.
Landy, Joshua. "SUNY Albany, Stanley Fish, and the Enemy Within." *Guardian*, 14 October 2010. arcade.stanford.edu/blogs/sunyalbany-stanley-fish-and-enemy-within.
Larsson, Stieg. *The Girl with the Dragon Tattoo*. Translated by Reg Keeland. New York: Vintage, 2011.
Las Casas, Bartolomé de. *An Account, Much Abbreviated, of the Destruction of the Indies*. Edited by Franklin Knight. Translated by Andrew Hurley. Indianapolis: Hackett, 2003.
Lavrin, Asunción. "Unlike Sor Juana? The Model Nun in the Religious Literature of Colonial Mexico." *Feminist Perspectives on Sor Juana Inés de la Cruz*, edited by Stephanie Merrim, 61–85. Detroit: Wayne State University Press, 1991.
Leibniz, Gottfried Wilhelm. *New Essays on Human Understanding*. Translated and edited by Peter Remnant and Jonathan Bennett. Cambridge: Cambridge University Press, 1981.
Lepore, Jill. "After the Fact: In the History of Truth, a New Chapter Begins." *New Yorker* 92, no. 6 (21 March 2016). newyorker.com/magazine/2016/03/21/the-internet-of-us-and-the-end-of-facts.
López de Úbeda, Francisco. *La pícara Justina*. Edited by Bruno Mario Damiani. Madrid: Studia Humanitatis, 1982.
Lorca, Federico García. *Canciones y primeras canciones*. Edited by Piero Menarini. Madrid: Espasa-Calpe, 1986.
Lozano, Cristóbal. *Historias y leyendas*. Edited by Joaquín de Entrambasaguas. Madrid: Espasa-Calpe, 1955.
Mann, Michael, and Tom Toles. *The Madhouse Effect: How Climate Change Denial Is Threatening Our Planet, Destroying Our Politics, and Driving Us Crazy*. New York: Columbia University Press, 2016.
Maravall, José Antonio. *La cultura del barroco: análisis de una estructura histórica*. Barcelona: Planeta, 2012.

- *Estudios de historia del pensamiento español, serie segunda: la época del Renacimiento*. Madrid: Ediciones Cultura Hispánica, 1984.
- *El mundo social de "La Celestina."* Madrid: Gredos, 1964.
- *Poder, honor y élites en el siglo XVII*. Madrid: Siglo XXI, 1979.
- *Teatro y literatura en la sociedad barroca*, 2nd ed. Barcelona: Crítica, 1990.

Márquez Villanueva, Francisco. *"Menosprecio de corte y alabanza de aldea" (Valladolid, 1539) y el tema aúlico en la obra de Fray Antonio de Guevara*. Santander: Publicaciones de la Universidad de Cantabria, 1999.

Mayhew, Jonathan. "José-Miguel Ullán: hacia una poética de lo visual." *Hispanic Issues On Line* 8 (2011): 222–9. cla.umn.edu/sites/cla.umn.edu/files/hiol_21_8_mayhew.pdf.

McGaha, Michael, trans. *Los empeños de una casa / Pawns of a House (A Mexican Baroque Fête)*. By Juana Inés de la Cruz. Edited by Susana Hernández Araico. Tempe, AZ: Bilingual Press, 2007.

Mendieta, Geronimo de. *Historia eclesiastica indiana*. Edited by Francisco Solano y Perez-Lila. Madrid: Atlas, 1973.

Miguel, Luis. "Amarte es un placer." *Amarte es un placer*, track 12. WEA Latina, 1999.

Molho, Maurice. *Cervantes: raíces folkóricas*. Madrid: Gredos, 1976.

"The Moral Limits of Markets: Live Interview with Michael Sandel." *Big Think*, 4 May 2012. bigthink.com/videos/the-moral-limits-of-markets-live-interview-with-michael-sandel.

Morozov, Evgeny. "The Perils of Perfection." *New York Times*, 3 March 2013. nyti.ms/14dmL2T.

Morris, James. "Simulacra in the Age of Social Media: Baudrillard as the Prophet of Fake News." *Journal of Communication Inquiry*, December 2020, dx.doi.org/10.1177/0196859920977154.

Nagesh, Ashitha. "People Think Donald Trump Is the Antichrist – and He's Bringing the Apocalypse." *Metro*, 10 November 2016. metro.co.uk/2016/11/10/people-think-donald-trump-is-the-antichrist-and-hes-bringing-the-apocalypse-6249004.

Nelson, Bradley J. "The Aesthetics of Rape, and the Rape of Aesthetics." *Hispanic Issues On Line* 8 (2011): 62–80. cla.umn.edu/sites/cla.umn.edu/files/hiol_08_04_nelson_the_aesthetics_of_rape.pdf.

Nietzsche, Friedrich. *Writings from the Late Notebooks*. Translated by Kate Sturge. Edited by Rüdiger Bittner. Cambridge: Cambridge University Press, 2003.

Noble, Safiya Umoja. *Algorithms of Opression: How Search Engines Reinforce Racism.* New York: NYU Press, 2018.
Nussbaum, Martha. *Not for Profit: Why Democracy Needs the Humanities.* Princeton, NJ: Princeton University Press, 2010.
O'Neil, Cathy. *Weapons of Math Destruction: How Big Data Increases Inequality and Threatens Democracy.* New York: Crown, 2016.
Ordway, Denise-Marie. "Facebook and the Newsroom: 6 Questions for Siva Vaidhyanathan." *Journalist's Resource*, 12 September 2018. journalistsresource.org/studies/society/social-media/facebook-siva-vaidhyanathan-news.
Orwell, George. *1984.* New York: Signet Classics, 1961.
Osterc, Lúdovik. *La verdad sobre las Novelas Ejemplares.* Mexico City: Facultad de Filosofía y Letras, 1995.
Parker, Patricia. "Fantasies of 'Race' and 'Gender': Africa, *Othello*, and Bringing to Light." *Women, "Race," and Writing in the Early Modern Period*, edited by Margo Hendricks and Patricia Parker, 84–100. London: Routledge, 1994.
Paskin, Willa, and David Marchese. "What's Real in 'Borat'?" *Salon*, 10 November 2006. https://www.salon.com/2006/11/10/guide_to_borat/.
Paz, Octavio. *Sor Juana Inés de la Cruz, o las trampas de la fe.* In *Obras completas*, 5:15–587. Mexico City: Fondo de Cultura Económica, 1994.
Perry, Mary Elizabeth. "Magdalens and Jezebels in Counter-Reformation Spain." In *Culture and Control in Counter-Reformation Spain*, edited by Anne Cruz and Mary Elizabeth Perry, 124–44. Minneapolis: University of Minnesota Press, 1992.
Poesse, Walter. "Utilización de las palabras 'honor' y 'honra' en la comedia española." In *Homenaje a don Agapito Rey. Trabajos publicados en su honor*, edited by Josep Roca-Pons, 289–303. Bloomington: Department of Spanish and Portuguese, Indiana University, 1980.
Polley, Sarah, screenwriter. *Alias Grace*, Part 6. Directed by Mary Harron. Netflix, 2017.
Poniewozik, James. "The Rise of Surreality TV." *New York Times*, 29 March 2017. nyti.ms/2ouWrTb.
Postman, Andrew. "My Dad Predicted Trump in 1985 – It's Not Orwell, He Warned, It's Brave New World." *Guardian*, 2 February 2017. theguardian.com/media/2017/feb/02/amusing-ourselves-to-death-neil-postman-trump-orwell-huxley.
Postman, Neil. *Amusing Ourselves to Death: Public Discourse in the Age of Show Business*, 2nd ed. New York: Penguin, 2005.

Prata, Elizabeth. "Genetic Modification and Dinosaurs." *The End Time*, 10 August 2010. the-end-time.blogspot.com/2010/08/genetic-modification-of-humans-animals.html.

Quevedo y Santibáñez Villegas, Francisco Gómez de. *Poesía completa*. Edited by José Manuel Blecua. Madrid: Turner, 1995.

Rabelais, François. *Le tiers livre des faicts et dicts heroiques du bon Pantagruel*. Œuvres complètes, edited by Pierre Jourda, 1:389–619. Paris: Garnier, 1962

"Read Sen. Jeff Flake's Speech Criticizing Trump." CNN, 17 January 2018. cnn.com/2018/01/17/politics/jeff-flake-speech.

Rodríguez de la Flor, Fernando. "Sacrificial Politics in the Spanish Colonies." Translated by Rose Seifert. *Reason and Its Others: Italy, Spain, and the New World*, edited by David Castillo and Massimo Lollini, 243–58. Nashville, TN: Vanderbilt, 2006.

Rojas Zorrilla, Fernando de. *La Celestina*. Edited by Joaquín Benito de Lucas. Barcelona: Plaza & Janés, 1984.

Rome, Adam. "DuPont and the Limits of Corporate Environmentalism." *Business History Review* 93 (2019): 75–99. doi:10.1017/S0007680519000345.

Rorty, Richard. *Achieving Our Country: Leftist Thought in Twentieth-Century America*. Cambridge, MA: Harvard University Press, 1998.

Rucker, Philip. "Sen. DeMint of S.C. Is Voice of Opposition to Health-Care Reform." *Washington Post*, 28 July 2009. washingtonpost.com/wp-dyn/content/article/2009/07/27/AR2009072703066.html.

Ruggiero, Guido. "Marriage, Love, Sex, and Renaissance Civic Morality." In *Sexuality and Gender in Early Modern Europe*, edited by James Grantham Turner, 10–30. Cambridge: Cambridge University Press, 1993.

Russell, Diana. "Preface." *Femicide: The Politics of Woman Killing*, edited by Jill Radford and Diana Russell, xiv–xv. Toronto: Maxwell Macmillan, 1992.

Sarlin, Benjy. "Comey Disclosures Leave Trump Alone on Island of Conspiracy Theories." NBC News, 21 March 2017. nbcnews.com/politics/white-house/comey-disclosures-leave-trump-alone-island-conspiracy-theories-n736101.

Sayers Peden, Margaret, trans. *Sor Juana, or, The Traps of Faith*. By Octavio Paz. Cambridge, MA: Harvard University Press, 1988.

Schramm, Percy. *Las insignias de la realeza en la Edad Media española*. Madrid: Instituto de Estudios Políticos, 1960.

Scott-Heron, Gil. *Now and Then …: The Poems of Gil Scott-Heron*. Edinburgh: Payback, 2000.

Shepherd, Jessica. "I Think, Therefore I Earn." *Guardian*, 20 November 2007. guardian.co.uk/education/2007/nov/20/choosingadegree.highereducation.

Sherwin, Richard. *Visualizing Law in the Age of the Digital Baroque: Arabesques and Entanglements*. New York: Routledge, 2011.

Shipley, George. "Garbage In, Garbage Out: 'The Best of Vidriera'." *Cervantes* 21, no. 1 (2001): 5–41. cervantesvirtual.com/obra-visor/cervantes-bulletin-of-the-cervantes-society-of-america--51/html/027938cc-82b2-11df-acc7-002185ce6064_15.html.

Singleton, Mack Hendricks, trans. and ed. *La Celestina*. By Fernando de Rojas. Madison: University of Wisconsin Press, 1958.

Smith, Dawn, trans. and ed. *Eight Interludes*. By Miguel de Cervantes. London: J.M. Dent, 1996.

Snyder, Timothy. "The American Abyss." *New York Times Magazine*, 9 January 2021. nyti.ms/35nixPu.

Starr, Barry. "Explosive Hypothesis about Humans' Lack of Genetic Diversity." *KQED Science Quest*, 17 March 2008. https://www.kqed.org/quest/474/explosive-hypothesis-about-humans-lack-of-genetic-diversity.

Sun, Lena, and Juliet Eilperin. "CDC Gets List of Forbidden Words: Fetus, Transgender, Diversity." *Washington Post*, 15 December 2017. wapo.st/2j7DbdS.

Suskind, Ron. "Without a Doubt." *New York Times*, 17 October 2004. nyti.ms/2jBfR9O.

Tate, Robert. "Mythology in Spanish Historiography in the Middle Ages and the Renaissance." *Hispanic Review* 22, no. 1 (1954): 1–18.

Teare, Chris. "Amusing Ourselves to Death with Donald Trump." *Forbes*, 14 May 2016. forbes.com/sites/christeare/2016/05/14/amusing-ourselves-to-death-with-donald-trump.

Thomas, Angie. *The Hate U Give*. New York: HarperCollins, 2017.

"Trump: 'My Primary Consultant Is Myself." *Morning Joe*, MSNBC, 16 March 2016. msnbc.com/morning-joe/watch/trump-my-primary-consultant-is-myself-645588035836.

"Trump Apocalypse Watch." *Slate*. 2016. slate.com/topics/t/trump_apocalypsewatch.html.

Trump, Donald J. Inaugural Address. *Politico*, 20 January 2017 https://www.politico.com/story/2017/01/full-text-donald-trump-inauguration-speech-transcript-233907

– "Remarks ... at the Veterans of Foreign Wars of the United States National Convention." *White House*, 24 July 2018. whitehouse.gov/

briefings-statements/remarks-president-trump-veterans-foreign-wars-united-states-national-convention-kansas-city-mo.
- "Remarks ... before Marine One Departure." *White House*, 9 November 2018. whitehouse.gov/briefings-statements/remarks-president-trump-marine-one-departure-23.

Trump, Donald, with Tony Schwartz. *Trump: The Art of the Deal*. New York: Random House, 1987.

"2006 White House Correspondents' Dinner." Master of ceremonies Mark Smith. C-SPAN, 29 April 2006. c-span.org/video/?192243-1/2006-white-house-correspondents-dinner.

Vaidhyanathan, Siva. *Anti-Social Media: How Facebook Disconnects Us and Undermines Democracy*. New York: Oxford University Press, 2018.
- *The Googlization of Everything (And Why We Should Worry)*. Berkeley: University of California Press, 2011.

Vattimo, Gianni. *Of Reality: The Purposes of Philosophy*. Translated by Robert Valgenti. New York: Columbia University Press, 2016.

Vega y Carpio, Félix Lope de. *El caballero de Olmedo*, 15th ed. Edited by José Manuel Blecua Madrid: Ebro, 1979.
- *Los comendadores de Córdoba*. In *Obras escogidas*, edited by Federico Carlos Sainz de Robles, 3:1226–59. Madrid: Aguilar, 1955.
- *El villano en su rincón*. Edited by Juan María Marín. Madrid: Cátedra, 1987.
- *Fuente Ovejuna*, 6th ed. Edited by Juan María Marín. Madrid: Cátedra, 1985.
- *Peribáñez y el comendador de Ocaña*. Edited by Juan María Marín. Madrid: Cátedra, 1995.

Vilas, Manuel. "Lorca Reloaded." *La vida de los otros*, edited by Enrique Vila-Matas, 9 January 2010. enriquevilamatas.com/escritores/escrvilasm3.html.

Vives, Juan Luis. *The Education of a Christian Woman: A Sixteenth-Century Manual*, translated and edited by Charles Fantazzi. Chicago: University of Chicago Press, 2000.

Vollendorf, Lisa. *Reclaiming the Body: Maria de Zayas's Early Modern Feminism*. Chapel Hill: University of North Carolina, Department of Romance Languages, 2001.

Voltaire. "On Absurdities and Atrocities." In *Les Philosophes: The Philosophers of the Enlightenment and Modern Democracy*, edited and translated by Norman Lewis Torrey, 277–8. New York: Capricorn, 1960.

Walley-Beckett, Moira, screenwriter. "Más." Directed by Johan Renck. *Breaking Bad*, season 3, episode 5. High Bridge/Gran Via, 18 April 2010.

"We Are the 99 Percent." Tumblr, 23 August 2011. wearethe99percent.tumblr.com/post/9289779051/we-are-the-99-percent.

Weller, Celia Richmond, and Clark Andrews Colahan, trans. *The Trials of Persiles and Sigismunda: A Northern Story*. By Miguel de Cervantes. Berkeley: University of California Press, 1989.

"What Life Means to Einstein: An Interview by George Sylvester Viereck." *Saturday Evening Post*, 26 October 1929. saturdayeveningpost.com/wp-content/uploads/satevepost/einstein.pdf.

Wheeler, John Archibald. "The Computer and the Universe." *International Journal of Theoretical Physics* 21, no. 6 (1981): 557–72.

White, Max. "Metro Detroit Man Allegedly Told CNN 'I'm Coming to Gun You All Down.'" *WXYZ Detroit*, 22 January 2018. wxyz.com/news/metro-detroit-man-allegedly-told-cnn-im-coming-to-gun-you-all-down.

Williamsen, Amy. "Engendering Interpretation: Irony as a Comic Challenge in Maria de Zayas." *Romance Languages Annual* 3 (1991): 642–8.

Wilson, Diana de Armas. *Allegories of Love: Cervantes's "Persiles and Sigismunda."* Princeton, NJ: Princeton University Press, 1991.

– "Uncanonical Narratives: Cervantes's Perversion of Pastoral." In *Critical Essays on Cervantes*, edited by Ruth El Saffar, 180–210. Boston: G.K. Hall, 1986.

Wollendorf, Lisa. *Reclaiming the Body: María de Zayas' Early Modern Feminism*. Chapel Hill: University of North Carolina Department of Romance Languages, 2001.

Wu, Tim. *The Attention Merchants: The Epic Scramble to Get Inside Our Heads*. New York: Vintage, 2016.

Yang, Jingxiang, Michael Ward, and Bart Kahr. "Abuse of Rachel Carson and Misuse of DDT Science in the Service of Environmental Deregulation." *Angewandte Chemie International Edition* 56, no. 34 (2017): 10026–32. doi.org/10.1002/anie.201704077.

Zabala, Santiago. "Trump's Call to Order: The Politics of Resentment." *Public Seminar*, 17 March 2017. publicseminar.org/2017/03/trumps-call-to-order.

Zayas, María de. *Novelas completas*. Edited by María Martínez del Portal. Barcelona: Bruguera, 1973.

Zimic, Stanislav. *Las novelas ejemplares de Cervantes*. Madrid: Siglo XXI, 1996.

- "*El retablo de las maravillas*, parábola de la mentira." *Anales cervantinos* 20 (1982): 153–72.

Zimmermann, Margarete. "The *Querelle des Femmes* as a Cultural Studies Paradigm." Translated by Gesa Stedman. In *Time, Space, and Women's Lives in Early Modern Europe*, edited by Anne Jacobson Schutte, Thomas Kuehn, and Silvana Seidel Menchi, 17–28. Kirksville, MO: Truman State University Press, 2001.

Žižek, Slavoj. *The Sublime Object of Ideology*. London: Verso, 1989.

Index

abortion, 37. *See also* women
Africa, 3–4, 6, 44
African Union, 4
AIDS, 149
airbrushing. *See* photo manipulation
Alemán, Mateo, 102, 129, 143
Alias Grace (series), 104–7. *See also* Atwood, Margaret
Almodóvar, Pedro, 23
AlterNet, 35
Althusser, Louis, 75, 116–17
"America First," 5. *See also* Trump, Donald
American Medical Association, 111
Anderson, Chris, 18
anti-Black racism, 3–4, 19, 45–9, 161. *See also* Black Americans; racism
anti-Semitism, 21, 67, 94, 123–4. *See also* Jewish people and religion
apocalyptic thought, 34–7, 39–49
Aquinas, Thomas, 27
Arabic language, 28
Arcadia. *See* Golden Age myth
Arcollas Cabezas, Joaquín, 164
Aristotle, 28
Armstrong Roche, Michael, 179n3
Asia, 44

Asociación para la Recuperación de la Memoria Histórica, 165
Atlanta, 6
Atwood, Margaret, 10, 13, 104, 107–8, 151–2. *See also* *Alias Grace*
augmented reality, 24–5, 47
Austria, 30
authoritarianism, 7, 17, 148
Aznar, José María, 162

Baena, Julio, 179n3
Balibar, Étienne, 19
baroque culture, 43, 45, 75, 115, 151; historiography, 36; neo-baroque, 149; prose, 78, 131; theatre, 54–5, 62, 68–9, 76–77, 111–12, 173n13; treatises, 39–40; verse, 109–10
Bateman, Jason, 50
Baudrillard, Jean, 28
BBC, 75
Beckett, Samuel, 26
Behar, Joseph, 123–4
Behar, Mariam, 123–4
Benjamin, Walter, 162, 166–7
Bergmann, Emilie, 93–4
Berkman Klein Center for Internet and Society, 156

Bible and biblical figures, 34, 37, 41, 43–4
Big Love, 57
Black Americans, 19, 22, 45–9, 56, 161. *See also* anti-Black racism; racism
Black Lives Matter, 46, 48–9, 56
Borat. See Cohen, Sacha Baron
Borges, Jorge Luis, 161
Breaking Bad, 51–3
Buffett, Warren, 54
Bush, George W., 8, 29, 161–2
Butler, Judith, 23

Calderón de la Barca, Pedro, 55–6, 66, 75–7, 111–12, 114–15
Canada, 20, 104
Carpenter, John, 48
Carreño de Miranda, Juan, 110
cartography. *See* mapmaking
Castiglione, Baldassare, 38–9
Castro, Américo, 66–7
Catholicism and the Catholic Church, 54, 61, 86, 115–16, 130–2; in early modern Spain, 18, 20, 36, 40–1, 54, 68, 93, 139–42; Inquisition, 20, 90, 101, 139, 144–5; in literature, 64–7, 69, 91, 126–7, 131–2, 139–40, 143–6. *See also* Christianity
Cato Institute, 152. *See also* Koch brothers
celiac disease, 44
censorship, 4–5, 11, 161
Centers for Disease Control and Prevention (CDC), 4–5
Central Intelligence Agency (CIA), 57
Cervantes, Miguel de, 20, 25, 98–101, 107, 157; *Don Quixote*, 121–4, 130–7, 139, 142, 146, 151, 161–2; *Entremeses*, 58–69, 151, 154–5; *Novelas ejemplares*, 122–8, 132–3, 151; *Persiles y Sigismunda*, 129–33, 137–47, 151; unique craft of fiction, 18, 21, 33, 45, 151–2. *See also Tía fingida, La*
Champier, Symphorien, 86–7
Chavez, Hugo, 161
Child, Lee (Jim Grant), 75
Childers, William, 179n3
children, 3, 36; as consumers of media, 12, 32; in literature and art, 106, 117, 146, 164–5; and mothers, 83, 94. *See also* Deferred Action for Childhood Arrivals (DACA); mothers
Christian Broadcasting Network, 37
Christianity, 28, 44, 54; in the United States, 34, 37, 41. *See also* Bible and biblical figures; Catholicism and the Catholic Church
citizenship, 12, 19–21, 47–8, 56, 97
Clapper, James, 5
Claramonte, Andrés de, 173n12, 175n6
climate change, 5, 8, 10, 152–3; and the United States, 17, 47, 149–50
Clinton, Hillary, 22, 29, 35, 128
CNN, 4, 6–7, 157
coal, 47
Cohen, Elizabeth, 4–5
Cohen, Leonard, 22
Cohen, Sacha Baron, 121–4
Colbert, Stephen, 8, 27, 45, 57, 123
colonialism, 40–2, 104
Conway, Erik, 153
Conway, Kellyanne, 8, 24, 148
Cooper, Bradley, 51
Corker, Bob, 7–8
Coulter, Ann, 3
Counter-Reformation, 54, 92–4, 129. *See also* Catholicism and the Catholic Church; Christianity
CSI (TV series), 166

Daily Show, The, 57
Davis, Nina Cox, 103
Deferred Action for Childhood Arrivals (DACA), 3, 6
Deggans, Eric, 51–2
Del Toro, Guillermo, 164–5
demagoguery, 38, 45, 123, 126–8, 153; in the United States, 157
democracy, 12, 19, 54, 157; in Spanish literature, 54, 56, 137; in the United States, 7, 17–18
denialism, 3, 5–6, 17, 27, 152–3
De Niro, Robert, 51–2
Department of Health and Human Services (US), 4
deportation, 4, 36–7, 124. *See also* immigration
Derrida, Jacques, 166
Descartes, René, 28
Dexter, 51–2
Diallo, Robin, 4
dramas de honor, 58, 62–3, 66–9, 173n13; as social propaganda, 54–6, 75–7, 95–6, 111–13
DuPont Industries, 153
dystopian literature and art, 8, 10, 45, 151–2

Easy Rider, 121
economic inequality, 52–3, 55–6, 157
education, 9–13, 48, 94, 153, 156; as determinant of behaviour, 19, 20, 26–7, 152; in literature, 59, 104, 107; post-secondary, 19, 124, 159–60, 182n1
Einstein, Albert, 152
El Salvador and Salvadorans, 3–4, 6
empiricism, 26–8, 31
End Time, The, 44
Enlightenment, 81–3, 108
Erasmus, Desiderius, 121
Estrella de Sevilla, La, 76, 173n12, 175n6

Europe, 35; in the early modern period, 23, 28, 84, 93, 124

Facebook, 18, 24, 155. *See also* social media
"fake news," 24, 28, 47, 156; and Donald Trump, 6–8, 17, 128, 148
Falwell, Jerry, 37, 41
Farley, Thomas, 4
fascism, 12, 164
Feffer, John, 35
Feinstein, Diane, 6
feminism. *See* women
Fichte, Johann Gottlieb, 82–3, 98, 108, 175n4
fiction, 18, 20–2, 33, 48, 108
Fish, Stanley, 160–1
Flake, Jeff, 7
Forbes, 11
Forcione, Alban, 132
Foucault, Michel, 82, 116
Fox News, 4, 6–7, 56–7, 157
France, 86–8
Frank, Thomas, 53–4
Friedman, Edward, 101
Fromm, Erich, 7–10, 149
Fuchs, Barbara, 179n3
fundamentalism, 19, 22–4, 26–32, 37, 124; of the market, 9–10, 157

Galadí Melgar, Francisco, 164
Galindo, Dióscoro, 164
gay rights. *See* LGBT people
genetics, 43–4
Georgetown University, 162
Gerli, E. Michael, 62, 90–1
Giuliani, Rudy, 148–9
Godfather, The, 75
GOD TV, 34
Goethe, Johann Wolfgang von, 22–3
Golden Age myth, 133–5, 137, 141–2
Góngora, Luis de, 109–10

Gossy, Mary, 90, 93
Gracián y Morales, Baltasar, 38–41, 178n6
Granada, 36, 84, 100, 163–4
Granovetter, Mark, 23
Grant, Jim. *See* Child, Lee
group behaviour, 23, 49, 56

Haiti, 3–4, 6
Hapsburg dynasty, 20, 36–7
Harrington, Alan, 9–10, 149–50, 157
Harvard University, 26, 156
HBO, 57
Heidegger, Martin, 26, 32
Hell on Wheels, 51
Heraclitus, 89
hermeneutics, 31–2
Hill, Anita, 81
homelessness, 24–5
homophobia. *See* LGBT people
honour play. See *dramas de honor*
House of Cards, 39
Hubbard, L. Ron, 28
Hulu, 10
humanities, 10, 12–13, 20, 159–61, 182n1
human rights, 4, 30, 56, 81–2, 161; in the United States, 48
Huxley, Aldous, 10–12, 151–2
hymens, 99

Idealism, 82. *See also* romanticism
immigration, 30, 37, 104; in the United States, 3, 6, 127
Inquisition. *See* Catholicism and the Catholic Church
insanity, 73, 83, 121–5, 136, 175n4
Into the Wild, 121–2
irony, 22, 132–3, 139–41, 162. *See also* fiction
Islam and Muslims, 30, 35–7, 43; in Spain, 21, 84, 162; in the United States, 6, 17, 20

Islamic State, 35
Italy, 98

Jackson, Michael, 166
James, William, 150
Jameson, Frederic, 177n43
Jerusalem, 41
Jewish people and religion, 21, 67, 94, 123–4
Jordan, Constance, 86–7
journalism, 11–12, 32, 38, 45–6; in confrontation with politics, 6–8, 17–18. *See also* media consumption
Juana de la Cruz, 107–18, 151, 155, 162, 178nn8–9
Juan Manuel, Don, 73–75

Kahr, Bart, 152
Kansas City, 148
Kant, Immanuel, 52–3
Katrina (hurricane), 161–2
Ketchum, Roy, 159
Khanna, Ayesha, 24
King, Stephen, 148–9
Koch brothers, 149–50, 152
KQED Science Quest, 44
Kritzman, Lawrence, 87–8

labour unions, 56
Lacan, Jacques, 31, 88, 117, 176n43
Lamar, Kendrick, 45
Landy, Joshua, 160–1
Larsson, Stieg, 78–9
Las Casas, Bartolomé de, 40, 172n21
Latin, 28, 61, 104
Lazarillo de Tormes, La vida de, 101–2, 107
Legion (TV show), 47–8
Leibniz, Gottfried, 21
León (Spain), 102–3
Lepore, Jill, 26–7, 29, 31
LGBT people, 19, 37, 56, 125; in art, 23, 57; in medicine, 4, 87

liberal arts. *See* humanities
liberalism, 5, 8, 22, 30, 37
Limitless, 51-2
literacy, 21. *See also* media literacy
lobbyists, 5
López de Úbeda, Francisco, 101, 103
Lorca, Federico García, 162, 164-6
Los Angeles, 24
Lozano, Cristóbal, 36-7, 41
Lynch, Michael P., 26, 31

Madonna (singer), 54
Madrid, 162
Mann, Michael, 153
mapmaking, 85
Maravall, José Antonio, 55, 75, 84-5, 161, 174n22; on honour, 68, 111; on *La Celestina*, 88-90
Marchese, David, 123
markets, 9-10, 18, 20, 149-53, 157
Marks, Grace, 104-7
masculinity, 82-3, 88, 94; in Spanish literature, 73-7, 103-4, 108-9. *See also* misogyny; patriarchy
Matos, Gregorio de, 41-2
Mayhew, Jonathan, 160-1
McEnany, Kayleigh, 8
McGuire, Paul, 34
McKinnon, Kate, 22
media consumption, 10, 20-4, 28, 46, 150-1. *See also* journalism; social media
media literacy, 20-2, 45, 48, 146-7, 166-7; and civic engagement, 12, 17, 158
medialogy, 10, 18-19, 23-4, 46-9, 107
medieval period, 28, 35-6, 73, 77; in contrast with later periods, 26, 84, 90, 176n23
Mendieta, Jerónimo de, 41-2
Merchants of Doubt (film), 153-4
metaphysics, 27, 33, 103

#MeToo, 81, 111. *See also* women
Mexico, 6, 17, 35, 37, 127; as New Spain, 109, 112, 115
Miguel, Luis, 74
misogyny, 73-83, 87, 90, 94, 121; combatted by Sor Juana, 108-11; and *La pícara Justina*, 101, 104; represented by Cervantes, 124-5, 151; in United States politics, 19, 149. *See also* patriarchy; Trump, Donald; women
Modamani, Anas, 24-5
Modern Language Association (MLA), 182n1
Molho, Maurice, 121-2
monarchy, 85, 96-7, 138-9, 175n4; in early modern Europe, 20, 37, 54-5, 123, 133, 141
Moreto y Cavana, Agustín, 112
Moriscos, 36, 123-4, 144-6, 162
Morozov, Evgeny, 24
mothers, 83, 93-4, 131, 163. *See also* children
Motorcycle Diaries, The, 121-2
Mozart, Wolfgang Amadeus, 160
Mr. Robot, 47-8
Mueller, Robert, 148
Mulye, Nirmal, 149
Muslims. *See* Islam and Muslims

Native Americans, 44
nativism, 127. *See also* immigration
NBC, 161
Nelson, Bradley J., 79
Netflix, 39, 104
New Spain. *See* Mexico; New World
Newspeak. *See* Orwell, George
New World, 40-1, 85
New York, 22, 47
New Yorker, 26
New York Times, 30, 48
Nietzsche, Friedrich, 26-7, 31
nihilism, 31

Noble, Safiya Umoja, 156
Norway, 3
Nostrum Pharmaceutical, 149
Nussbaum, Martha, 160

Obama, Barack, 5, 35, 43, 47
Occupy movement, 52–3.
  See also economic inequality
O'Neil, Cathy, 156–7
Orestes, Naomi, 153
Orwell, George, 4–8, 10–12, 148–9, 151
Osterc, Lúdovic, 125
Oxford English Dictionary, 38
Ozark, 50–2

Paré, Ambroise, 87
Parker, Patricia, 87
Paskin, Willa, 123
pastoral literature, 133–6, 146
patriarchy, 83, 87–8, 94, 108; in literature, 73–80, 117
Paz, Octavio, 115–16
Peaky Blinders, 75
Penn State University, 153
Perot, Ross, 9
Perry, Mary Elizabeth, 92–3, 176n35
Philip III of Spain, 36, 103, 145–6, 175n8
photo manipulation, 45, 47, 110–11
Pícara Justina, La, 101–7, 109, 143, 151, 177n11
picaresque literature, 98, 101–7, 129, 133, 143; and motherhood, 94; and stock characters, 146
Plato, 28
Poe, Edgar Allen, 78
Poesse, Walter, 173n13
Poniewozik, James, 48
Postman, Andrew, 11–12
Postman, Neil, 10–12
postmodernism, 26–8, 31–2, 43, 161, 166; in politics, 19

Prophecy Depot Ministries, 34
Pryor, Richard, 45

Quevedo, Francisco de, 40
Quinze joies de mariage, Les, 86

Rabelais, François de, 87–8
racism, 19, 45–9, 56, 156, 161; in Cervantes's writing, 124, 126–7, 151; and Donald Trump, 4, 149, 157. See also anti-Black racism; anti-Semitism; Philip III of Spain; Trump, Donald
Radcliffe, Anne, 78
Rather, Dan, 18
reality, 24–33, 121–2, 135–7, 157–8, 164; manipulated, 5–9, 39; perceived, 12, 17–22, 45–8, 73, 128, 146–7. See also media literacy
reality TV, 11, 17, 37, 57
refugees, 24–5, 46–7, 49.
  See also immigration
republicanism, 19
revenge, 52–4, 56–7, 69, 89–90, 113
Robertson, Pat, 37, 41, 161
Rodríguez de la Flor, Fernando, 40–1
Rojas, Fernando de, 88–93, 98, 112
Rojas Zorrilla, Francisco de, 76
Romanticism, 22–3, 122
Rome, Adam, 152–3
Romero, George, 47
Rorty, Richard, 19, 30
Rothman, Emily, 4
Rove, Karl, 8, 18, 29
Ruggiero, Guido, 98
Russell, Diana, 78–9
Russia, 8, 51, 127–8

Salon (website), 123
Salus, Bill, 34, 37, 41
Samsung, 23
Sanchez, Boris, 157

Sandel, Michael, 9
Sanders, Sarah, 8
San Francisco, 24
Sarlin, Benjy, 18
Saturday Night Live, 22
Schiff, Adam, 148
Schramm, Percy, 175n8
Scott-Heron, Gil, 46
Seagal, Steven, 75
700 Club, The, 37
Shakespeare, William, 73
Shepherd, Jessica, 182n6
Sherwin, Richard, 146
Shipley, George, 122, 124, 127
Shkreli, Martin, 149
social media, 11, 21–4, 48, 126, 155–7; and Jean Baudrillard, 28
Sons of Anarchy, 51
Spacey, Kevin, 39
Spadaccini, Nicholas, 60
Spain, 162, 175n8; and apocalypticism, 43, 45; archetypes in early modern Spain, 62; civil war, 164–5; propaganda in early modern Spain, 18, 20–1; representations in historiography, 36–7, 39–1; representations in literature, 123–4, 129–30, 133, 139–42, 144–6; and social changes, 84–5, 88; social illusions in early modern Spain, 54–6, 64, 66–9, 75, 77, 151, 155; women in early modern Spain, 93–8, 101, 108–9
Spanish language and Spanish-language literature, 12–13, 58–9, 111, 115, 159–60, 173n13
Spears, Britney, 54
Spicer, Sean, 8, 24
Stalin, Josef, 7–8
STEM (science, technology, engineering, and mathematics) fields, 10, 31–3, 152–3, 156–7; and censorship, 4–5, 24
stop-and-frisk program, 47
suicide, 23, 137
Suskind, Ron, 8, 29
syphilis, 93, 106

Tate, Robert, 37
Tea Party movement, 52
Teare, Chris, 11
television, 11, 46, 50–3, 75, 150; television dramas, 35, 47–8. *See also* reality TV
Teresa de Jesús, 109
terrorism, 6, 24, 43, 46, 57; terrorist attacks in Spain, 37, 162; terrorist attacks in the United States, 6, 33, 37
Thelma and Louise, 121–2
theocracy, 10
Thomas, Angie, 104
Thomas, Clarence, 81
Tía fingida, La, 98–9
#TimesUp, 111. *See also* women
Todd, Chuck, 148
Toledo (Spain), 36, 103
Toles, Tom, 153
torture, 10, 57, 78–9
totalitarianism, 10, 12
Tower, Troy, 174n22, 175n5, 177n3, 178n1, 179n5
transgender people. *See* LGBT people
True Blood, 57
Trump, Donald, 3–12, 17–22, 81, 127–8, 148–50; and apocalypticism, 35–7; and fantasy, 38–9, 47; and lies, 27–8, 43–5, 157–8; and misogyny, 107, 111; Trumpism, 49, 52. *See also* demagoguery; "fake news"; misogyny; whiteness
Trump Apocalypse Watch, 45

Trump University, 127
24 (series), 56–7
Twitter, 3, 6, 8, 148, 157

United Nations, 4
United States, 3–10, 17–24, 35–8, 47–9; corporate behaviour, 52, 149, 152–3; and education, 159, 182n1; and gender discrimination, 81; and political motivation, 56; 2016 election, 11, 17, 22, 26, 35, 45, 81, 127–8, 156; 2020 election, 6, 20, 28, 48, 127–8, 157. *See also* democracy; terrorism
universities. *See* education: post-secondary

Vaidhyanathan, Siva, 155–6
Vattimo, Gianni, 26–7, 31–3
Vega y Carpio, Lope de, 60, 62–3, 67, 75–6, 177n44; *El caballero de Olmedo*, 95–7; *Los comendadores de Córdoba*, 173n13; *El villano*, 173n12
Veterans for Foreign Wars, 148
Vilas, Manuel, 165–6
Visigoths, 36–7
Vives, Juan Luis, 91, 93–5, 100
Vollendorf, Lisa, 79
Voltaire, 157
voter suppression, 48

Ward, Michael, 152
Washington Post, 3, 35
West, Kanye, 161–2
western films, 75
West Virginia, 47
Westworld, 47
Wheeler, John, 32
whiteness, 37, 47–8, 54, 56, 157. *See also* racism; Trump, Donald; United States
Wilson, Diana de Armas, 141, 179n3
women, 19, 23, 117, 161; in literature and television, 45, 61–2, 73–81, 90–111, 114–15, 125; in media, 81; in philosophy and natural philosophy, 82–4, 86–8; and sexual assault, 35, 37, 55; women's equality, 30, 56. *See also* misogyny
Wu, Tim, 150–1, 153

Yang, Jingxiang, 152

Zabala, Santiago, 17, 32
Zayas y Sotomayor, María de, 107, 151–2, 155; *Desengaños amorosos*, 77–80, 111; *Novelas amorosas y ejemplares*, 99–101
Zimic, Stanislov, 65, 125
Žižek, Slavoj, 116–17, 173n9, 176–7n43
zombies, 34–5, 47, 156–7